WHOLE WORLD IN AN UPROAR

WHOLE WORLD IN AN UPROAR

Music, Rebellion, and Repression 1955–1972

Aaron J. Leonard

Published by Repeater Books

An imprint of Watkins Media Ltd

Unit 11 Shepperton House

89-93 Shepperton Road

London

N1 3DF

United Kingdom

www.repeaterbooks.com

A Repeater Books paperback original 2023

1

Distributed in the United States by Random House, Inc., New York.

ISBN: 9781914420924

Ebook ISBN: 9781914420931

Sections of this book are drawn from work published previously on *Truthout.org*:

"Newly Unearthed FBI File Exposes Targeting of Folk Singer Dave Van Ronk," Aaron J. Leonard, *Truthout*, July 8, 2018.

"FBI Tracking of Bob Dylan and Suze Rotolo Foreshadowed Future Abuses," Aaron J. Leonard, *Truthout*, September 1, 2019.

Printed and bound in the United Kingdom by TJ Books Limited

For My Comrades — Past & Present

CONTENTS

As can be seen in the title, this book covers the decade of the 1960s and the key years surrounding it. I do this in keeping with the historical concept of "the long Sixties," where the basis and resolution for this extraordinary period extended beyond the calendar decade.

Abbreviations

BPP	Black Panther Party
CORE	Congress of Racial Equality
CP/CPUSA	Communist Party USA
DNC	Democratic National Convention
ECLC	Emergency Civil Liberties Committee
FPCC	Fair Play for Cuba Committee
HUAC/HCUA	House Committee on Un-American Activities
IS	Internal Security — FBI investigation
NAACP	National Association for the Advancement of Colored People
PLP/PLM	Progressive Labor Party / Progressive Labor Movement
SDS	Students for a Democratic Society
SI/ADEX	Security Index / Administrative Index (potential detention list kept by the FBI)
SNCC	Student Non-Violent Coordinating Committee
SCLC	Southern Christian Leadership Foundation
SWP	Socialist Workers Party
VVAW/WSO	Vietnam Veterans Against the War / Winter Soldier Organization
YIPPIE	Youth International Party

PREFACE

Several years ago, I had an idea for a book to examine how the FBI targeted progressive and radical artists in the Sixties as part of a larger imperative to gain control of the social tumult of that period. At the time, the effort led to a dead-end. After undertaking initial research, I discovered the files to accomplish this either did not exist or would not be made available. So, I put the idea aside and went to work on *The Folk Singers & the Bureau,* with its focus on the left-wing folk singers and the FBI in the 1940s and 1950s. With that book behind me, I found myself again drawn toward the "Sixties book," but was still confronted with the problem of the dearth of FBI material.

Then it occurred to me. Unlike with the partisan folk music artists of the Forties and early Fifties, who were grouped around the Communist Party USA (CPUSA), the radical and progressive artists of the Sixties emerged from the ashes of the "old left." As such, they did not associate or identify with the CPUSA or any other hierarchical left-wing organization. Because of this, they were by and large not internal security targets of the FBI. That did not, however, mean they were not targets of repression. While not the purview of the FBI, they instead were confronted by forces embedded in the wider socio-political structure — whether that be the television censor, immigration authority, intolerant Christian, scolding politician, right-wing musician, or hostile journalist. To tell that story, I needed to draw on not only any relevant FBI files, but also on the abundance of material from the media of the day, the extensive corpus of music journalism, and the ever-growing body of memoirs of the prime actors of the period.

In the end, this book turned out to be a different one from that originally conceived. It also marks a departure, to a degree, from my work so far, with its primary focus on the FBI and radicals in the last half of the twentieth century. Nonetheless, it tells a story I think needs telling. Not just of music and repression, but a version of the Sixties where rebellion and upheaval lie at the heart of events. To have passed through that time — or in my case, to have come of age in those years — is to have lived through a revolution of a kind. And while the debate continues as to its lasting significance, my hope is that this work will contribute to an understanding of an overlooked component operating in that cyclonic past.

Aaron J. Leonard
Spring 2022

INTRODUCTION

We have the power to shape the civilization that we want.
— Lyndon Johnson, May 1964.[1]

Look, the world is being turned upside down.
— Mao Zedong, 1965.[2]

Jim Morrison had something in mind when he took the stage in Miami in March 1969. Having consumed a fair amount of alcohol, he thought he would channel the provocative sensibilities of avant-garde art into the evening's show. His bandmate, drummer John Densmore, explained Morrison's state of mind:

> [H]e went to see Julian Beck and Judith Molina of The Living Theater and was inspired because they wore minimal clothes and were going up the aisles saying, "No passports, no pieces." It was pretty wild stuff. Jim tried to inject it into the Miami concert, and he was inebriated, so it wasn't so successful.[3]

That lack of success was on full display when the band moved into their song "Touch Me." Morrison, who had been making calls from the stage such as "Let's have a revolution," began a faux striptease and is reported to have said, "Do you wanna see my cock?" The police — who would later claim Morrison exposed himself — wanted to arrest him on the spot, but fearing a riot, held back.[4]

Unable to take him into custody, acting police chief

Paul Denham told the media that they had produced two warrants against Morrison: one for indecent exposure, another for the "use of obscene languages [*sic*]." The Chief then continued, revealing the police's lack of evidence, "we were waiting, hoping, to get pictures that were taken during the performance."[5]

Pictures or not, the authorities were worried about the impact on local youth. The Miami CBS television affiliate made a special effort to interview local young people, who denounced the event, calling it "shocking" and "uncalled for." None of those youths, however, had actually been at the show. One young woman — who had — revealed that Morrison wasn't the only one having trouble with the police: "It seemed like very many people were under the influence of drugs [...] everyone, a lot of people were getting busted."[6]

The guardians of south Florida's youth responded quickly. Within weeks of the show, they organized a "Rally for Decency" at the Orange Bowl, to stand as a rebuke to the decadence of the Doors. During the event, "Teenage speakers gave three-minute talks on God, parents, patriotism, sexuality and brotherhood." As for the entertainment, it was retrograde. Among the celebrities appearing was former Miss Oklahoma, Anita Bryant — soon to be a prominent anti-gay activist. She was joined by mainstream comedian, and Richard Nixon golf partner, Jackie Gleason. For music, the attendees heard the safe harmonies of "The Lettermen."[7] The event hit all the right notes for those at the top of the political establishment. After the concert, Richard Nixon wrote to one of the organizers, "I was extremely interested to learn about the admirable initiative."[8] Jackie Gleason was so pleased that he foretold of a movement taking shape, saying, "I believe this kind of movement will snowball across the United States and perhaps around the world."[9]

As if to actualize Gleason's prediction, right-wing forces worked to take the Miami experience nationwide, holding a similar rally in Alabama the following month. Ten days after that, another rally was held in Baltimore. It ended in a riot.[10] Such was the state of things in the United States in the final years of the 1960s.

Rebellion, Repression, and Art

One cannot understand the trouble Jim Morrison got into in his short, wild, and creative life, without understanding the period in which he flourished. The upsurge of the Sixties, and the music it produced, was made possible in no small way by the churning of titanic forces operating within and beyond the borders of the United States. The Cold War, the Sino-Soviet split within that, and the continued tearing up of the previous century's colonial system, elicited internal changes within the US, from the long-delayed ripping up of the American South's apartheid state, to the country's first major military defeat in Vietnam. This was the *terra firma* for unprecedented upheaval: urban insurrections, massive protests, the rejection of established norms, and the quest for an alternative culture.

It was under these circumstances that a new music emerged. The art being inseparable from the social upheaval, or perhaps better said, the upheaval manifesting itself within the art. In that regard, the social turmoil made otherwise impossible things possible.

In discussing Crosby, Stills, Nash & Young's song "Ohio," music writer Dorian Lynskey makes the point that it is "perhaps the most powerful topical song ever recorded."[11] To which could be added, it was a song that could not have been written were it not for the killing of four students at Kent State by the National Guard. Put starkly, the song was paid for in blood. No less can be said of Nina Simone's

"Mississippi Goddam," Bob Dylan's "With God on Our Side," Phil Ochs's "Santo Domingo," and no small number of others. The music that came forward in this period was "special" because so much human suffering and experience went into its realization.

It was not, however, only upheaval and the consequent creativity that was in play. Throughout this period, there was myriad and varied repression leveled at those creating this art. While most commentary on the music of this period focuses on the trials and tribulations of different artists — their personal choices, muses, relationships with their record companies and managers, etc. — what was discovered in researching this book was how these artists also had to contend with the relentless pushback from "the powers that be," in manifold forms, in order to produce their work.

In that respect, one is struck by how everyone from the Beatles to Bob Dylan, Johnny Cash, Miriam Makeba, Phil Ochs, to Pete Seeger, and many others, confronted at critical points forces highly motivated to keep them or their work out of the public square. It was only through meeting the challenges thrown at them that their art was realized, or failing that, constrained, if not abandoned entirely.

What to Leave In / What to Leave Out?

The reader will notice that the bulk of this book focuses on the folk revival of the late 1950s and early 1960s, rumblings in R&B and jazz, and the revolution in rock that took place in the decade of the 1960s. While there are some references to other genres, they are minimal. This was a choice made out of a desire to make the case for music and repression largely among more widely known artists — not to diminish the intensity of attacks, or importance of the contributions of those not referenced. Even with that criterion, not everyone gets mentioned. Also, the aim of this work was not to present an encyclopedic account of every example of political content by every artist that entered into the fray — there are many fine books in this regard, and they are a point of reference for this work. Further, this book does not attempt to document the totality of repressive or censorious activity that was leveled. That would be a long, unwieldy, and a not very compelling project. Rather, the aim is to show, through select examples, how the radical music of the Sixties was birthed amid unprecedented upheaval and systemic repression.

This, then, is the story of the Sixties, told as the escalating contention between the forces of the status quo in a country sitting at the pinnacle of power — and intent on remaining so — and the forces it unintentionally set loose who opposed them. And it is the story of the artists, called to operate "far beyond their rightful time," who had to contend amid these extraordinary circumstances, producing works of wonder in the process.

CHAPTER 1
EISENHOWER'S GRAVE DIGGERS (1955–1960)

American houses last for more than 20 years, but, even so, after twenty years, many Americans want a new house or a new kitchen.
— Richard Nixon to Nikita Khrushchev, 1959[1]

This is the story of America. Everybody's doing what they think they're supposed to do.
— Jack Kerouac, *On the Road*, 1957[2]

When the chart-topping folk-pop group the Weavers took the stage of Carnegie Hall on Christmas Eve, 1955, the performance was stellar, the selections wonderful, and the atmosphere convivial. As good a show as it was, however, it was too late. The Weavers' moment as a national phenomenon had passed.

Several forces conspired against the group. They had been chased from the public square by a combination of blacklisting, the work of government informants, and the panting media who branded them a communist front. The quartet — Pete Seeger, Lee Hays, Ronnie Gilbert, and Fred Hellerman — had topped the charts in the opening years of the decade, but by the end of 1952 had called it quits. The Carnegie concert was a comeback, one of several revivals that were successful on a certain level, but the mainstream acceptance the group accessed between 1950–1952 was no longer available to them. Not only had political forces conspired against them, but pop music was moving on in a multitude of different directions.

By the latter part of the 1950s in the United States, there was a cultural flowering. Not only was there the emergence of rock 'n' roll, there was the iconoclastic poetry of the Beats, radical rumblings in jazz, and the ascent of the folk music revival. Taken as a whole, this was a cultural insurgency, one met with hostility by the forces in control of Cold War American culture.

The Beats

Among the most controversial of these insurgents were the Beats, a group of post-war artists and intellectuals such as writer Jack Kerouac, poet Allen Ginsberg, and author William S. Burroughs. What distinguished them from the mainstream literary culture of the time was their alienated aesthetic. This was no better articulated than in Ginsberg's poem "Howl!" with its haunting opening: "I saw the best minds of my generation destroyed by madness, starving hysterical naked…"[3] It should not be surprising, then, given the overall conservative and anti-communist consensus of the era, that the movement and individuals within it would come under attack.

Most famously they were the target of a direct assault on one of the preeminent Constitutional freedoms: freedom of the press. Specifically, Shigeyoshi "Shig" Murao was arrested on June 3, 1957, by an undercover San Francisco police officer, after selling him a copy of *Howl* at City Lights Books. In turn, Lawrence Ferlinghetti, owner of the store, was arrested for publishing the poem. The two were put on trial in the fall of that year, charged with disseminating obscene literature.[4] While they were ultimately cleared, with Superior court judge Clayton W. Horn ruling the poem was not obscene, the media attention on the trial sent a clear message to the larger mainstream of US society that there was something inappropriate about the Beats.

For their part, the FBI took note. In a memo from September 1963 in Allen Ginsberg's file, they wrote, "No investigation pertinent to your inquiry has been conducted by the FBI concerning the captioned individual [Allen Ginsberg]." It continued, referencing the obscenity trial noting, "Subject of name check [Ginsberg] described as a 'Beat' poet who was author of *Howl and Other Poems*."[5] Ginsberg, in other words, was on the FBI's radar.

It is worth noting that the FBI correctly refers to Ginsberg as a "Beat" poet, a term which would be cast aside by the mainstream culture in favor of the derogatory term "beatnik." The Beat name itself was one that had been coined by Kerouac. As Allen Ginsberg explained:

> The phrase "Beat Generation" rose out of a specific conversation with Jack Kerouac and John Clellon Holmes in 1950–51 when discussing the nature of generations, recollecting the glamour of the "lost generation." Kerouac discouraged the notion of a coherent "generation" and said, "Ah, this is nothing but a beat generation!"

Disregarding that explanation, *San Francisco Chronicle* journalist Herb Caen would catalyze the corruption of the term, instead calling the Beats "Beatniks." Caen's construction was a conflation of the Beat moniker with Sputnik, the satellite launched by the Soviet Union. He initially used the term "Beatnik" in his column "Around the Town" on April 3, 1958, referencing a club which he referred to as "a hangout for the bearded Beatnik Generation." He was so pleased with his wordplay that he repeated it in another column that month and twice more in June.[6]

Whatever Caen's intentions, the term hit at a moment when the US was particularly stung by advances in the Soviet space program. As a result, a willing media, unhappy with the anti-social Beats and quick to seize on any opportunity to ridicule their Soviet enemy, embraced the term, which had the benefit of conflating the Beats with communism. This was so successful that it effectively replaced the correct moniker for that cultural movement.

Jazz, the Red Scare, and Black Freedom

The Beats were particularly associated with the jazz music of the era, Jack Kerouac's *On the Road* in particular was brimming with passion for the music.[7] Jazz occupied an important position in US society, being a musical form created within the United States by African American artists. As such, it would be a site of creative ferment in the movement for Black freedom. It was also, however, manipulated as a tool for advancing the US's Cold War agenda.

During the Second Red Scare, there were a number of artists that drew the attention of the FBI. Among them were Nat King Cole and Duke Ellington, both of whom had FBI files. In Cole's case, this was out of the suspicion that he had been a member of the Communist Party and the short-lived Communist Political Association — something the Bureau appear to have never established.[8] The file also contains reports of Cole being the object of a racist attack in 1956 — his assailants rushing the stage and knocking him down during a concert. The attack was orchestrated by members of the white supremacist White Citizen's Council, leading Cole to cancel his subsequent shows in the South.[9] All in all, however, the FBI found nothing worth pursuing, and his file ends in 1961.

Duke Ellington also landed on the FBI's radar because of past communist associations. Specifically, his performances for the Artists' Front to Win the War and the National Council of American-Soviet Friendship during WWII. Ellington, however, would put a clear distance between himself and any perceived ties to communism. This made him respectable enough in the eyes of the powers that be that, on his seventieth birthday in 1969, he was honored at the Nixon White House.[10]

Louis Armstrong was also an object of FBI attention, though not for perceived communist affiliations, but more for his international travel.[11] Part of that travel was sponsored by the US State Department — most notably a visit to Africa in 1960–61 — in its efforts to erect a cultural counter to that of the Soviet Union by sponsoring the tour of jazz musicians. Both Armstrong and Dizzy Gillespie had participated in US State Department tours.[12] Pointedly, Gillespie, who had gone to Europe in 1956, refused to take part in the government's official briefings, saying he "wasn't going to apologize for the racist policies of America."[13] While such a position is admirable, it suggests a view on the part of such artists of being able to participate on their own terms. Given the exigency of the Cold War, that was more illusion than reality.

Someone with no such illusions was jazz saxophonist Sonny Rollins. This came through in his 1958 album *Freedom Suite*, whose title song was a musical statement for liberation. As Rollins would say on the record's liner notes:

> How ironic that the Negro, who more than any other people can claim America's culture as his own, is being persecuted and repressed, that the Negro, who has exemplified the humanities in his very existence, is being rewarded with inhumanity.[14]

One of Rollins's collaborators on *Freedom Suite*, Max Roach, would soon follow in his footsteps. In 1959, he began working with singer-songwriter Oscar Brown on an album that would become *We Insist: Max Roach's Freedom Now Suite!* That album also included Abbey Lincoln, whom he would marry in 1962, along with tenor saxophonist Coleman Hawkins and drummer Babatunde Olatunji. The album's cover, Black men sitting at a white lunch counter, was unambiguously defiant.[15]

Finally, there was jazz bassist Charles Mingus, who recorded "Fables of Faubus," ridiculing the governor of Arkansas, Orval Faubus, who called out the National Guard to stop the 1957 integration of Little Rock Central High School. The lyrics consisted of a call and response, asking who is the most ridiculous, with the answer being Faubus. That was too much for Columbia Records — they released the song without the lyrics.[16]

Rock 'n' Roll

While the Beats and progressive jazz artists represented one kind of rebellious cultural movement, they were rarefied to a degree that they could be marginalized by the media and others — relegated to the intelligentsia. Another cultural convulsion which animated a huge section of youth could not, that being the first wave of rock 'n' roll. It was in the mid-1950s that Elvis Presley, Little Richard, Fats Domino, Jerry Lee Lewis, Chuck Berry, Buddy Holly, and others burst onto the scene with this electrifying music.

Rock 'n' roll posed a peculiar challenge to the standing order. While the early artists who made up its cohort did not have backgrounds in left-wing politics, nor was their lyrical content political in any conventional sense, they were nonetheless controversial. First, their music challenged white supremacist social norms by embracing Black musical styles and popularizing them among white youth. Beyond that was the music's sexuality, coded as it was, which challenged the dominant puritanical mores of the United States. For these reasons it was met with scorn — similarly to how jazz was vilified as "the Devil's music" in the 1920s.[17]

Presley & the FBI

Of all those who emerged in this period, none was more prominent than Elvis Presley, a cultural persona whose actual musical influence is overshadowed by the dominant culture's canonization of him. Given that, it is noteworthy that the FBI kept a file on Presley. While the Bureau did not view him as a national security threat, their attention was called forward because of the moral panic conjured up by rock 'n' roll.

The concern over Presley comes through in a correspondence from a writer describing himself as a "newspaper man, parent, and former member of Army Intelligence Service." The writer informed the Bureau of his "conviction that Presley is a definite danger to the United States":

> Presley's actions and motions were such as to rouse the sexual passions of teenaged youth. One eyewitness described his actions as "sexual self-gratification on the stage." [...] It is known by psychologists, psychiatrists, and priests that teenaged girls from the age of eleven, and boys in their adolescence are easily aroused to sexual indulgence and perversion by certain types of motions and hysteria, the type that was exhibited at the Presley show.[18]

Not content to leave things at that, the writer relays gossip that Presley fan clubs degenerate into sex orgies, before concluding, "From eye-witness reports about Presley, I would judge that he may possibly be a drug addict and a sexual pervert. In any case I assume he bears close watch."[19] In Presley's case, the writer had little to fear, as he would soon become safe enough for the mainstream. However, the focus on the sexual mores exhibited by artists would be a running battle in the years to come.

Elvis vs Mexico

While Presley's FBI file is not a record of an investigation against him as a target, it does reveal how the Cold War was omnipresent throughout this musical upsurge. The file contains an extensive report on how Presley ran afoul of authorities after news outlets in Mexico City reported on Presley saying racist things about Mexican — and African-American — women. According to the FBI, Presley was reported to have said, "he would rather kiss three negresses rather than one Mexican girl." As incendiary as the comment was, the Bureau thought "it would almost appear contrived." Contrived or not, it sparked a campaign to prevent playing Presley records "over any Mexican radio station." Further, the rumored remarks led to university students planning a protest in a downtown Mexico City park "where ELVIS PRESLEY music, magazines, and recordings will be publicly burned."

As the FBI suspected, the incident appears to have been fabricated. According to Herbe Pompeyo of Polygram Records in Mexico City, a "'high-up Mexican political figure' wanted to contract Presley for a private party, for which he sent the performer a blank check to fill in as he wished." According to Pompey's account, Presley returned the check, thereby offending the politician, who retaliated by concocting the derogatory story.[20] While incontrovertible evidence of this account is lacking, if true, it would not be the last time that a high-profile pop star encountered the wrath of the ruling class of a developing country over a perceived snub, as the Beatles would learn a few years later in the Philippines — and they too would see their records burned in the US.

Amongst all this, the Cold War was never far from the center of things. As the FBI, reporting on the incident, noted, "The Communists quick to ban rock-and-roll dancing from Mexican Communist youth social functions, may try to spark the bonfire meeting in the plaza, but even the Communists may not stop rock-and-roll in Mexico."[21] While the Bureau may have scorned Presley and the moral corruption they felt he represented, if people like him created problems for the communists, well, so much for the good.

Alan Freed's Transgression

While Elvis Presley called up negative attention in some quarters, he was largely allowed to go about his career. Alan Freed, however, was another matter.

Alan Freed is the man credited with popularizing the term "rock 'n' roll." As a disc jockey in Ohio, he was among the first to promote the music. And while he is now hallowed in the Rock and Roll Hall of Fame as the "boundary-smashing, trend-setting evangelist of rock and roll," when he was alive, he was relentlessly pursued by the US government, which hounded him till his death.[22]

Along with playing rock 'n' roll music on the radio, Freed also promoted it in live events, one of which led to his first confrontations — Freed faced criminal prosecution for a concert in Boston in May 1958.[23] The show, held at the Boston Arena, attracted six thousand people. While the concert itself proceeded without incident, in its wake several people were reported to have been robbed or assaulted by teenagers who attended the show. The authorities called it a riot. In response, Boston Mayor John B. Hynes banned future rock shows in any of the city's public auditoriums.[24] In the Boston case, the charges against Freed for incitement to riot and "inciting unlawful destruction of real and personal property" were eventually dropped. Unfortunately, it was not the end of his legal troubles.

Office Memorandum • UNITED STATES GOVERNMENT

TO : Mr. DeLoach   DATE: 12/2/59

FROM : M. A. Jones

SUBJECT: DISC JOCKEY "PAYOLA" SCANDAL;
ALAN FREED, NEW YORK
"ROCK & ROLL" PROMOTER

      As a result of the current Congressional hearings concerning unethical practices in the entertainment industry, wide public attention has been focused upon the practice of some radio and television disc jockeys of accepting "payola" to promote certain recordings. Among the disc jockeys prominently mentioned in the "payola" scandal has been Alan Freed, the New York radio and television personality who has been credited with originating the term "rock and roll."

"GO, MAN, GO"

      From the outset of this scandal, Freed has orally denied being a party to any "improper" practices; however, he was fired late last month by New York Radio Station WABC for refusing to sign an affidavit to the effect that he had never accepted "payola" or otherwise been involved in conflicts of interest. In addition, his contract with WNEW-TV was terminated last week "by mutual consent." Before parting company with WNEW-TV, however, disc jockey Freed did sign a statement denying that he had ever been guilty of "improper practice" while employed by that television station.

BANNED IN BOSTON

      Despite the loss of these two jobs, Freed claims he has plenty to do--including offers to consider from other stations and scheduled appearances with his rock and roll road shows. It is a safe assumption, however, that Freed will not consider any radio or television offers from Boston or take his road show near that city.   REC-61 MCT-2

      In May, 1958, the wrath of responsible citizens of Boston descended upon Freed when one of his rock and roll road shows in that city was followed by a teen-age riot. According to newspaper reports, during one of his rock and roll shows in the Boston Arena on Saturday night, May 3, 1958, Freed asked that the auditorium lights be lowered. The auditorium electricians, however, did not lower the lights but, instead, pointed at a police sergeant who was standing nearby. At this point, Freed is alleged to have blurted into the microphone, "I guess the

(continued on next page)
GWG:jss (7)

A report in Alan Freed's FBI file

More dire for Freed was his role as a target in what the media branded the "payola scandal" — a scheme whereby DJs were given money to play certain records. Freed and fellow disc jockey Dick Clark were singled out; Freed would be pursued legally, while Clark was largely given a pass.[25]

Behind the "scandal" was a struggle between Broadcast Music Inc. (BMI), who represented the "young, racially mixed writers of R&B and rock 'n' roll," and the American Society of Composers, Authors, and Publishers (ASCAP), representing older established artists, with the latter attempting to check the rising power of the former.[26] ASCAP, according to Michael James Roberts, had instigated the hearings to make the case that demand for rock 'n' roll was being artificially created by DJs. In that sense, this was a battle emerging from technological advances wherein musicians — who used to be able to perform live on the radio — saw their livelihood imperiled by recorded music.[27] In that respect, the "scandal" was less about moral corruption, and more about who was going to make money in the music business.

All of this, however, was wrapped up in the pushback against a cultural expression that was upsetting to the white supremacist order that demanded an iron wall separating Black and white.[28] Not only did white and Black youths attend Freed's concerts, but, as a matter of principal, he refused to play the sanitized cover versions of popular records by Chuck Berry or Little Richard, re-recorded by mainstream white artists such as Pat Boone. Through such actions, Freed was upsetting the status quo.[29]

Given that, it is little surprise who the FBI — though not directly involved in the case — sided with:

Undoubtedly Alan Freed has an intense dislike for the Director [J. Edgar Hoover] because of statements which the Director made to the prominent newsman Aaron G.

Benesch in May 1958, a few days after the Boston rock-and-roll riot. In an article regarding his interview with the Director, Mr. Benesch wrote, "FBI Director J. Edgar Hoover said today Rock 'n Roll is a corrupting influence on America's youth. The famous chief of the world's foremost law enforcement agency denounced rock 'n roll riots like the recent one in Boston as 'inexcusable.'"[30]

In the end, it was the Payola scandal that pushed Freed out of the public square. He would eventually be charged with twenty-six counts of commercial bribery. While he was able to escape prison with a six-month suspended sentence, he was dropped from his high-profile radio spot on New York's WABC, as well as its television station WNEW, where he had a show called "The Big Beat."[31]

For all intents and purposes, it was the end of his career, though not the government's pursuit of him. In 1964, the IRS claimed Freed had evaded taxes on $37,920 — money they say was garnered through the payola scheme. At the time of the tax action, Freed was living in Palm Springs, broke and suffering from uremia and cirrhosis, brought on by alcoholism. He died in 1965 at the age of forty-three, before those charges were resolved.[32]

Riot Around the Clock

The measures leveled at Alan Freed are better understood against the backdrop of the rebellion the music set loose. In 1955, when the film *Blackboard Jungle* — a caution against juvenile delinquency, which prominently featured the Bill Haley and the Comets song "Rock Around the Clock" — was released, it created a sensation. At Princeton University, a minor riot broke out when students blared the song from record players, prompting the school to launch an investigation. In Memphis, authorities went further, banning the movie entirely. According to the city's eighty-eight-year-old chief censor, Lloyd Binford, the problem was the intransigence: "[T]he teenagers start off bad [...] I thought they would reform. But they are just as bad at the end."[33] Binford, it should be noted, was a hard-core segregationist, who likely would have been uncomfortable with the prominent role of Black actor, Sidney Poitier, in the film. The film was also removed from the Venice Film Festival when the US Ambassador to Italy, Clare Booth Luce, said she would not attend the festival if it was screened.[34] The trouble generated by the song, however, was just beginning.

A year later, the song was included in the film *Rock Around the Clock*, which showcased Bill Haley and the Comets, along with the Platters and Alan Freed. On its release in the spring, there were numerous incidents. In Minneapolis, "youngsters marched out and snake-danced down a leading thoroughfare, breaking store windows." Similarly, "Police intervention also was necessary to quiet disorderly juveniles" in a theatre in La Crosse, Wisconsin."[35] In Newport, Rhode Island, the film was banned at the enlisted men's club after what was described as "a beer-bottle throwing, chair-swinging riot."[36]

In other parts of the world, as newspapers reported, "teen-agers have wrecked motion picture houses, assaulted policemen and danced in wild mobs through the streets."[37] On the European continent, in the Belgian town of Mons, authorities banned the film after "Youths stormed the police station with eggs and tomatoes" after police "broke up a rock 'n' roll session in the streets."[38] In Cuba, still under the pro-US dictator Fulgencio Batista, the country's Minister of Communications called the music "immoral and profane," and banned it from television.[39] Similarly, in Iran, a country four years out from a CIA coup that had removed its elected prime minister, Mohammad Mosaddegh, rock-and-roll dancing was banned as "harmful to health."[40]

In attempting to make sense of these incidents, the *Manchester Guardian* suggested that, ultimately, anthropologists might be needed to study the matter. Short of that, they mused, it could be "an echo in staider surroundings of tribal dances to the drum, or the slogans to which dervishes revolve..." before suggesting the music gave rise to "a certain amount of auto-intoxication."[41] From the distance of decades later, such commentary reads as almost satirical, and not a little racist. The concern, however, had a validity, suggesting that the force unleashed by this musical form might just get a good deal more out of hand.

Precipitous Decline

After its astonishing arrival, the first wave of rock 'n' roll receded rapidly. While the moves against Freed, law enforcement efforts, and assaults from the media played their role, several other factors conspired to knock the wind out of the phenomena.

In the case of the biggest star to emerge out of this wave, Elvis Presley suffered a more or less self-inflicted wound. In the late Fifties, Presley was draft age, subject to mandatory military service. Rather than take measures to avoid or minimize service, he chose, in 1958, to be inducted, saying it is "a duty I've got to fill, and I'm going to do it." While he continued to release pre-recorded material, it significantly diminished his presence on the pop scene at the peak of his career.[42] His stint in the military coincided with a trajectory already in play of turning Presley into a high-value commodity, particularly as a star in profitable mainstream films. The effect was decisive. A *New York Times* film critic hit things squarely when reviewing Presley's first post-Army film, 1960's *G.I. Blues*: "Whatever else the Army has done for Elvis Presley, it has taken that indecent swivel out of his hips and turned him into a good, clean, trustworthy, upstanding American young man."[43]

Another voluntary exit from rock 'n' roll was undertaken by the African-American artist Richard Penniman, aka Little Richard. Penniman had topped the charts in 1955 and 1956 with ecstatic and bawdy songs such as "Good Golly Miss Molly" and "Tutti Frutti." However, in 1957, just as he was topping the charts, he had a religious epiphany after a plane trip to Australia. As a result, he stopped doing rock 'n' roll and would not return to secular music until 1962 — at which point the music scene had fundamentally changed.[44]

Among those who exited tragically was the brilliant singer-songwriter, twenty-two-year-old Buddy Holly. Holly's career had only just begun, with hits such as "Rave On" and "Peggy Sue," when he died in February 1959, along with eighteen-year-old Latino rocker Richie Valens, in a plane crash after their show in Clear Lake, Iowa.

There were also exits due to scandal. The piano rocker Jerry Lee Lewis, who had been a major presence with songs such as "Great Balls of Fire" and "Whole Lotta Shakin' Goin' On," ran afoul of the mainstream when the twenty-two-year-old Lewis married his thirteen-year-old cousin, Myra Gale Brown. The ensuing scandal effectively ended his career until he reemerged as a country act later in the 1960s.

Similarly, Chuck Berry would be arrested in December 1959, charged under the Federal Mann Act — which makes it a crime to transport someone over state lines for the purposes of sex. In Berry's case, it involved a fourteen-year-old girl. He would serve three years in federal prison. Regardless of the disturbing nature of Berry's offense, the experience of prison had a detrimental effect on him. As singer Carl Perkins remarked, "[I] Never saw a man so changed. He had been an easygoing guy before, the kinda guy who'd jam in dressing rooms, sit and swap licks and jokes. [But] in England he was cold, real distant and bitter. I figure it was mostly [because of] jail."[45]

Disentangling the impact of personal decisions, tragic events, and repressive initiatives in the decline of the first wave of rock 'n' roll is near impossible. What is clear is that this musical movement was met with considerable hostility — tolerated only to the degree that it could reap enormous profits. This was a circumstance that would change little in the coming years.

The Folk Revival

While there was a radicalism to early rock 'n' roll, it was a radicalism more flowing from style than anything else. To the degree it supported and reinforced the burgeoning Black freedom movement — albeit unconsciously — it was quite radical. Similarly, to the degree the music had an effect at chipping away at the walls of a dominant stultifying culture, it was also subversive. That said, there was little to nothing politically radical about rock 'n' roll. True, when Elvis appeared on *The Ed Sullivan Show*, censors worked to minimize his gyrating torso out of a puritanical conservatism, but as a bold socio-political statement, it said very little.[46] This is even more true regarding the music's lyrical content, which rarely broached topics beyond love and sex, a convention that still dominates pop music.

A more complicated phenomenon existed in another cultural eruption of the late Fifties: the folk revival. Folk music came into the mid-1950s strongly tainted by its association with the Communist Party, via people such as Pete Seeger, Woody Guthrie, Alan Lomax, and others. As country singer Tex Ritter pointed out, in the late Forties and early Fifties:

At one time I called myself a folk singer. It got to the point there for a few years where it was very difficult to tell where folk music ended and Communism began. So that's when I quit calling myself a folk singer. It was the sting of death if you were trying to make a living.[47]

Of those who retained that taint were Lee Hays and Pete Seeger, who started the Weavers in 1949, along with Ronnie Gilbert and Fred Hellerman, while they were still in the Communist Party's orbit.[48] As the Forties gave way to the Fifties, they were able to move into the commercial mainstream, breaking into the top ten between 1950 and 1952 with songs such as the Lead Belly standard "Irene" and Woody Guthrie's "So Long, It's Been Good to Know You." Despite having put distance between themselves and the Communist Party, in 1952 they became targets of the Second Red Scare and were locked out of radio and the most important performance venues in the country.

Notably, they also came under fire from the left as well. In early 1952, *Sing Out!* magazine ran an editorial entitled "Can an All-White Group Sing Songs from Negro Culture?", which questioned the Weavers for doing so. Irwin Silber, editor of *Sing Out!*, followed that with a piece saying the group did "a disservice to the struggle against the blacklist by conducting their professional lives in such a way as to alienate their most powerful allies in such a struggle — the Negro people."[49] It would not be the last time that Silber, under the claim of championing equality, would point his pen at artists in a vulnerable position, who were breaking new ground, for not adhering to the narrow path he thought they should be on.

Gateway Singers Fail to Breakthrough

While the Weavers presented a challenge for the ideological strictures of the more doctrinaire on the left, a group called the Gateway Singers checked all the appropriate boxes. The group was made up of Lou Gottlieb, Travis Edmondson, Jerry Walter, and Elmerlee Thomas — an African-American woman, making them a rare mixed quartet. While the group released several records for Decca, they never broke through in the way the Weavers did.

One barrier to breaking through was CBS television's refusal to have them appear on *The Ed Sullivan Show* — reportedly because of their multi-racial makeup.[50] However, while race may have been a factor, it was likely not the only one. The group's ties to the Communist Party — Lou Gottlieb alone would accumulate a 425-page FBI file — would have made them a non-starter for a show that, as we will see, carefully vetted such things.[51]

The Gateway Singers' history also contains a troubled backstory. The singer Barbara Dane — a former Communist Party member who later married Irwin Silber — had created the group. However, she was asked to leave when others learned she was a *persona non grata*, having been expelled by the CP. In what Dane would later describe as a good amount of chutzpah, they asked her to recommend a replacement. Dane, showing considerably more dignity than her detractors, suggested Thomas.[52]

Pursuing Pete Seeger

In 1950 and 1952 respectively, the House Committee on Un-American Activities (HUAC) called blues singer Josh White and folk singer Burl Ives to testify. In White's case, they were satisfied enough by his appearance, in which he denounced communism, that they did not ask that he identify people he knew who may have been communists. In Ives's case, they were less restrained, compelling him to identify several people who attended Communist Political Association meetings with him in the mid-1940s.[53] In the same period, the Committee obtained testimony from former FBI informant Harvey Matusow, who had worked with the music popularization organization People's Songs, which had ties to the Communist Party. Matusow in turn named everyone he could who were associated with the communist folk milieu, including Fred Hellerman, Ronnie Gilbert, Lee Hays, and Pete Seeger, among others.[54] As a consequence of that testimony, Lee Hays and Pete Seeger would also be called to testify in front of HUAC, though not until 1955.

Hays, who appeared first, invoked his Fifth Amendment privilege against self-incrimination. Seeger, however, took the more adversarial tack of claiming privileges under the First Amendment. Unfortunately for him, this was not recognized by HUAC. As a result, his refusal to answer questions led to charges of contempt of Congress. This was something the FBI took note of in their voluminous file on Seeger:

> On 2/13/57 AUSA ROBERT W. BJORK, SDNY advised SA WILLIAM E. FOLKNER that the Federal Grand Jury in NYC had returned a True Bill against the subject for contempt on 2/8/57 and he expected further action in the immediate future.[55]

The crux of the government's pursuit of Seeger came down to the fact that, despite having dropped his membership in the Communist Party in 1949, he had never denounced communism. As a result, he would be pursued, both legally and in the press, well into the next decade.

Harry Belafonte

The taint of communism also followed someone on the cusp of becoming a major celebrity. Harry Belafonte would ultimately break out in 1956 with the release of his album *Calypso*, but this only happened *after* he distanced himself from former friends by going on record as standing against communism.

Belafonte's entry into the mainstream came with his appearance in 1953 on *The Ed Sullivan Show*, then known as *The Toast of the Town*. His appearance took place only after he was able to overcome accusations leveled at him in the anti-communist publication *Counterattack* — started by three former FBI agents and backed financially by the anti-communist Alfred Kohlberg[56] — in its November 11, 1951 issue. In its mention of Belafonte, they wrote that while he "may have been new to many in the TV audience," he was known "by many Communists and fellow travelers," particularly at functions of the Committee for Negro Arts — a left-wing Black advocacy group, which they described as "the Party's Negro cultural front, since the start of the Korean War."[57] Given that the Second Red Scare was at its height in 1951, this was dangerous company to be associated with.

Further complicating things for Belafonte was the fact that Ed Sullivan was a huge supporter of *Counterattack* — before becoming a staple of Sunday night television, he had been a newspaper columnist and a voracious anti-communist.[58] In advance of the 1950 publication of *Red Channels* — a report issued by *Counterattack* which listed prominent figures in radio and television with communist ties — Sullivan dedicated a column heralding its imminent release. In it, he described the report as "a bombshell" about to be "dropped into the offices of radio-TV networks." He then bragged, "the Commies and 'reliables' won't have much success in knocking down" its credibility.

Aside from hyping the report, the column revealed Sullivan as an adjunct for *Counterattack*. As he wrote, "[Ted] Kirkpatrick [the managing editor of *Counterattack*] has sat in my living room, on several occasions, and listened attentively to performers eager to secure a certification of loyalty." In other words, Sullivan was directly involved in vetting the patriotic bona fides of entertainers being judged by *Counterattack*.

All of which suggests that the story Belafonte recounts about appearing on Sullivan's show is less than candid. In his telling, he was able to convince him in a private meeting, "man to man," on why he should be allowed to appear. Writing in his memoir, he describes telling Sullivan:

> I am not a communist. But I don't need to admit that. And if someone else were to ask that I would say it is none of your business. I don't think the onus is on me — I think it's on you to explain why you feel the need to judge in this cruel and unfair way the artists you have on your show. As for me, I have a choice: stop speaking out against racism and other issues I feel strongly about, which I won't do, or accept the consequences. I'm prepared to do that.[59]

While one can appreciate Belafonte's position, and his recollection generally squares with his personal integrity, the reality was that, for him and anyone else, more would be required than simply a frank conversation. For Belafonte, or any target of *Counterattack*, to get off their list, they needed to either prove the claims were false or publicly denounce and distance themselves from communism. In that respect, Belafonte's meeting with Sullivan met some criteria in as much as he said he was not a communist, and he was able to appear on the show in 1953.

That does not, however, seem to have been the end of things. *Counterattack* again targeted Belafonte in January 1954, after which he appears to have approached them directly with a statement. It is not clear if this was oral or written, but Belafonte's views were published in the newsletter's February 12, 1954 issue. In it, Belafonte was described as "a Roman Catholic, a Negro, and an American [who] hates Communism and everything it stands for." According to the newsletter, Belafonte acknowledged some left-wing associations in the past, but made clear he would "exercise extreme care in his future associations." That appears to have been sufficient for the organization to "clear" Belafonte. His name did not come up in their newsletter again.[60]

All of which explains why there is ambiguity over Belafonte in regard to the Red Scare. While he did not appear before HUAC, or "name names," he *did* have to publicly denounce communism.

As Belafonte recalled:

> A lot of people on the left turned against me, because they thought there was no way I could get on the Sullivan show if I hadn't talked to the Committee, or whatnot. I had to live for a long time with the pain of rejection from people who were in the same camp.[61]

Here Belafonte conflates testifying in front of HUAC — which he did not do — with publicly denouncing communism through *Counterattack* ("or whatnot"), which he did. This was likely the reason some saw his behavior as disagreeable. While one can sympathize with his predicament — no one should have been put in such a position — by acceding to the terms set by the anti-communists, he gave them strength in their attacks in their repressive efforts. The point, it need be said, is not to judge

Belafonte for actions from long ago, but to underscore the pressures brought to bear and the implications of various actions taken.

The Kingston Trio

Unlike the Gateway Singers, Pete Seeger, and Harry Belafonte, the Kingston Trio arrived on the scene free of prohibitive racial or political controversies. John Stewart, Nick Reynolds, and Dave Guard — three clean-cut, smooth-singing folk musicians — started out as a white calypso act (hence the name) before transitioning to folk music. Their breakthrough came at the end of the decade with songs such as "Tom Dooley" — number one on the Billboard charts in 1958 — followed by the 1959 hit "The MTA," a satirical song about a transit hike in Boston.

The group deliberately applied lessons learned by the Weavers and Pete Seeger *to avoid* controversy. As Nick Reynolds recalled, "We decided that if we wanted to have our songs played on the airwaves, we'd better stay in the middle of the road politically."[62] This was something they did aggressively.

For example, they changed the lyrics to "The MTA" to avoid association with the Progressive Party — the song had originally been written to support their mayoral candidate, Walter A. O'Brien. They also offered a satirical spoken word intro, which further muted any political import. This made sense for them, given the song's origins, having been written by Bess Lomax and Jacqueline Steiner, the former being one of the Almanac Singers and a long-time Communist Party partisan. In their defense, Reynolds explained, "everything in those days was controversial. This was the McCarthy era. Who knows who would come knocking on your door?"[63] While such was not without truth, it was not especially brave.

Paradoxically, while the group was not willing to risk being politically controversial, they were comfortable — given it was socially acceptable — to be racist. As *New York Times* folk music critic Robert Shelton wrote in an album review, "the apogee of bad taste is their version of the Mexican song 'Coplas,'" which "degenerates into a vehicle for ridiculing Mexicans and even Chinese!" Shelton, if anything is restrained, the song being replete with mock Mexican accents and other racists tropes.[64]

On the whole, while the group's popularization of a music that would otherwise have been lost to a wider population was critically important to what would come, that they had to compromise so much in order to do so speaks to the ominous constraints in place.

Things to Come

The Kingston Trio were welcomed into the mainstream, but they would soon be joined by artists who would not compromise in similar ways and would transform the mainstream in the process. Among them was Joan Baez, who would become a key figure in the Boston folk scene. Similarly, Odetta Holmes, an African-American woman originally from Alabama who had been performing throughout the Fifties, would be building a career which would hit full flower in the ensuing decade. Also, there was Carolyn Hester, a folk singer from Texas, who gave Bob Dylan his first recording opportunity playing harmonica on her debut album.[65] And there was Dave Van Ronk, who, after a turn in the Merchant Marine, then as a jazz musician, was all in with folk music. Van Ronk would become an influencer in the larger folk scene, and as such, an essential force in what was to come.

The bellwether of all this would be the first Newport Folk Festival, conceived by George Wein as a complement to the

Newport Jazz Festival, which he began in 1954. Originally, Wein had thought to add some folk acts to the 1959 Jazz Festival, but as things developed, a full-on folk festival emerged, showcasing Odetta, Pete Seeger, the Weavers (which at that point included Erik Darling, who had replaced Seeger), Joan Baez, and the Kingston Trio. Aiding Wein in organizing the festival was Albert Grossman, who was Odetta's manager.[66] Newport would become at once an incubator and seismograph of where things stood on the cutting edge, not just of folk music, but youth-oriented popular music more broadly.

CHAPTER 2
THE GREAT FOLK SCARE (1961–1963)

I am not opposed to the wonderful symphony concerts, bands, quartets, or chamber music. What I am against is these fellows that come from miles away to display the most terrible costumes, haircuts, etc. and who play bongo drums and other weird instruments attracting a weird public.
— NYC Parks Commissioner Newbold Morris, 1963[1]

The kids should continue to sing anywhere they damn well please.
— Izzy Young[2]

Pete Seeger greeted the media the best way he knew how: by singing. The press conference, called in advance of his trial for contempt of Congress for refusing to answer the House Committee on Un-American Activities' questions, was held at New York's Park-Sheraton Hotel. While he declined to talk about the specifics of the upcoming trial, he did explain that the Committee had been curious about three of his songs. Giving the press something to write about, he proceeded to sing them: first was an *a cappella* version of the "Hammer Song," written with fellow Weaver, Lee Hays; then "Wasn't That a Time," which Congress had grilled Hays about during *his* testimony in 1955; and finally a banjo-accompanied version of Huddie "Lead Belly" Ledbetter's "Midnight Special." The press seemed duly placated, with the *New York Times* correspondent noting Seeger's rhythms "had newsmen tapping their toes."[3]

Seeger's performance for the press came at a moment when the Cold War was transforming from the hard terms set at the end of World War II into something even more complex and perilous. It was a situation that would come to impact every element of US society.

A Moment of High Danger

It is a popularly held opinion that the first years of the 1960s were a period of great hope and boundless optimism. The standard narrative holds that forty-three-year-old John F. Kennedy, the youngest ever US president, was on track to guide the country and lead the world to a far more equal, scientifically dynamic, and peaceful place. Consequently, his assassination less than three years into his presidency is seen as the signal event demarcating two Sixties: the peaceful and optimistic decade and the one beset by violence and disorder. [4] The reality, of course, is otherwise. While Kennedy was despised by elements of the political establishment, particularly on the far-right, that did not change the fact that he was a Cold Warrior of the first order. As a result, the Kennedy years were among the most dangerous in human history. Understanding this is in no small measure critical to understanding why the 1960s were what they were.

Kennedy was sworn in as President on January 20, 1961. Within weeks of assuming office, he approved a plan, initiated by his predecessor, Dwight Eisenhower, to overthrow the popular government of the island nation of Cuba. This happened after forays by the US at working with the new regime — Castro even garnered a friendly interview with Ed Sullivan in January 1959 — and it was deemed to be a threat to the United States.[5] The military scheme, which came to be known as the Bay of Pigs invasion, was a disaster from start to finish. When the invaders — CIA-trained anti-Castro Cubans — landed at la Bahía de Cochinos (the Bay of Pigs) on April 17, they immediately came under fire, with Cuban planes sinking two of their escort ships and destroying half of their air support. The operation was a military and political disaster for Kennedy and the CIA, which constructed the scheme.[6]

Events in Cuba were the backdrop for what would be the most dangerous episode of the Kennedy years: the Cuban Missile Crisis, in which the US and the USSR squared off over the Soviets deploying nuclear missiles in Cuba. It was a crisis that walked a razor's edge of nuclear war. In the end, Kennedy and Khrushchev were able to pull back from the brink, negotiating a resolution wherein the Soviets would remove their missiles, with the promise that the US would not attempt an invasion of Cuba — and with the US secretly agreeing to remove its missiles from Turkey. In this way, a nuclear exchange was avoided. Things, however, had come closer to nuclear war — where both countries would have suffered unimaginable losses — than at any other time in the nuclear era.[7]

In the wake of the crisis, both sides moved to avoid nuclear confrontation, but the standoff put a higher premium on other conflicts. This included Vietnam, where Kennedy's support of the assassination of the President of South Vietnam, Ngô Đình Diệm, on November 2, preceded his own assassination four weeks later.

While pundits and historians endlessly argue over Kennedy's relative greatness, his legacy appears to be far more problematic than conventional wisdom holds. Specifically, his administration set the stage for the escalation in Vietnam, unending efforts against Cuba, and multiple aggressions to thwart communism, from Santo Domingo to Jakarta. All of this played a huge role in the turmoil that followed.

From Old Left to a New Left

It was amid all this that China and the USSR would wholly break with one another, disrupting the world order that had been in place since 1949. On one level, the schism was doctrinal. The Chinese communists took issue with Khrushchev's policy of "peaceful coexistence," his denunciation of Stalin, and what they perceived as an accommodating view toward the West. They would later go further, claiming the USSR had restored capitalism.[8] The Soviets, in turn, defended their positions and felt the Chinese Party was unduly and harshly attacking them and undermining the unity of the world communist movement — of which *they* were the head.[9] While all this was framed in Marxist-Leninist terminology, the stakes were geopolitical — would there be one socialist bloc, or two?

The Sino-Soviet schism sharply impacted the radical left, whose small size belied its influence in setting terms and moving the goalposts in political events. When Khrushchev denounced Stalin in 1956, he precipitated a rolling crisis for the CPUSA — already under unrelenting repression from the Second Red Scare — causing multiple fractures and thousands of exits. When the smoke cleared, the Communist Party retained organizational cohesion, but it was no longer the force it had been in earlier decades. The vacuum this created laid the basis for forces to develop that were far more radical than the CPUSA had ever been. Among these was the Progressive Labor Movement, organized by former party members who had been expelled in 1961 over doctrinal differences.[10] Unlike the other split-offs from the Communist Party, Progressive Labor would come to represent the Maoist current in the US — giving it greater legitimacy than its small numbers would suggest.[11]

It would be a harbinger of other radical elements in the New Left that would come to fruition later in the decade.

Also underway was a shift toward more militancy in the Black freedom movement. Starting in July 1960, students sat in at whites-only lunch counters in Greensboro, North Carolina. In the wake of these actions would emerge the Student Non-Violent Coordinating Committee (SNCC), who would lead the Freedom Rides in 1961, traveling on segregated interstate buses into the deep South and confronting hyper-violent white supremacists.[12] While SNCC's origins were in a multinational, non-violent framework, by mid-decade their leadership was confronting those limits and was moving in more radical directions.[13]

It was also in 1962 that Students for a Democratic Society (SDS) issued a statement, named after its place of authorship: Port Huron, Michigan. Drafted in the context of an extremely dangerous period of the Cold War, it was a call for students to step into activism: "If we appear to seek the unattainable, it has been said, then let it be known that we do so to avoid the unimaginable."[14] One of the things that set SDS apart from its forebears — and this was also true of SNCC — was in its breaking with the McCarthy-era legacy in its refusal to ban communists. That measure would widen its reach but ultimately contribute to its undoing.[15] SDS was nonetheless a magnet for radical youth. Its membership, at its peak, would approach a hundred thousand, and it would be an incubator for more radical ideologies.

In short, the terms on the left in the early Sixties had altered dramatically. Largely due to Khrushchev's denunciation of Stalin, and the subsequent Sino-Soviet schism, there was no longer a formidable united communist pole, let alone a COMINTERN. In the US, that fragmentation meant that the Communist Party — while always small relative to the larger population — no longer dominated the far left. In its place was fragmentation, contention, and disorientation. All of which was baffling to those in power, most of whom were proceeding, either through ignorance or opportunism, as if things were as they had been a decade earlier. This can be seen in how they responded to the folk revival that was capturing the imagination of a new generation.

The Great Folk Scare

It was anarchist singer-songwriter Utah Phillips who coined the phrase "the Great Folk Scare," slang shorthand for the folk revival of the late Fifties and early Sixties.[16] The spirit of the term is one of ridicule, coinciding with a view that claims of communist affiliation were the ravings of an overly paranoid state. This was part of a mounting pushback against the Red Scare, which was being challenged in ways unheard of ten years earlier.

When HUAC convened hearings in San Francisco to investigate communists in California, there was organized resistance both by those called to testify and students opposed to the hearings. Things took a dramatic turn when, in an action raising images of civil right demonstrators in the Deep South, police turned fire hoses on those trying to gain entrance into the hearings, washing them down the steps of City Hall. The incident, which came to be called the "HUAC Riot" — "riot" being the misnomer used for a police attack — would lead to a HUAC-produced propaganda film titled *Operation Abolition: The Story of Communism in Action*, which cast the incident as one rife with communist provocation. However, organizers pushed back, with the ACLU producing its own account of events, portraying the police response as the reason for the violence.[17]

HUAC Chairman Edwin Wills would later complain that the San Francisco episode "was probably the worst incident in the history of the committee."[18] Unfortunately for him, it served as a signal by an emerging movement which was ready to forcefully challenge not only the committee, but a good deal else.

The "Beatnik" Riot

By the early Sixties, the folk revival that had arisen in the previous decade had become a national movement, the epicenter of which was Greenwich Village in New York. The revival brought forward an unprecedented array of artists: people such as Tom Paxton, Phil Ochs, Bob Gibson, Carolyn Hester, Dave Van Ronk, Ian and Sylvia, and, of course, Bob Dylan. Along with the professional musicians were thousands of youthful disciples, many of whom would gather in Washington Square Park. As civil disorders go, what would come to be called "the Beatnik Riot" was modest, but like the HUAC riot before it, it signaled more contentious encounters to come.

Washington Square Park had been a gathering place for folk enthusiasts since the 1940s, and the tradition had continued into the 1960s, where, on Sunday afternoons, people would come to jam, others to listen, and others just to hang out. The scene, compared to other parts of the city, was wide open — people could mix, whether Black, gay, Beat, or otherwise, and not be seen as outsiders. In the words of Village resident and author James Baldwin, it was "the place of liberation."[19] This delighted some, but annoyed and even incensed others. Among those not happy with the scene was the city's cultural commissioner Newbold Morris, who tried to ban music from the park.

Unsurprisingly, Morris's initiative was not welcomed by those using the park to play and listen to music. In response, they organized protests, with Israel "Izzy" Young — who had established a business and gathering spot for folk aficionados on MacDougal Street called The Folklore Center — and Art D'Lugoff — owner of the folk club "The Village Gate" — playing prominent roles.[20] While the city had issued permits for music since the late Forties, in 1961 they issued an internal memo changing the policy. As a result, when Young requested a permit for "folk-singing with stringed instruments" every Sunday in April, the city flatly rejected the request.[21] In response, Young and others went to the park to demonstrate. The result was several hours of confrontation. As the *Village Voice* reported, "a few of the officers reacted as if they had 1917 Union Square Bolsheviks as adversaries." What followed was a melee with police knocking down demonstrators, amid "shoving, kicking, and wrestling." The police would end up arresting ten people. At least twenty were injured, including three police officers.[22]

The incident was covered in the New York press, who denounced the protesters and defended the police with blaring headlines, such as the *New York Times*, "FOLK SINGERS RIOT IN WASHINGTON SQ.," and the *New York Mirror,* "2000 BEATNIKS RIOT IN VILLAGE."[23] According to the *Times*, "at the height of the battle, hundreds of young people, many of the boys with beards or banjos and many of the girls with long hair and guitars, fought with fifty police across the square."[24] This image of bearded beatniks was echoed by New York University professor F. Thrasher, who criticized the singing in the park by a "degenerate beatnik rabble," with "absolutely NO regard for the moralities of normal, decent people." Charles Rao, president of an Italian-American organization in the Village, offered praise to Newbold's repressive initiative: "[W]e wish to compliment you in the action to do away with the ridiculous display of beatnicks [*sic*] in Washington Square Park which degrades this fine community."[25]

Despite such support, the protests continued, leading to

a court ruling in July by the Appellate Division of the State Supreme Court, which struck down an earlier decision which had upheld the ban. As a result, the city was forced to back off. New York Mayor Robert Wagner agreed to let singing continue, though "on a controlled basis," that being between 3 and 6pm on Sundays, and then only in a certain section of the park.[26]

On a surface level, the issue in Washington Square was a matter of a public space colliding with residential sensibilities. But what made it more than that was the specific targeting of folk music, Beat sensibility, the mixing of people of different colors and backgrounds, and the assemblage's disregard for mainstream conventions. In that respect, it was an opening skirmish in what would later become fierce contention between the mainstream and a counterculture.

Seeger on Trial

While the Communist Party USA was not the threat it had been when its members had numbered in the tens of thousands, it remained anathema, a group with a hostile ideology seen as an agent of a foreign power.[27] Which explains why Pete Seeger, no longer a party member, but someone who refused to denounce the party, was pursued legally.

In March 1961, Seeger finally came to trial for his refusal in 1955 to answer the questions of the House Un-American Activities Committee.[28] Seeger, rather than invoking his Fifth Amendment privilege against self-incrimination, argued that as an American, he could not be forced to answer questions he did not want to. As he told the Committee, "I do not want to in any way discredit or depreciate or depredate the witnesses that have used the fifth amendment [...] I simply feel it is improper for this committee to ask such questions."[29] Had he invoked the Fifth, he likely would not have faced legal action — though doing so carried the inference of guilt, true or otherwise.

All of which resulted in a trial in March 1961.[30] Seeger maintained the same position he had in 1955. When speaking to the press a week before the trial, he said, "I feel that I have never done anything of a conspiratorial nature and I resented being called before the committee just because my opinions differed." Given such a view, he did not fare well. After a three-day trial, he was convicted on all ten contempt charges. He was then sentenced to a year in prison.[31]

The hostility of the court toward Seeger was apparent at sentencing. The judge, assuming the role of HUAC interrogator, asked him, "Would you want to tell me now, if you are or have ever been a member of the Communist Party?" When Seeger declined, the judge denied bail and remanded him into custody. It was only because of a ruling by the Appeals Court that Seeger was allowed to remain free while he awaited a further hearing.[32] Free or not, he was still blacklisted. Soon after the conviction, WQED in Pittsburgh canceled a performance he was to give to children.[33]

Fortunately for Seeger, however, elements of the Red Scare were beginning to thaw. A year after his conviction, the US Court of Appeals overturned the decision on a technicality, due to the fact that the indictment did not correctly define the authority of the subcommittee to conduct the hearings. In their ruling, they said:

He did not rely on the Fifth Amendment but couched his refusals in terms of "improper" and "immoral." His irrelevant self-serving replies were more than obvious because no one had asked him concerning his religious or political beliefs or how he had voted in an election. However, these answers probably come forth from a (in my opinion only misguided) personal conception of private rights rather than from a desire to be contemptuous of his country or the subcommittee.[34]

In the Court's view, "Seeger was a layman whose mind might well have been concentrating on new songs rather than new legislative enactments."[35] The result was that Seeger's legal troubles were largely behind him, but this did not mean he was welcome again in certain influential quarters.

Hootenanny

Working to capitalize on the folk music craze, ABC television launched a musical variety show in April 1963 called *Hootenanny*, showcasing artists such as the Chad Mitchell Trio, Judy Collins, Ian and Sylvia, and a good many others. While the show was willing to embrace the folk music trend, it drew the line when it came to allowing Pete Seeger to perform on his own terms. As the *New York Times* described, "Television's belated interest in folk singing, however, is accompanied by one disquieting note. Apparently, Pete Seeger's private political concerns continue to keep him off all network shows of folk singers."[36] Seeger, who, arguably more than anyone who would appear on the show, was key to the folk revival, was being kept off *Hootenanny* because of his political background. As a result, some artists, such as Bob Dylan, Dave Van Ronk, and the Kingston Trio, boycotted the show — though Seeger himself encouraged people to seize the opportunity to appear.[37]

There was in this a certain complexity — though not much of one. Given Seeger was no longer facing charges, ABC agreed to consider his appearing, but only if he signed a "sworn affidavit as to his past and present affiliations." In other words, much like HUAC and the judge in his trial, they were once again asking, "Are you now or have you ever been a member of the Communist Party?"[38] His FBI file includes the details:

> The April 16, 1963 edition of "The Worker" contained an article which reflected that the subject was being "blacklisted" by the American Broadcasting Company (ABC) Television Show "Hootenanny," scheduled to debut on April 6, 1963, for refusing to sign the "regular television Loyalty Oath." This article described the "Television Loyalty oath" as an anti-communist loyalty oath, and further stated that "the anti-Communist loyalty oath questioning of performers and blacklisting those who dare to uphold their liberties as guaranteed by the Bill of Rights, is based on the old McCarthy dodge of ferreting out "Communists" among folk singers.[39]

Seeger would not appear on national television for another six years.

Trouble for the Chad Mitchell Trio

Unlike Seeger, the Chad Mitchell Trio, whose lineup in 1963 was Chad Mitchell, Joe Frazier, and Mike Kobluk — later iterations would include John Denver — did not carry the stigma of past communist affiliations. They did, however, write songs of biting satire, including one about the John Birch Society — an anti-communist, far-right political advocacy group — with the inimitable line: "Fighting for the right to fight the right fight for the Right." During their performance at Chicago's Drake Hotel, a patron, Harold W. Simpson, took issue with the group's song "Alma Mater," which ridiculed the racist governor of Mississippi, Ross Barnett. When Simpson took a swing at Frazier, a scuffle ensued, but the hotel refused to call police on someone considered a prominent socialite. When the group then stopped their show, and canceled their remaining two performances at the hotel, they called the police on the man. When cops arrived, Simpson then started throwing things at the group, and was arrested. Once in custody, he then had Frazier arrested on a cross-complaint. While both were quickly bailed out, it underscored the volatility of a certain kind of song.[40]

Watching Dave Van Ronk

Whether branded communist or not, the fact was that most of the artists in the folk revival were not members of any left-wing organizations. Such, however, was not the case with Dave Van Ronk, who, because of his political affiliations, was a longtime subject for the FBI. Van Ronk first appears in their files in 1958 as a member of the Young Socialist League, then affiliated with the Socialist Party. His file then traces his subsequent membership in the Socialist Workers Party (SWP) and then the Workers League — two Trotskyist entities.[41]

While a highly political person, Van Ronk did not do "protest songs." This was not out of any abiding principle, but for aesthetic reasons. As he wrote, "It did not suit my style, and I never felt that I did it convincingly." All of which is ironic, because in contrast to people such as Bob Dylan and Phil Ochs, who were not in such organizations, and whose repertoire included a good deal of overtly political music, Van Ronk *was* part of the organized left.

It was these politics that drove the FBI to him. While Bureau reporting on Van Ronk in the late Fifties is sparse, it picks up considerably in the early 1960s. For example, after the FBI received a report on an SWP branch meeting in St. Louis, one of the members — an informant — describes an encounter with Van Ronk.

[He] said that he had been in recent contact with a singer who was making an appearance in St. Louis' Gaslight Square. His last name was RONK or RUNK. He was a young man from New York City who obviously represented the minority voice of the SWP as he was rather critical of FARRELL DOBBS, [a leader of the SWP]. He seemed to feel that the SWP should do more insofar as infiltration of union organizations.[42]

While the identity of the informant is unknown, what is striking is the level of coverage — the FBI having unique insight, not only into the SWP, but also into Van Ronk's travels and specific political views.

Dave Van Ronk, 1962
Credit: Van Ronk FBI File

File No. 100-136446-7&5

Date Received 2/7/63

From _____
(Name of Contributor)

_____
(Address of Contributor)

By John E. HEGARTY
(Name of Special Agent)

To Be Returned   Yes ☐
                  No ☒

—3 to SI unit

Description:
photographs of
DAVID VAN RONK taken
at am SWP election Rally
held on 11/26/62 at Central
Plaza, NY, NY.

SEARCHED ....INDI
SERIALIZED ....FILED

Credit: Van Ronk FBI File

47

Van Ronk's tenure in the SWP would be relatively brief. As his file explains, he was part of a faction — called the [Tim] Wohlforth Group — that felt the SWP was not sufficiently radical. As a result, they were expelled. Those who left, including Van Ronk, went on to form the American Committee of the Fourth International, which would later become the Workers League.

While Van Ronk's SWP membership was brief, the interest the FBI had in him was not — his SWP membership led him to being added to the Bureau's Security Index, which was essentially a preventative detention list. This happened in the spring of 1963, and he would remain on that list into the Seventies, when the Security Index was renamed the Administrative Index (ADEX).[43]

The Lost Seaman's Papers

Van Ronk's Trotskyist affiliations would impact him in ways both seen and unseen. Perhaps the sharpest example is in his decision to not pursue a career as a merchant seaman.

In the film *Inside Llewyn Davis,* modeled loosely on Van Ronk's life, there is a plot line involving the lead character's attempt to renew his union card so he could work again in the Merchant Marine, only to discover his papers have been thrown out. That story was derived from Van Ronk's experience of being robbed and having his seaman's papers stolen. According to Van Ronk, he decided to forego replacing the documents — and give all his energy to folk singing — because "It might take six months or a year before I could get a new set and ship out again [...] Furthermore, with my politics and all my Commie friends, it had been a small miracle I was given them at all."[44]

TREASURY DEPARTME
UNITED STATES COAST GUARD

ADDRESS REPLY TO:
COMMANDANT
U.S. COAST GUARD
HEADQUARTERS
WASHINGTON 25, D.C.

ƆIN
Ser: 0112
11 July 1963

Honorable J. Edgar Hoover
Director, Federal Bureau of Investigation
Washington 25, D. C.

Attention Liaison Section

Dear Mr. Hoover:

The below named Subject is a holder of a U. S. Merchant Mariner's
Document issued pursuant to Executive Order 10173, as amended, and
Parts 6 and 121, Title 33, Code of Federal Regulations. As files
of your Bureau reflect information which may indicate the desirability of denying Subject a document through the hearing procedures of
33 CFR 121.19, it is requested that the Coast Guard be advised, if
possible, of the identity of the informants referenced in the enclosure
hereto, and further, if your Bureau would interpose an objection to the
Coast Guard interviewing any identified informant.

SUBJECT: VAN RONK, David Ritz
D&POB: 6/30/36, Brooklyn, N. Y.
FBI NO. 100-136446

Sincerely yours,

LCDR, U. S. Coast Guard
Acting Chief, Intelligence Division
By direction of the Commandant

Encl: (1) Availabilities
      (2 copies)

REC- 22 100.449146-5

EX.-112

10 JUL 1963

*Letter from the head of Coast Guard Intelligence regarding
denying Dave Van Ronk replacement seamen's papers*

Van Ronk's misgivings were well-founded. One of the things the Bureau did in researching Van Ronk's background was to review his recorded work. In doing so, they learned, "Subject has made several record albums. The cover of one of the albums reflects that subject in the past has been a merchant seaman."[45] Discovering this, they passed the information on to the Coast Guard's Intelligence Division, who in turn asked FBI head J. Edgar Hoover if he might supply witnesses who could testify to the "desirability of denying Subject a document through hearing procedure."[46] Hoover obligingly responded by offering the services of the Special Agent who "observed the subject [Van Ronk] entering the SWP headquarters."[47]

In the end, there was no hearing, only because Van Ronk had moved on. However, his apprehension about being able to get replacement papers, because of his political background, was well grounded — it is quite likely he would have been denied. In that sense, it was the US government that pushed him in the direction of being a lifelong folk singer.

The Hammer Song

The larger problem in the efforts by the FBI and others to proscribe any communist taint from US society was that the folk revival was so popular that it was manifesting itself firmly in mainstream culture — evidence of which comes through in a scheme by Bob Dylan's manager Albert Grossman.

In 1961, Grossman approached Van Ronk with a proposal. As he recalled:

> Albert had taken a good long look at the Weavers clones in their preppy outfits, and he decided there was an opening for a group that was hipper than that — more musically

sophisticated, with a contemporary feel — so he was scouting local talent with this in mind. One day we ran into each other on MacDougal, and he said he had a proposition for me: he was putting together a trio, and he had two people already, and he needed a third."[48]

That group turned out to be Peter, Paul and Mary, consisting of Peter Yarrow, Mary Travers and Noel "Paul" Stuckey, who filled the spot that Van Ronk declined. It is left for speculation what political and musical controversy Peter, Dave, and Mary might have produced.

As things turned out, one of the hits the group had was a version of the Weavers' "Hammer Song" — a Seeger-Lee Hays composition written in the heat of the first Smith Act trial of eleven communist leaders in 1949.[49] (Trini Lopez also had a hit with a rock 'n' roll version of the song a year later.[50]) One can only imagine the consternation of the anti-communists at seeing such a pariah song — albeit one that, in the early Sixties, spoke more to the civil rights movement than the anti-communist Smith Act — in the top ten. That said, they would soon have far more songs to worry about than those passed down from the 1940s.

CHAPTER 3
THE UNWELCOME ARRIVAL OF BOB DYLAN
(1963–1964)

A song satirizing the John Birch Society was barred from Ed Sullivan's television show on Sunday night by the Columbia Broadcasting System, which said it was controversial.
— *New York Times*, May 1963[1]

No one can say anything honest in the United States. Every place you look is cluttered with phonies and lies.
— Bob Dylan, 1963[2]

When Bob Dylan released his breakthrough album, *The Freewheelin' Bob Dylan,* in May 1963, many saw it as a revelation. Others, however, saw it as a problem. Depending on how one saw the arrival of Dylan says a lot about where someone would fall out as the disruptions and dislocations of the 1960s unfolded. Ironically, Dylan himself would not be radically engaged in the most incendiary years of the decade he helped define, his most radical period occupying just over thirty-eight months from the release of *Freewheelin'* to his motorcycle accident in July 1966. Regardless, his arrival said much about not only how Dylan was seen by the guardians of American culture, but how they would respond to those who followed him.

The origin myth of Bob Dylan reads something like this. He arrived in New York City in the cold of the winter of 1961, paid a pilgrimage to the hospital where his then idol Woody Guthrie was slowly dying of Huntington's Chorea, proceeded to busk and hustle his way through the Greenwich Village folk scene before being discovered by *New York Times* folk music critic Robert Shelton, and was then picked up by legendary Columbia music producer John Hammond, who worked with Dylan on his first, and unremarkable, eponymous record, before striking gold in 1963 with the breakout masterpiece, *The Freewheelin' Bob Dylan*, soon after becoming a living legend who continues to occupy the pop consciousness of millions. All of which is true, plus or minus a few details, but something essential is missing. Bob Dylan arrived on the scene amid the red-hot embers of the Second Red Scare, and he was, for a time, part and parcel of a left-inclined resurgence in music that was relentlessly opposed by the powers that be. If, in the end, Dylan made his way through to the mainstream, he did so by leaving aside overt political controversies for more nuanced ones.

At the moment "he became," however, there was no small amount of energy directed at keeping him marginalized. That he was ultimately not constrained is testament not only to his extraordinary talent, but to the social tumult that allowed him to realize his genius.

Dylan Comes to New York

Dylan, nineteen years old, arrived in New York in January 1961. His first years in the city brought him into intimate contact with the Old Left, with people such as former Communist Party members Woody Guthrie, Pete Seeger, Sis Cunningham, and Gordon Friesen, and the then-Trotskyists Dave Van Ronk and Terri Thal. In late 1961, Dylan's breakthrough came with his meeting John Hammond, who had already caught his eye in the studio where the young Dylan was playing harmonica for the Texas folk artist Carolyn Hester.[3]

Things vaulted ahead further when *New York Times* critic Robert Shelton reviewed Dylan's performance at Gerdes Folk City. In a review titled "Bob Dylan: A Distinctive Folk Song Stylist," Shelton wrote that "his music-making has the mark of originality and inspiration."[4] For an unknown folk singer in the crowded environment of the early 1960s Greenwich Village folk scene, Shelton's review was akin to turning a high-voltage floodlight on Dylan.

Shelton himself was a curious character, having an unclear relationship to the Old Left. In 1956, he was called to testify in front of the Senate about his communist affiliations. The problem was that the Senate was actually looking for a Willard Shelton, who also worked at the *New York Times*. Despite the mistake, Shelton refused to cooperate, garnering a contempt citation. He would spend many years contesting the charge, and faced prison, before the matter was finally dropped.[5] While the exact reasons for his decision to not cooperate are unclear, his failure to do so, in the face of imprisonment, speaks volumes about his adherence to principles.

Freewheelin'

Despite Shelton's review and Hammond's support, it was not until 1963 that Dylan fully arrived on the national scene with *Freewheelin'*, which contained the classic "protests songs" — the popular moniker attached to any music of social criticism — "Blowin' in the Wind," "Masters of War," "Oxford Town," "Talking World War III Blues" and "A Hard Rain's A-Gonna Fall." The album also included quite a bit else, including the love songs "Don't Think Twice, It's All Right," and "Girl from the North Country." More than a few of these would become classics, most notably "Blowin' in the Wind," when Peter, Paul and Mary — the group created by Dylan's manager, Albert Grossman — had a hit with the song that same year.

What happened to Dylan's political sensibilities between his first album, whose only trace of politics was in "Song to Woody," his paean to Woody Guthrie, and the second, is a matter of conjecture — though it was a period where he began writing his own songs at a feverish pace, upending in the process what his peers in the folk milieu thought possible. In that regard, Ian Tyson tells of how "Dylan came running in one day in about 1962 and he said, 'Hey, you've got to hear this great song I've written,' and we said 'Written? What do you mean written? Everybody thought he was nuts. You don't write folk music.'"[6]

That aside, what is known is that he was surrounded by highly political people trying to influence his thinking. For example, Dave Van Ronk — who Dylan was close to in this period — has said:

> I was always trying to recruit him, but Bobby was not really a political person. He was thought of as being a political person and a man of the Left, and in a general sort of way, yes, he was, but he was not interested in the true nature of the Soviet Union or any of that crap. We thought he was hopelessly politically naïve, but in retrospect he may have been more sophisticated than we were [laughs ironically].[7]

Van Ronk's explanation is helpful as far as it goes, but a comment by Sylvia Tyson offers insight into the influence his peers exerted on him:

The thing most people don't realize about Bob Dylan is that he has a kind of photographic memory for things. He literally remembers everything he's ever heard or seen. I've had him recall conversations we had a year earlier word for word. So he has a wealth of material to draw from in his songwriting. It's how he gleans from this, how he synthesizes all this, how he put it together that is his real talent.[8]

For a brief while, Dylan was immersed within a very political crowd — by choice — and that could not but have had a profound impact on how, and what, he chose to write about.

Among this circle was his girlfriend, Susan Elisabeth "Suze" Rotolo. Rotolo was the daughter of Mary and Gioachino Pietro (known as "Joachim" or "Pete") Rotolo, both of whom had been active with the Communist Party USA. As such, they all were subject to significant FBI attention. Rotolo landed on the Bureau's radar because of her participation in a youth group called Advance, the forerunner of the Communist Party's "DuBois Clubs" — named after W.E.B. Du Bois. It was because of such ties that the Bureau flagged her when she applied for a passport to travel to Italy with her mother in early 1961, several months before she met Dylan.

Rotolo herself was never a member of the CP, as she explained, "I knew I could never sign on to any political organization. It wasn't in my nature to follow a party line. I would participate, but I would never join anything."[9] So while she would work with a group like Advance, she was not a cadre in a Marxist-Leninist organization.[10] But member or not, her associations drew the FBI's attention and they would maintain a file on her throughout the 1960s. It was not, however, just Rotolo who garnered attention.

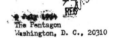

The Pentagon
Washington, D. C., 20310

I, ⬛⬛⬛⬛⬛ born ⬛⬛⬛ at St. Louis, Missouri, a resident of ⬛⬛⬛⬛⬛⬛⬛⬛⬛⬛⬛⬛⬛⬛⬛⬛⬛⬛ presently assigned as Special Agent, FBI Sub-Section, Operations/Administration Section, Investigations Desk, Counterintelligence Branch, Security Division, Assistant Chief of Staff for Intelligence, Department of the Army, The Pentagon, Room MB 870, do freely and voluntarily, without promise of benefit or threat or use of force or coercion, proceed under oath to state the following:

On 7 July 1964, while performing my normal duties of reading FBI reports for Investigations Desk, I was reading an FBI Letter to the Director, Bureau of Intelligence and Research, Department of State, dated 2 July 1964, Subject: Student Committee for Travel to Cuba, when I found mentioned in this letter, one Susan Elizabeth Rotolo, born 20 November 1943 in New York City, New York, residing at 106 Avenue B, New York, New York, previously residing at 263 West End Avenue, New York, New York, a theater designer.

Susan Rotolo is the ⬛⬛⬛⬛⬛⬛⬛⬛⬛⬛⬛⬛⬛⬛ nee ⬛⬛⬛ on her mother's side. My wife was fairly close to Susan Rotolo up to about 1956. During the last five years my wife and I have not seen Susan Rotolo at all. Three of those years we spent in Berlin, Germany, where I was assigned with the United States Army. In 1962, before we returned to the United States, while we were residing in Berlin, we received a letter from Susan Rotolo who was then attending school in Italy. We did not reply to her letter. We have had no contact with Susan Rotolo since our return from Berlin in November 1962.

Last year we heard, through family channels, that Susan Rotolo was dating Bob Dylan, the folk singer. In 1963 Columbia Records issued a Bob Dylan recording, and Susan Rotolo appears in a photograph with Dylan on the jacket cover. Since Christmas, 1963, Susan Rotolo has allegedly broken off her relationship with Dylan, according to members of my wife's immediate family.

Prior to my departure for Germany in September 1959, I saw Susan Rotolo occasionally during short visits to her family's home, then in Jackson Heights, Queens, New York, New York. My wife and I, while we were hunting for an apartment in New York during the Summer of 1958, stayed with Susan Rotolo's family for a few days, but, to the best of my knowledge, Susan Rotolo was away at a summer camp. I first met Susan Rotolo in the Summer of 1956, during a short weekend visit in New York. At that time I was attending Boston University, Boston, Massachusetts.

I was married in February, 1957. We resided in New York City from June 1957 until approximately March 1958. We occasionally visited with Susan Rotolo and her family. I saw her for the last time around March 1958. My wife possibly saw her during the 1959 Christmas holidays before leaving to join me in Berlin.

My wife's family considers Susan Rotolo something of a beatnik. She returned from Italy sometime in 1963. Since then she has either resided alone or with her older sister, ⬛⬛⬛⬛⬛⬛⬛ Susan Rotolo is a theater scene designer.

0 JUL 24 1964

FBI report on Suze Rotolo's relationship with Bob Dylan

Because of her FBI monitoring, we know Bob Dylan was also on the Bureau's radar — in entries such as "during 1963, the subject [Suze Rotolo] frequently associated with Robert Dylan, a folksinger." Dylan is also mentioned in regard to the *Freewheelin'* cover, with its iconic image of Dylan and Suze walking in the February chill on Greenwich Village's Jones Street. An affidavit from July 1964, by an employee of the Department of the Army — defined as being "presently assigned as an FBI special agent" — describes how he came across Rotolo's name while going through FBI documents. He in turn submitted a report to the Bureau, writing, "my wife was fairly close to Susan Rotolo up to about 1956." He then tells of how:

> [L]ast year we heard, through family channels that Susan Rotolo was dating Bob Dylan, the folk singer. In 1963 Columbia Records issued a Bob Dylan recording, [*Freewheelin'*] and Susan Rotolo appears in a photograph with Dylan on the jacket cover.[11]

The agent's report closed, noting that, "according to my wife's immediate family," Rotolo "has allegedly broken off her relationship with Dylan." All of which is instructive as to the myriad ways the FBI was gathering intelligence, first by having a "liaison" agent working within Military Intelligence, then by the serendipity of family connections.

Rotolo's file would eventually grow to 174 pages — modest by FBI standards, but voluminous given how little it was predicated on. It would remain open until 1974.

The FBI Hootenanny Hopping

While Dylan is referenced multiple times in Rotolo's file, he does not show up in Dave Van Ronk's — though the two were close in that period. The file does, however, show the FBI visiting the club where both Dylan and Van Ronk performed:

> On 2-6-63 inquiry was made at Gerdes Folk City 11 W. 4th St., NYC re subject. It was ascertained that subject was not currently appearing nor scheduled to appear in the near future. However, subject has appeared as a Folk Singer at that establishment in the past.[12]

In similar fashion, the Bureau reported, "On 12/13/63, REDACTED who has furnished reliable information in the past, personally provided a written statement to SA REDACTED," which described a benefit in Philadelphia for the miners of Hazard Kentucky where the "folk singers were: Phil Ochs and REDACTED."[13]

That the Bureau was poking around in Philadelphia and at a Village nightclub in pursuit of Ochs and Van Ronk is rather astonishing. That said, by the end of the year, the FBI would open a file on Dylan himself.

The Ed Sullivan Show

While Dylan was crossing the FBI's radar, if vicariously, he came under direct targeting in the private sphere. This occurred when he sought to perform his song ridiculing the ultra-right — "Talkin' John Birch Paranoid Blues" — on *The Ed Sullivan Show*, which he had been slotted to appear on following the strength of the Shelton review and imminent release of *Freewheelin'*. Unfortunately, the powers that be at CBS took issue with his choice.[14] After a successful rehearsal, Dylan was told by Sullivan's son-in-law, Bob Precht, that he would have to choose another song. Dylan was uncompromising, responding, "No; this is what I want to do. If I can't play my song, I'd rather not appear on the show."[15]

While press reports attribute the decision to ban the song to television censors, there was likely more going on in the background, not the least of which was Sullivan's track record as an aggressive anti-communist. It is hard to imagine Sullivan, and those of his mindset, not being put off by a song that mercilessly ridiculed anti-communism. This might also explain why, while it was reported Dylan would be asked back later, he never appeared on the show.[16]

This incident, in turn, impacted the imminent release of *Freewheelin'*. In the wake of the controversy, lawyers at Columbia Records, which was owned by CBS — concerned about a libel suit from the right-wing organization — instructed that the song be pulled, despite the fact that copies had already gone out. Regardless, the record company ordered a new pressing, removing it from the album.[17] It would only make an official release in 1991, when Dylan's first "bootleg" set included a version from his Carnegie Hall performance of October 1963. In introducing the song, Dylan angrily tells the audience, "There ain't nothin' wrong with this song."[18]

Black Freedom

Dylan's year of wading into deep political waters was just getting started. In July he was warmly welcomed at the Newport Folk Festival, where, among other things, he sang, "With God on Their Side" in a duet with Joan Baez. The show closed with Dylan, Baez, Pete Seeger, Peter, Paul and Mary, and the Freedom Singers on stage to perform "We Shall Overcome."

The Freedom Singers (Bernice Johnson, Rutha Harris, and Charles Neblett) were a fund-raising group for SNCC, composed of members who had been involved in the civil rights struggle in Albany, Georgia — where, from the fall of 1961 to the summer of 1962, activists confronted the Jim Crow power structure. Freedom Singer member Cordell Reagon described how the songs they developed in that period, such as "Ain't Gonna Let Nobody Turn Me 'Round" and "Oh Freedom," "became a major way of making people who were not on the scene feel the intensity of what was happening in the South."[19]

Following Newport, Dylan performed "When the Ship Comes In" — with the enemies of justice being "drowned in the tide" — at the March on Washington in August. He also performed "Only a Pawn in Their Game," about the murder of civil rights worker Medgar Evers, as told, provocatively, from the stand of the white man who killed him."[20] The performance came amid his recording *The Times They Are A-Changin'*, which was to be the peak of Dylan's phase as a "protest singer."

Joan Baez and Bob Dylan at the 1963 March on Washington
Credit: Rowland Scherman — US National Archives & Records Administration

Broadside... *Newsweek*

While Dylan was not allowed to perform "Talkin' John Birch" on *The Ed Sullivan Show,* and as such was not then able make his debut in front of a national television audience, *Newsweek* magazine ran a feature on him in their November 4, 1963 issue. The article was a high-profile hit piece. Its opening set the tone:

> He sticks his skinny frame into blue jeans and wrinkled shirts, and he talks hip talk, punctuated by obscenities. His singing voice scratches and shouts so jarringly that his success, at first, seems incredible.[21]

It then proceeded to debunk claims Dylan was estranged from his parents and revealed his birth name as Robert Zimmerman. The article also made clear, contrary to what Dylan told Oscar Brand in a radio interview, that he was not "raised in Gallup, New Mexico." Nor had he "traveled in the carnival since he was 13 years old..."[22]

The magazine was essentially on a mission to let the American public know the artist was projecting a biography more fanciful than real — an issue, it should be said, which was of far less importance than the music he was producing. *Newsweek*, however, was merciless:

> Why Dylan — he picked the name in admiration for Dylan Thomas — should bother to deny his past is a mystery. Perhaps he feels it would spoil the image he works so hard to cultivate — with his dress, with his talk, with the deliberately atrocious grammar and pronunciation in his songs.

But the article saved its most consequential attack for last. Citing "a rumor," they wrote that Dylan did not write

"Blowin' in the Wind." At the time, the song was a major hit for Peter, Paul and Mary and, in the words of Robert Shelton, was "probably the most artistic and certainly the most popular" of songs Shelton called "Northern freedom songs."[23] *Newsweek* instead suggested the song was written by a New Jersey high school student. In their telling, "several Millburn students claim they heard the song from [the student Lorre] Wyatt before Dylan ever sang it."[24] Such hearsay was the thin evidence sent out nationwide. It was a potentially career-ruining slur.

The consequences were immediate. According to Robert Shelton, the article "threw Dylan into a depression for months [and] resulted in him breaking off nearly all contact with his parents and brother for years." It also "turned [Dylan] from an accessible subject into a cagey game-player who toyed with interview questions, who developed the outrageous 'anti-interview,' saying shocking, even deleterious things, things he often didn't believe."[25]

While the line Shelton draws between the *Newsweek* article and Dylan's later behavior is debatable, if not easily dismissed, it serves as a marker for the contentious two-and-a-half-year period which followed, one that resolved in Dylan's retreating from the public stage for the most tumultuous years of the Sixties.

The Kennedy Assassination

On November 22, little more than two weeks after the *Newsweek* article, John F. Kennedy was assassinated in Dallas. On December 13, Bob Dylan received an award from the Emergency Civil Rights Committee. Things did not go well.

Problems arose when Dylan, who had been drinking throughout the ceremony, gave a rambling acceptance speech that reads more as an out-loud, unfiltered internal monologue, rather than a thought-through statement of views, let alone the expected thank you at an awards ceremony. In part, he said:

> So, I accept this reward — not reward *[laughter]*, award on behalf of Phillip Luce who led the group to Cuba which all people should go down to Cuba. I don't see why anybody can't go to Cuba. I don't see what's going to hurt by going any place. I don't know what's going to hurt anybody's eyes to see anything. On the other hand, Phillip is a friend of mine who went to Cuba. I'll stand up and to get uncompromisable about it, which I have to be to be honest, I just got to be, as I got to admit that the man who shot President Kennedy, Lee Oswald, I don't know exactly where — what he thought he was doing, but I got to admit honestly that I too — I saw some of myself in him. I don't think it would have gone — I don't think it could go that far. But I got to stand up and say I saw things that he felt, in me — not to go that far and shoot. *[Boos and hisses]*

Before ending his remarks, he scolded the crowd for booing, "Bill of Rights is free speech," and saying he accepted the award "on behalf of James Forman of the Student Non-Violent Coordinating Committee and on behalf of the people who went to Cuba." That too was met with boos as well as applause.[26]

UNITED STATES DEPARTMENT OF JUSTICE

FEDERAL BUREAU OF INVESTIGATION

New York, New York
December 30, 1964

In Reply, Please Refer to
File No.
BuFile 100-435482
NYfile 100-144460

DECLASSIFICATION AUTHORITY DERIVED FROM:
FBI AUTOMATIC DECLASSIFICATION GUIDE
DATE 04-07-2011

Re: Susan Elisabeth Rotolo

Susan Elisabeth Rotolo, who is also known as Sue Rotolo, Susyn Rotolo, Susan Elizabeth Rotolo, and Susan Justine Rotolo, was born November 20, 1943, at Brooklyn, New York, to Joachim Rotolo and Mary Pezzati. She resides in apartment 4A at 106 Avenue B, New York, New York. She is occupied as a freelance artist, student, and theater scene designer. The subject completed high school in New York City in 1960, attended the New School For Social Research in New York City during 1962, and also enrolled in the Academy of DeBell Art at Perugia, Italy, in 1962. During 1963 and 1964, she attended sporadically at the School of Visual Arts, 209 East 23rd Street, New York, New York.

Rotolo is described as a white female, five feet six to seven inches tall, approximately one hundred and ten pounds, long light brown hair, and is single. She usually appears in the style of an unkempt "beatnik" type. She has traveled abroad on U.S. Passport number B-135413.

In answer to an inquiry directed to her by the School of Visual Arts seeking an explanation for her frequent absences from classes in 1963 and 1964, the subject replied to the questionnaire by saying that she had been absent frequently because she was "mentally unbalanced", and indicated that she would try to do better.

Confidential sources, who have furnished reliable information in the past, have advised as follows regarding the subject:

Copy to S S N Y
by routing slip for
☒ info ☒ action
date
by

100-43-482-
RECD 358

DEC 31 1964

This document contains neither
recommendations nor conclusions
of the FBI. It is the property
of the FBI and is loaned to your
agency; it and its contents are
not to be distributed outside

69 JAN 6 1965

65

During 1958, the subject attended Camp Kinderland. At that time, her father was deceased, and her mother, Mary, a member of the Communist Party sometime during the period of 1939 to 1951, was listed as her guardian.

> A characterization of Camp
> Kinderland appears in the
> Appendix hereto.

During 1959, the subject was a girlfriend of Eugene Dennis, Jr., son of Eugene Dennis, then publicly known as National Secretary of the Communist Party, USA.

In 1961, the subject's name and address appeared on a list maintained by the headquarters of Advance Youth Organization, 82 Second Avenue, New York, New York.

> A characterization of Advance
> Youth Organization appears in
> the Appendix hereto.

During 1963, the subject frequently associated with Robert Dylan, a folksinger.

> Robert Dylan, self-employed as a
> folksinger, appeared on December
> 13, 1963, at the 10th Annual Bill
> of Rights Dinner held by the
> Emergency Civil Liberties Committee
> (ECLC), at the Americana Hotel, New
> York City. At this dinner, Dylan re-
> ceived the Tom Paine Award given each
> year by the ECLC to the "foremost
> fighter for civil liberties". In his
> acceptance speech, Dylan said that he
> agreed in part with Lee Harvey Oswald
> and thought that he understood Oswald,
> but would not have gone as far as
> Oswald did.

> A characterization of the ECLC
> appears in the Appendix hereto.

In June, 1964, the subject, as a member of a group known as the Student Committee For Travel to Cuba (SCTC), departed from New York and traveled to Cuba in defiance of U.S. Government travel restrictions. She returned from Cuba on August 14, 1964, and has since made statements to the press

in praise of the Cuban Government. The subject has continued her activities in the SCTC and related activity with the Progressive Labor Movement (PLM) since her return from Cuba.

> Characterizations of the the
> SCTC and PLM appear in the
> Appendix hereto.

FBI report on Bob Dylan's ECLC speech

Apology or not, the speech had repercussions. Among other things, the incident found its way into the FBI's files — by way of his girlfriend Suze Rotolo. As a report in her file noted:

> ROBERT DYLAN, self-employed as a folksinger appeared on December 13, 1963 at the 10th Annual Bill of Rights Dinner held by the ECLC at the Americana Hotel, New York City. At this dinner, DYLAN received the Tom Paine Award given each year by the ECLC to the "foremost fighter for civil liberties." In his acceptance speech DYLAN said that he agreed in part with LEE HARVEY OSWALD and thought that he understood OSWALD but would not have gone as far as OSWALD did.[27]

What is striking about the column is that it reads as though Lewis were at the dinner, though he never says as much, nor does he cite any source for what is a very detailed description of the event. So either he failed to mention his attendance — his byline has him in Washington, the dinner was in New York — or he received a rather detailed report from an unnamed source.

All this might be explained by the fact that Lewis had a friendly relationship with the FBI. An FBI memo from October 1963, which listed anti-communist writers "who have proved themselves to us," includes journalists such as Paul Harvey of ABC News, Victor Riesel of the Hall Syndicate, and Fulton Lewis Jr. of King Features Syndicate.[28]

That particular mystery might be answered by information in the FBI file on Bob Dylan, which recent governmental releases show *was* created. Specifically, there is an FBI report on the Emergency Civil Liberties Committee, which includes a table of contents listing for a report on the dinner. Unfortunately, the actual report is not included in that document, though there is a notation on the informant — coded as T-3390-S — who supplied information on Dylan.[29] Beyond that, there is a report from January 1964, which references a file on Dylan himself, though there he is called "Bobby Dyllon."[30] Bob Dylan, in other words, was a subject of a more particular kind of FBI attention.

While most writing on Dylan in this period focuses on his personal decisions and behavior, what is clear in looking at the concentrated events in his most political period is that he confronted a considerable amount of scrutiny and hostility. He was ridiculed in the media, kept from performing certain material on television, and had his spontaneous remarks used to justify the opening of an FBI file. Dylan, in other words, was up against more than he realized. In this, he was not alone.

CHAPTER 4
MISSISSIPPI, HARLEM, HAVANA... GODDAM! (1964)

It is very appropriate that from this cradle of the Confederacy, this very heart of the great Anglo-Saxon Southland, that today we sound the drum for freedom as have our generations of forebears before us time and again down through history.
— George Wallace[1]

I'll tell you what freedom is to me. No fear!
— Nina Simone[2]

In the late spring of 1964, Black marchers demanding desegregation in St. Augustine, Florida, were set upon by organized racists. News accounts reported how the marchers were attacked with "flailing clubs and pounding fists." The attack was especially brutal in singling out women and girls:

> In one instance, a representative of a national news magazine attempted to protect a 13- year-old girl who was trembling and seeking shelter in a row of bushes. Her dress had been ripped away and blood was running from a bruise on her shoulder. "Let that gorilla go!" shouted three white rioters who tried to seize the girl from the correspondent.[3]

Martin Luther King would later claim that it was only the non-violence of protestors that "saved the city from a bloody night of terror" — a specious claim considering that some among the marchers had fought back that day, leading at least three of their racist attackers to exit the demonstration via ambulance.[4]

This episode, coming amid the high point of the non-violent movement for civil rights, was not an outlier. On June 9, Black youths in Tuscaloosa, Alabama, shouting "we want freedom," engaged in what press reports called "a bloody clash with police" when city officials refused to let them carry out a protest march against segregation. As one press account noted, "Angry Negroes inside a church threw bottles, rocks, and even chairs" at police surrounding the church where the group had assembled.[5]

Violence and Non-Violence

Events in Jacksonville and Tuscaloosa underscored an aspect of the early Sixties that is generally given short shrift. The non-violence of most organized civil rights forces was never "no violence" — to the contrary, it hinged on the violence of the racists and reactionaries, who, once so engaged, so the theory went, would lead to their defeat morally and in the realm of public opinion.

Such a philosophy is made clear by no less than Martin Luther King's role model, Mahatma Gandhi, who took this to extremes. For example, writing about Jews and Palestine in 1938, he said:

The calculated violence of Hitler may even result in a general massacre of the Jews by way of his first answer to the declaration of such hostilities. But if the Jewish mind could be prepared for voluntary suffering, even the massacre I have imagined could be turned into a day of thanksgiving and joy that Jehovah had wrought deliverance of the race even at the hands of the tyrant.

In like manner, he offered advice to the British in 1940, then under bombardment from Germany, "You will invite Herr Hitler and Signor Mussolini to take what they want of your beautiful island, with your many beautiful buildings. You will give all these but neither your souls, nor your minds."[6]

While King never showed affinity for such monstrous logic, his core philosophy sprang from that template. As he said in 1960:

> As I delved deeper into the philosophy of Gandhi my skepticism concerning the power of love gradually diminished, and I came to see for the first time that the Christian doctrine of love operating through the Gandhian method of nonviolence was one of the most potent weapons available to oppressed people in their struggle for freedom.[7]

Regardless of the best intentions of King and other proponents of non-violence, the reality on the ground was that challenging one hundred years of Jim Crow and the legacy of centuries of slavery was always going to involve violence — on both sides — and a considerable amount of it at that. And this was not only the case in the South. By the summer of 1964, there would be rioting taking aim at the police in what was considered the capital of Black America — Harlem.

Barbara Dane

It was against such a backdrop that popular music produced some of the most abiding and incendiary songs of the era. One of the artists who embodied the best of these insurgent artistic elements, though she never broke into the mainstream, was Barbara Dane. Dane's commanding blues singing was able to take flight because of her commitment to social justice and willingness to break social barriers.

Barbara Dane, 1957
Credit: BLDP

Dane, a member of the original incarnation of the Gateway Singers, but who had been kicked out because of her expulsion from the Communist Party (see Chapter 2), would be active in the civil rights movement, undertaking, among other things, a path-breaking collaboration with the Chambers Brothers.[8] One of the songs on that collaboration, "It Isn't Nice," dealt directly with the tactics used to challenge white supremacy — and how in doing so they were leaving behind more restrained protest. As Dane said:

> Malvina Reynolds' powerful words, written after she herself had participated in the San Francisco Palace Hotel Sit-Ins [an anti-discrimination protest[9]], has helped change the history of hundreds of young people there who kept on insisting on their rights even when the "old-heads" of the established civil rights groups told them "It Isn't Nice," and it has a special and personal meaning for them. I felt that the same sense of courage and commitment was what I wanted to pass on to the young Mississippians and other students working in the South where I was going to sing at Freedom Schools and mass meetings that summer.[10]

As the song explained, when you deal with "men of ice", you can't deal with them nicely, and that is the price of freedom. That sentiment was a current in the civil rights movement, best expressed by the front-line activism of SNCC, but one that would begin to inform protest in other realms as well.

Dylan Retreats

Bob Dylan, who had drawn so much energy from the Black freedom struggle, and in turn infused energy back into it, was by 1964 turning away from direct ties to activism. In a free verse poem to *Broadside Magazine*, he offered an explanation of sorts, but it was more a testament to those who would remain on the front lines. Referring to people such as Tom Paxton, Barbara Dane, and Johnny Herald (of the Green Briar Boys), Dylan wrote "they are the heroes"

> they are the ones that lose materialistically
> ah yes but in their own minds they dont
> an that is much more important

it means much more we need more
kind a people like that people that cant go against their
conscience
no matter what they might gain.[11]

Dylan's testimonial is a good exposition of a certain kind of artist operating in this period, who paid a price for refusing to "go against their conscience," and either avoided or were kept out of the mainstream as a result. They nonetheless played an important role, being in the vanguard, despite the sacrifices that involved. It was not, however, a space Dylan wished to occupy.

The British Invasion

While people like Dane, Peter, Paul and Mary, Tom Paxton, Joan Baez, Phil Ochs, and early Dylan had been at the burning core of the folk music explosion, as popular as some of them became, they would not garner the attention of the music that was about to hit.

The Beatles, who had formed in Liverpool, England, in 1960, took four years before crossing the Atlantic to play for the US audience. Their entry into the US "market" officially came in February 1964, when conservative Ed Sullivan, comfortable with the group's well-scrubbed, if long-haired, bona fides, introduced them to a screaming American public. What followed was a massive media hype — leveraging real fan excitement — anointed as "Beatlemania."[12]

That same year, Red Skelton welcomed the Rolling Stones to his comedy variety show. Unlike Sullivan, however, the right-wing Skelton took the opportunity to take a swipe at the group, ostensibly about their looks, remarking that "England must have socialized haircuts."[13] The Cold War sensibility behind that "joke" indicated the larger animosity by the US cultural establishment at the British Invasion.

Lost in the haze of the nostalgia that now enshrines the Beatles' *Sullivan Show* appearances is the fact that, during their first American visit, they were ridiculed by significant elements of the mainstream media. *New York Times* critic Jack Gould played a particularly aggressive role in this. Responding to a video segment of the group that had run on *The Jack Paar Show*, he predicted that Beatlemania will be seen "in the United States as dated stuff."[14] When the band appeared on *The Ed Sullivan Show* the following month, Gould wrote another column, this time denigrating the group by writing: "The boys hardly did for daughter what Elvis Presley did for her older sister or Frank Sinatra for mother." He went on to insult their looks, claiming their haircuts were like those of "Captain Kangaroo." His final point took a shot at the UK, claiming the group was exemplary of "Britain's comeback as an international influence, they followed established procedure for encouraging self-determination in underdeveloped areas."[15]

For his part, right-wing pundit William F. Buckley turned the hostility up to eleven, writing, "The Beatles are not merely awful, I would consider it sacrilegious to say anything less than that they are godawful." Buckley's "critique," as over the top as it was — one imagines he thought he was being funny — suggested a deeper problem he saw coming into focus. As he wrote, "If our children can listen avariciously to the Beatles, it must be because through our genes we transmitted to them a tendency to some disorder of the kind."[16]

Breaking Down Barriers

Complain as these critics did, the new wave of musicians getting a hearing was growing — and they were doing so by popularizing musical forms long kept from the white mainstream. None of this was obvious in the moment, as Elijah Wald writes: "the idea that English rockers were steering white Americans to authentic African American traditions would become commonplace of rock history, but very few people were making that case in 1964 or 1965."[17] The artists doing so, however, did seem to have an appreciation of this. As George Harrison would later say, "If there was no Lead Belly, there would have been no Lonnie Donegan; no Lonnie Donegan [who recorded Lead Belly's "Rock Island Line"], no Beatles. Therefore no Lead Belly, no Beatles."[18]

Not only did groups like the Beatles and the Rolling Stones revive earlier rock 'n' roll, with covers of songs by Little Richard, Buddy Holly, and Chuck Berry — the Animals did what neither Bob Dylan or Dave Van Ronk were able to do, breaking through the American top forty charts in 1964 with their version of "House of the Rising Sun" — presaging "folk-rock" in the process. British artists such as John Mayall, the Yardbirds, and the Stones also embraced various strains of African-American blues music. This in turn made room for US acts such as the Paul Butterfield Blues Band and, later, Johnny Winter and the Allman Brothers Band — with the Allman and Butterfield bands being racially integrated.

While there were elements of cultural appropriation in this, the embrace of this music from the outside mainly had the effect of elevating and promoting the original artists — people such as Lightning Hopkins, Son House, Rev. Gary Davis, Muddy Waters, Blind Willie McTell, Robert Johnson, and Memphis Minnie — including inviting those still alive and active on their tours. All of which served as an auxiliary force in breaking down the rigid racial order that had been enforced since the abandonment of Reconstruction.

St. Augustine and the AFM

The events in St. Augustine described at the start of this chapter took place less than a month before Congress passed the Civil Rights Act, making discrimination based on race illegal. This was a major blow to the apartheid setup in the US South. Law or not, segregation was still very much in place when the Beatles were set to play that September, in Jacksonville, forty-five minutes north of St. Augustine.

The group, whose popularity was at a high point, took the position that they would not play when they learned that the Gator Bowl was a segregated venue. As John Lennon said, "We never play to segregated audiences and we aren't going to start now. I'd sooner lose our appearance money." In this instance, officials backed off, and the concert went off as planned. It was, however, a foretaste of problems the group would encounter when they toured the country two years later.[19]

Another area of contention for the group would come from the American Federation of Musicians (AFM) when the union's leadership decided to push back against the popularity of the Beatles and other British musical acts, which they felt undermined "American" musicians. The AFM had formed in 1898 as part of the American Federation of Labor. The union served as representative of professional musicians, such as those in orchestras, back-up bands, musicians who perform for television, and others.[20] The union leaders, feeling threatened by the artists coming to the US from Britain, responded to the Beatles' wildly successful US tour in 1964 by asking the US Labor Department and the Immigration and Naturalization Service to ban any future tour by the band. They specifically challenged the group's artistic uniqueness, seeking to downgrade their visa status to H (ii), or "No unique talent." In the union's view — or better said, the union's leadership — there was nothing about the music of the Beatles, and others coming from Britain, that could not just as easily be produced by American musicians. When word of the scheme became public, Beatles fans mounted an opposition which forced the union to back off. It was not, however, the last time the union undertook efforts to keep a British invasion band from performing in the US.[21]

Mississippi Goddam!

While the civil rights struggle was raging in Florida, activists were also targeting Mississippi in what was called Mississippi Freedom Summer, which included a major effort to register Black people to vote. The campaign was beset by violence, with churches burned and businesses near where civil rights workers were located bombed.[22] Press reports told of six Black people being killed in the six months leading up to the campaign, with others, in a chilling throwback to slavery, being flogged.[23] Events reached a crescendo in August with the discovery of the bodies of James Chaney, Andrew Goodman, and Michael Schwerner, who had been working as staff members of the Congress of Racial Equality, registering people to vote.[24] The three had been murdered by a gang of racist whites.

It was out of the intensity of this summer's events that the classically trained pianist Nina Simone emerged as an incendiary voice for Black freedom, ultimately finding her voice in popular, rather than classical music. Incensed by the racist bombing of a Black church in Birmingham the previous year that killed four young Black girls, Simone composed the blistering "Mississippi Goddam." The song, set deceptively to a jaunty show tune, was a searing indictment of what was happening. According to Simone:

This is a song I wrote during the time the four little kids

were bombed in Alabama [...] and it was conceived, though, during the time when James Meredith was finally getting into the University of Mississippi. And I was beginning to get angry then. First you get depressed, then you get mad. And when these kids got bombed, I just sat down and wrote this song. And it's a very moving, violent song 'cause that's how I feel about the whole thing.[25]

Nina Simone 1965
Credit: Ron Kroon / National Archives (Netherlands)

What stood out about the composition, in contrast to the mainstream popularization of non-violence, was its articulation of rage. At one point in the song, Simone proclaims that the whole country is full of lies and those perpetuating such foul acts were "all going to die and die like flies."

Just as Billie Holiday is forever identified with her version of the anti-lynching song "Strange Fruit," "Mississippi Goddam" stamped Simone's political persona. While her fiery politics would limit what she could accomplish in the professional mainstream, it made her an icon of the Black freedom movement.[26]

Cuba

As if events playing out in the US were not enough, in the Caribbean, the government of the United States was contending with its failure to prevent an independent regime from consolidating power in Cuba.

The US political establishment, initially wary of Fidel Castro and the Cuban revolution, became outright hostile to it when it aligned with the USSR.[27] In contrast, a section of the left and progressive population in the US were energized by it and mobilized to counter US moves against the country. While the Cuban Missile Crisis had diminished the possibility of invasion, in its wake the US instituted a punishing, all-encompassing embargo on trade. Following up a year later, the Kennedy administration instituted a ban on all travel to the country. That action was seized on by activists as a way of protesting the administration's overall anti-Cuba policy.

Among the first efforts to challenge that ban was the sending of a delegation to visit the island under the name Student Committee to Travel to Cuba. One of those it attracted was Bob Dylan's former girlfriend, Suze Rotolo. Rotolo's role in a press conference by the delegation on their return from the visit was dutifully documented by the FBI:

> Miss Rotolo said the only opposition to Premier Fidel Castro that the group encountered among Cuban workers was expressed freely by some waiters and bartenders in hotels. She referred to them as gusanos, or worms, as the Castro regime calls its opponents. "These gusanos are not supported," she said. "There can be open criticism of the regime. As long as they keep it to talk they are tolerated as long as there is no sabotage."[28]

By this point, Rotolo and Dylan were no longer together, and Dylan himself was disengaging from political activism. Nonetheless, Rotolo's file — aside from being exemplary of how the US intelligence apparatus was operating — shows the manifold interconnections between the overall political situation and the cultural milieu. This is even more pronounced in the character of one of the overtly political artists of the era — Phil Ochs.

Phil Ochs

Phil Ochs came out of the same folk scene as Bob Dylan and Joan Baez, but more than any other artists of his caliber, he assumed the position of radical social critic. This was on sharp display in regard to Cuba and his talking blues song, "Talking Cuban Crisis." In it, he sarcastically described how, "when President John [Kennedy]" started to speak, we knew right away he "wouldn't be weak," and that the US was going to teach the Russians a lesson "for trying to upset the balance of power." All this reads as bold, accurate, and highly informed, suggesting that the US was not the good guy in the Cuban Missile Crisis — leaving aside whether there were *any* good guys.[29] Complex figure that he was, Ochs was said to have been shattered by Kennedy's assassination, but his personal grief seems to not have affected his political stand; in fact, the month after the assassination, he insisted he be allowed to play the Cuba song at a concert in the Village's Gaslight Cafe.[30]

Phil Ochs, 1975
Credit: Chip Berlet

Ochs was not reaching audiences anywhere near the scale of Dylan, Baez, or Peter, Paul and Mary, but the people he *was* reaching were listening closely, as a 1966 profile in *Melody Maker* makes clear:

Phil Ochs is possibly the most controversial songwriter in America today, not excluding Dylan. He can write the most vicious political songs but gets angry at anyone who tries to turn songwriters into propagandists [...] He is virtually banned from American radio and TV programmes, because he refuses to play down his political material, but his last *In Concert* album got into the American charts virtually on the basis of word-of-mouth recommendation alone.[31]

Not only was Ochs not heard on US radio or seen on TV, but it was in this period that the FBI opened a file on him. Noting that he was a "beatnik type," the report flailed around trying to get a bead on the artist:

The reader is drawn to conclude that OCHS himself is a guitarist and folk singer. An article on page 42 of the same issue of "Mainstream" entitled "Off the Record" by JOSH DUNSON describes PHILIP OCHS as a "topical songwriter." NYO [New York Field Office] Indices reflect no information concerning PHILIP OCHS.[32]

The Bureau, in other words, was not able to shoehorn Ochs into a narrower category because he was not organizationally affiliated — though he would help form the non-organization organization, the Yippies!

Ochs's complicated outlook is perhaps best expressed in his "Power and the Glory," a kind of reworking of Guthrie's "This Land is Your Land," though with a sharper edge. The song does not simply describe the wonder of the US landscape and declares the power of its freedom, but rails against those who see "law is their weapon" and "treason" is their cry.[33] No wonder, then, his file would remain open into the Seventies.

Harlem Riot, July 16–22

The summer of 1964 saw the Drifters riding high on the charts with "Under the Boardwalk," as were the Beach Boys

("I Get Around") and the Dixie Cups ("Chapel of Love"). There was, however, something else happening in pop music — if hiding in plain sight. The Impressions had a hit with the Curtis Mayfield song "Keep on Pushin'" — which those properly tuned-in understood to be a call to continue to struggle. Among other things, it was listed as the #2 most requested song in Atlanta that summer and was said to have been the number one sing-along for the Freedom Riders.[34] Also, in June, Martha and the Vandellas released "Dancing in the Street," written by William "Mickey" Stevenson, Ivy Joe Hunter, and Marvin Gaye. A celebration of summer, it became an anthem for the civil disorders intimately bound up with what summer in the city came to mean in the 1960s.[35] To understand this, one need look no further than Harlem, NYC, that July.

The spark for the Harlem riot did not happen in Harlem, but in the Upper Eastside neighborhood of Yorkville on July 16. It was there that James Powell, a fifteen-year-old Black youth, was attending summer school when he and his friends got into a confrontation with an apartment superintendent.

The super is said to have been hosing down the sidewalk and, after words with Powell and two friends, turned the hose on the youth. In turn, NYPD lieutenant Thomas Gilligan, in plain clothes at a nearby radio shop, snapped into action and proceeded to chase Powell into the building. After a few minutes, Gilligan walked out, Powell never did, having been shot dead by the off-duty policeman. What followed was a confrontation in which students threw bottles and cans at the "300 steel-helmeted" officers dispatched to the scene. While the police were able to get the upper hand that day, that was not the end of things.[36]

The killing happened on a Thursday morning. The following Saturday, there was a protest rally in Harlem that concluded with a march to the local precinct. That action in turn became a confrontation after police moved on protestors. What followed was a melee between police and the crowd, who responded to the police's actions by throwing bricks, bottles, and rocks.[37]

March in Harlem During the 1964 Riots
Credit: Dick DeMarsico, New York World Telegraph & Sun

Malcolm X, who had recently left the Black separatist Nation of Islam, characterized the aggressive actions of the police as "outright scare tactic[s]," before adding that they would not work "because the Negro is not afraid."[38] That lack of fear was manifested in the fact that the turmoil lasted six days and included breaking windows, looting, and setting certain local businesses on fire. When the rebellion ended on July 22, one Black resident had been killed and another one hundred had been injured. Additionally, 450 people were arrested and around $1 million in property damage was reported.[39]

In the riot's wake, the authorities singled out Bill Epton, a Korean war veteran and member of the Maoist Progressive Labor Movement (later the Progressive Labor Party).[40] Epton was arrested under a New York State criminal anarchy statute for giving a speech during the disturbance, based on the evidence of a Black NYPD detective who had infiltrated PLM. As a result, he was convicted and given a year in prison — after losing all appeals, he was forced to serve out the sentence.[41]

The move against Epton and Progressive Labor was of a piece of the authorities' repressive attention aimed at that group in their early years — when they were the most radical communists on the scene. However, it also presaged the way the criminal justice system and intelligence apparatus would later target political radicals, such as members of the Black Panther Party, former SNCC activists such as Stokely Carmichael and James Forman, prominent members of the New Left, and those embracing Maoism and other revolutionary doctrines.[42]

Legislation and Freedom

On July 2, 1964, President Lyndon Johnson signed into law the Civil Rights Act, aimed at ensuring equal rights for Black people in the United States. In most popular accounts, this is recorded as a key turning point and accomplishment of the Black freedom struggle. Events in Harlem, which broke little more than two weeks after that legislation was signed into law, belie the legislation's import.

Within events in Harlem was a spirit of rebellion, the edge of which eluded the comprehension of authorities. An analysis in the *New York Times* is instructive in that respect. The piece offered the view that, for Black youth in New York, "a voter registration campaign, a picket line, or an economic boycott mean very little." By contrast, "the teen-aged guerrillas have found in a stone, a brickbat, or a wine bottle full of gasoline a potent weapon of protest against the System, and that they are delighted with it."[43]

While Martha Reeves's song embodied the spirit of the youth of Harlem, it is worth pointing out that one artist at least, Phil Ochs, wrote directly about the event. In his song "In the Heat of the Summer," on 1965's *I Ain't Marching Anymore*, he proceeded to indict the scolding press, chastise the mayor, and proclaim that people had been "down for too long," and it was time to "make somebody listen."

Rumblings in Times Square and Sproul Plaza

In August, a group of around sixty people organized by the May 2 Movement (affiliated with Progressive Labor Movement) and Youth Against War and Fascism (affiliated with the Workers World Party) rallied in New York's Times Square to oppose the escalating war in Vietnam. Notably, one of those taking part was PLM's Phillip Luce — who Bob Dylan had mentioned in his ECLC remarks. Luce was singled out in the *New York Times* as "a well-tailored young man with a red mustache" under federal indictment for having visited Cuba in defiance of the State Department's travel ban. That aside, as things unfolded, the demonstration was broken up by "mounted policemen and patrolmen using nightsticks." The demonstration would seem a historical footnote except for the fact that it signaled, both in determination and brutality meted out, much more to come.[44]

Such was even more the case on the other coast, where authorities at UC Berkeley moved to restrict what kind of politics could be promoted on campus. In September 1964, the university administration, citing rules that only allowed the Republican and Democratic parties to solicit on campus, announced it would strictly enforce a ban on all other activity. The triggering event was the arrest of Jack Weinberg for setting up a CORE table on campus, leading to a standoff when hundreds of students surrounded the police car he was being held in, demanding his release.[45] What ensued was an electrified Free Speech Movement that stretched throughout the academic year, with sit-ins, protests, and mass arrests.[46] In a defining moment of the struggle, Mario Savio — who had been a civil rights volunteer that summer in Mississippi — gave a speech to students assembled in Sproul Plaza on December 3, 1964:

> There is a time when the operation of the machine becomes so odious, makes you so sick at heart, that you can't take part; you can't even passively take part, and you've got to put your bodies upon the gears and upon the wheels, upon the levers, upon all the apparatus, and you've got to make it stop.[47]

Savio's speech would become iconic, not the least for its heralding of protest that went beyond passive resistance, toward an active one. In the ensuing years, Berkeley would be ground zero for this. After the speech, Joan Baez — who, true to her conscience, would be in the middle of some of the most consequential protests of the era — led the crowd in singing "We Shall Overcome," before joining students who entered the hall to sit in.[48]

The authorities were not pleased, and vigorously denounced the actions of the students and their supporters. One of those speaking out was Robert D. Wood, then head of KNXT in the Bay Area. In a television editorial, he inveighed, "There is no excuse on earth for the type of demonstrations fostered by the beard and sandal crowd at Berkeley." In response, he offered that such actions "should be dealt with quickly and severely to set an example for all time for those who agitate for the sake of agitation."[49] While Wood would soon leave the station, it would be to assume a more powerful position as an executive at CBS television, where he would play an even more significant repressive role.[50]

Change Gonna Come

As good as Nina Simone was, she did not have the same size audience as the enormously popular Sam Cooke. Cooke had built a career as a pop star after abandoning work with the gospel group the Soul Stirrers. During the early years of the 1960s, he was riding the top of the charts with songs like "Chain Gang," "Shake," "Cupid," and "Twistin' the Night Away" all landing in the top ten of the Billboard charts.[51]

Sam Cooke, 1966
Credit: RCA Publicity Photo

Cooke's success was a result of a combination of wonderful singing, amazing songwriting, and business savvy. As popular as he was, he was still an African-

American in a country that was still white supremacist. Cooke was born in Clarksdale, Mississippi, but moved with his family to Chicago when he was two, insulating him from the brutality and humiliations of the Jim Crow South. As his career took off, however, failing to tour the South was not an option.[52]

Cooke's status became abundantly clear when he tried to check into a hotel in Shreveport, Louisiana. Unbeknownst to him, the Holiday Inn, where he had made a reservation, was a whites-only hotel. As a result, when he went to register on the morning of October 8, he was told there were no vacancies.[53] Incensed by the obvious racism, Cooke reportedly went to the parking lot, along with his wife, brother Charles, and manager S.R. Crain, and repeatedly blew the car horn and yelled against the blatant discrimination. Meantime, the police had been called to the alternate hotel Cooke and his entourage had driven to. There, Cooke and the others were arrested. While the group was quickly released on bail, the racist sting of it remained.[54]

That incident occurred little more than a year before Cooke was shot to death in Los Angeles on December 11, 1964, at the Hacienda Motel in South Los Angeles. Cooke, who had been at a bar earlier in the evening, had picked up a twenty-two-year-old Asian-American woman, Elisa Boyer, and taken her back to the motel. From there the only account is that of Boyer, who claims she fought off an attempted rape and seized a moment when Cooke had gone into the bathroom to grab her and Cooke's clothes and ran out of the room. Cooke, in turn, wearing only his remaining sport jacket, went to the hotel manager's office, thinking the woman was inside. He was then shot dead by the manager, Bertha Franklin.[55]

Both Franklin and Boyer were later cleared of any criminal culpability by a coroner's inquest. A year later,

Boyer was arrested in a prostitution sting — suggesting her encounter with Cooke was more transactional than amorous. At least one theory holds that Franklin was working in league with the woman and her pimp in order to rob Cooke — which would explain why Boyer chose to run off with Cooke's pants, in which he had a wad of cash — rather than just running out of the room, which she claimed to have done out of fear. The whole incident reads as sordid, with few plausible innocent explanations. Nonetheless, some suggest a conspiracy behind the killing, an effort to take down and disgrace a successful Black man.[56] As seductive as such a theory is, evidence is lacking.

While Cooke's killing appears — short of evidence showing otherwise — to be a case of the fraught nature of interacting with the criminal sub-culture, it does not negate the fact that, at the end of his life, Cooke was taking a strong stand with those struggling for Black freedom.

Cooke is said to have written his most important song, "A Change Is Gonna Come," in early 1964. This was around the same time that he famously met with Malcolm X and Muhammad Ali (then Cassius Clay) after Ali's victory over Sonny Liston in February 1964.[57] Given the Bureau's attention to the Nation of Islam, it seems likely the FBI was keeping a file on Cooke as well — indeed, one of their files references a "REDACTED negro recording star from Los Angeles," saying he was probably a Muslim "because of his friendship with Malcolm," the most likely person being Cooke.[58] In a response to a request for Cooke's file — which did apparently exist — the FBI would only say the file "had been destroyed." [59]

Legacy

Cooke's song "A Change Is Gonna Come," was released as the B-side of the single "Shake" days after his funeral. It is at once a broadside against Jim Crow, with a lyric describing going downtown to the movies and always encountering someone "telling me, don't hang around," but in hymn-like fashion, singing a "change is gonna come." Cooke is said to have been moved to write the song after hearing Dylan's "Blowin' in the Wind." As Peter Guralnick wrote, Cooke "was so carried away with the message, and the fact that a white boy had written it, that he was almost ashamed not to have written something like that himself."[60] Saying that, with "A Change Is Gonna Come," Cooke took a step further than Dylan — he was not simply asking a question, but envisioning transformation.

CHAPTER 5
READY TO GO ANYWHERE (1965)

What is needed if social order is to reign is that the mass of men be content with their lot. But what is needed for them to be content, is not that they have more or less but that they be convinced they have no right to more.
— Emile Durkheim[1]

Chaos is a friend of mine. It's like I accept him; does he accept me?
— Bob Dylan[2]

As the United States moved into 1965, for the keen observer it was becoming increasingly clear that the country was headed to a place beyond the conservative conformity the dominant culture had been comfortably nestled in. On the surface, things seemed to be operating in a familiar framework. The Beatles were still in their "cute" phase, and shared the space with the likes of the *Mary Poppins* soundtrack and Lorne Greene — of the popular television show *Bonanza* — who had a number one with "Ringo." US troops deployed in Southeast Asia were still referred to as "advisers," and the civil rights movement continued under the banner of non-violence.

The surface calm was illusory. As the year progressed, Alabama became the site of shocking violence, and Black people in Watts exploded in what was at that point the biggest urban uprising ever. US global power was confronted by challenges in the Dominican Republic, Indonesia, and Vietnam. Meantime, the Beatles — cute or not — were setting off in a different musical direction, folk music was moving into the pop mainstream, albeit fusing with rock, and Bob Dylan was vaulting in a radically different direction — and in so doing, confronting resistance from the left and the right.

Santo Domingo

On April 28, Lyndon Johnson, fearing a communist takeover in the Dominican Republic, dispatched four hundred Marines to the country's capital, under the pretext of "protecting Americans." Two days later, the Marines were joined by members of the US Army's 82nd Airborne, bringing the invasion force to 6,200.[3] At issue was a military junta that had seized power in a coup from the democratically elected government of Juan Bosch, nineteen months earlier, and a group of constitutional rebels, which included communists, that attempted to take power back.

An analytical piece in the *New York Times* made clear the stakes in the Dominican Republic, writing that the United States

is determined there shall be no spread, especially in the Caribbean, of regimes oriented to or controlled either by Moscow or Peking; and that the end has come of the evangelistic and faltering United States policy which assisted Castro to power in Cuba and led to the calamitous episode of the Bay of Pigs.

In other words, there would be no dithering — the US would intervene, and it would intervene as hard as necessary to prevent another Castro. Anyone looking to understand the real reason the US would come to invest so much in

Vietnam need look no further than what was being said about the Dominican Republic.[4]

Phil Ochs and US Imperialism

While today the Dominican intervention is overshadowed by the morass of Vietnam, it was, and remains, a momentous episode. As such, it called forth a song by Phil Ochs, "Santo Domingo," with images of crabs scuttling to take flight as the Marines set foot on the beaches of the capital city.

"Santo Domingo" was part of a set of incendiary songs included on Ochs's 1965 record, *I Ain't Marching Anymore*, including — as well as the title track: an indictment of US wars over the country's history — "Here's to the State of Mississippi," which called out that state's reputation for vicious white supremacy, and "Draft Dodger Rag," about resistance to conscription. But if Ochs's lyrics were provocative, his public statements were more so. In a profile in the *Detroit Free Press* that October, he explained his views about Vietnam:

> The heroes of the underdeveloped countries and my heroes are the revolutionists of today — men like Ho Chi Minh in Vietnam and Che Guevara and Castro in Cuba. I think we should be supporting the Viet Cong instead of fighting it. I don't consider Ho my enemy and I'd rather go to jail than fight him.[5]

Ochs was far out front on such matters. Not surprisingly, he garnered pushback, as can be seen in a letter to the editor in the *Baltimore Sun*:

> Sir: I understand that the Board of Education is allowing a so-called folksong concert to be held at Baltimore Polytechnic Institute on February 28. Is it their idea of an

educational program to allow Phil Ochs and other people of questionable political backgrounds to get up on a stage and preach their philosophies of socialism and agrarian reform in the guise of folk song to an audience of impressionable young people?[6]

The writer concluded his missive with a threat: "I must personally condemn their judgment here and if the people of Baltimore allow this program to be held they must face the consequences." Notably, the same editorial page included a letter from an Ochs defender: "I think we owe five minutes of our time in thinking instead of acting in ignorance."

All this was happening at a time when the movement against the war in Vietnam was moving beyond a concern only for the far-left toward one taken up by elements of the liberal mainstream. Among other things, a march of 35,000, the largest up to that point, took place in Washington, DC, highlighted by the participation of Dr. Benjamin Spock and Norman Thomas. The march, held on November 27, was in turn attacked by political authorities. In the words of Georgia Governor Carl Sanders, it did "more to help the Communists than anything I know of today."[7]

Buffy Sainte-Marie

Scottish folk singer Donovan Leitch had a minor hit in 1965 with the song "Universal Soldier" — whose lyrics decry militarism and call for an end to war. It was written by the Canadian-born indigenous woman, Buffy Sainte-Marie.[8] While not as thoroughly political as Ochs, Sainte-Marie occupied a rare space in this period — especially in decrying the treatment of Native people. As she put it in a 1967 interview, "All I can do is prevent this leprous part of American history from being covered up anymore. I'm just trying to let some sunlight in."[9]

Buffy Sainte-Marie, 1968
Jack de Nijs / National Archives (Netherlands)

Sainte-Marie too was a target of the authorities, reporting
that the FBI compiled a thirty-page, highly redacted file on
her. In it are reports of radio stations being commended for
not playing her music. As she would tell one interviewer,
"It was ridiculous — they had letters from people in the
file asking the FBI if they had a file on me."[10] She was
also apparently targeted in other ways: "[A] broadcaster

announced they received letters of commendation from the White House for having suppressed my music."[11]

While the specific interest the FBI had in Sainte-Marie is unclear — and the length of the file suggests it was more modest than some — it nonetheless underscores a certain point. As she later described, "It's not like they tell you they're gonna deny your rights or trample your freedom or gag you — they just do it."[12] To which could be added, in this period there was a multitude of times when those targeted did not even know it was being done to them.

Johnny Cash

Another artist who discovered that wading into certain waters could lead to background suppression was Johnny Cash. In 1964, Cash was riding high on the charts with songs such as "I Walk the Line" and "Ring of Fire." Because of his success, his record company, Columbia, allowed him to record an album thematically centered on issues of native Americans. The album, *Bitter Tears: Ballads of the American Indian*, was conceived and created by Cash — inspired in part by his then mistaken belief that he was part Cherokee. Regardless of this mistake, he was appalled by the conditions of the country's indigenous population. But when Columbia let him record the album, they did little to promote it. According to filmmaker Antonio D'Ambrosio, although Columbia

> honored the contract to ship a minimal amount of records for sale, they undertook a type of "soft censorship" where they did no promotion and just ignored its existence. And of course, many radio stations just refused to play it.[13]

In response, Cash promoted the album on his own:

He bought back thousands of copies of the record, penned a protest letter that he placed as an ad in *Billboard* magazine, stuffed the letter inside each record, and traveled around the country hand delivering the record to radio stations and asking them to give it a chance.

In his letter, he laid down a challenge: "DJs, station managers, owners, etc., where are your guts?"[14]

In the end, Cash had success with a single from the album, "The Ballad of Ira Hayes," a song about the Pima Indian and Marine who helped raise the American flag on the Japanese island of Iwo Jima — ironies abound — but who died forgotten and disparaged. The song was written by Peter La Farge, a folk singer from New Mexico — and part of the Sixties folk revival — who had a keen interest in the conditions of Native people and claimed, though it is unconfirmed, to have a heritage linked to the Narragansett tribe in New England.[15]

Cash was privileged that, given his success, he could do such things, but the fact that he *had* to do such things is revealing of the difficult terrain anyone making stinging socially conscious music would confront.

From Selma to Montgomery to the Audubon Ballroom...

On March 7, a civil rights march of around six hundred people, led by John Lewis of the Student Non-Violent Coordinating Committee and Hosea William of the Southern Christian Leadership Conference, planned to march from the central Alabama city of Selma to the state capitol in Montgomery. Setting out on the march, they crossed the Edmund Pettis Bridge, named after a Confederate general and Grand Dragon of the Ku Klux Klan. With TV news cameras rolling, police proceeded to beat the marchers and violently break up the demonstration. The incident, soon to be called "Bloody Sunday," is now considered a turning point in the civil rights movement — the last straw leading to the Civil Rights Act of 1965.[16] The event would later be enshrined in music with a release the following year by the pop gospel group the Staple Singers, in the title song of their album *Freedom Highway*.[17]

While the Civil Rights Act was hailed in certain quarters as testament to the strategy of non-violence, Malcolm X — who by 1965 had left the constraints of the Nation of Islam — had a different view. As he told the *New York Times*, "It is criminal to teach a man not to defend himself when he is the constant victim of brutal attacks."[18] Tragically, Malcolm himself was the object of a brutal attack, murdered while he spoke in the Audubon Ballroom in New York's Washington Heights, less than two weeks before the incident at the Edmund Pettus Bridge. While his assassination was enmeshed in controversy, fodder for endless conspiracy theorizing, what is not controversial is that his ideology of militant self-defense was ahead of its time. It would come to dominate the second half of the decade.[19]

Pointedly, it was down to jazz saxophonist Archie Shepp to eulogize Malcolm in music. This he did on his 1965 album *Fire Music* in "Malcolm, Malcolm, Semper Malcolm," with its ominous, mournful, angry intro: "We are murdered in amphitheaters."[20]

... to Watts

Malcolm's fiery spirit was on full display in the African-American community of Watts in Los Angeles. After what would usually have been a routine police stop, this time of an alleged drunk driver, the neighborhood exploded into six days of rioting, with massive fires, Molotov cocktails, sniper fire, and the dispatch of thousands of National Guard troops. When the hostilities subsided, thirty-four people would be dead, 1,032 injured, and 4,000 arrested. Along with this was the destruction of 1,000 buildings and properties, totaling $40 million in damages.[21] It was, at the time, the worst riot of its kind ever seen in the United States.

Watts Burns 1965
Credit: New York World Telegram

Watts set authorities scrambling to understand what was happening. The *New York Times* could offer only that "There were as many theories as there are sociologists today on why a depressed residential area was ripped [by violence] for three nights by rioting Negroes."[22] Underneath the confusion was a ruling class, which had counted on the more socially safe tactics of Martin Luther King and civil rights legislation to end the most egregious treatment of Black people in the US and bring about a more inclusive social order. What they discovered instead was that certain phenomena, once set in motion, could no longer be controlled. In that respect, no less than Lyndon Johnson is said to have offered the clarifying insight: "[W]hen you put your foot on a man's neck and hold him down for three hundred years, and then you let him up, what's he going to do? He's going to knock your block off."[23]

Events that had been set loose, starting with *Brown v. Board of Education* in 1954, continued to deliver deeper levels of social anomie — and there was no going back. In amongst all this was a musical shift, one that went beyond "We Shall Overcome." During the turmoil in Alabama, Nina Simone performed "Mississippi Goddam" in Montgomery on March 25, in front of ten thousand people. After the performance, she was introduced to Martin Luther King, to whom she declared, "I'm not nonviolent!" King is said to have responded cordially, "That's OK, sister. You don't have to be." This was fortuitous. After all, Simone was not asking for permission.[24]

"Turn! Turn! Turn!"

In another musical realm, a song with Pete Seeger's imprint inserted itself into the mainstream by way of the Byrds. The group, who had a hit in early 1965 with Bob Dylan's "Mr. Tambourine Man," followed it with Seeger's "Turn! Turn! Turn!" The song, which Seeger had adapted from the Bible's book of Ecclesiastes, was received largely as a call for peace, with its closing line saying, "I swear it's not too late."[25] It is worth pointing out, however, that the verse constitutes a multitude of examples of dialectical opposition — many of which are hardly peaceful, from casting away stones (at what exactly?), to gathering them, to the even more dire "A time to kill." In that respect, it was far more in tune with the times than a casual listen suggests.

The Byrds had deep roots in folk music — particularly David Crosby, Gene Clark, and Jim "Roger" McGuinn. However, they represented a step further into an emerging counterculture. As a result, they were met with a less-than-welcoming bewilderment. One critic noted, "They adopted Prince Valiant haircuts, which make them look as if they were wearing hairy cloth hats."[26] That said, the group was not "political" in an agitprop way, their subversion residing in their lack of conforming to middle-class sensibilities. It is thus little surprise that they came under scrutiny for the perceived drug subtext of songs such as "Eight Miles High" and their cover of Dylan's "Mr. Tambourine Man" — the former alleged to be about being "high," the latter rumored to be about a drug dealer — neither of which was true.[27]

Bob Dylan — 1965

By 1965, Bob Dylan had moved into another universe relative to where he had been a year earlier. Not only had he made a definitive break with overt protest songs — much to the chagrin of certain of his former champions on the left — the new songs he was creating were unlike anything that had heretofore existed in pop music, and they were reaching a larger audience than Dylan ever had before.

Dylan made the shift with his 1964 release *Another Side of Bob Dylan,* which, while still in the folk style of singer and acoustic guitar, was saturated with songs about putting distance between himself as any kind of spokesman for larger causes. This comes through tellingly in "My Back Pages" — where he criticizes himself for believing that "life is black and white." It can also be heard in the love song "To Ramona," where he describes a former lover as having been "fooled into thinking" that a "finishing end is at hand." Similarly, with "It Ain't Me Babe," another ostensible love song, he expresses the limits of his commitment, unwilling to "die for you and more." It is possible that the love songs simply mean what they say, but given his break with the politics of the moment, it is hard to not also hear something else.

While there was a letting go, or even a distancing from politics in these songs, some among the politically inclined saw the change in direction as capitulation, if not downright betrayal. One of the most famous expressions of this came after Dylan's performance at Newport in 1964 when Irwin Silber published an open letter in *Sing Out!*. In it, he took Dylan to task:

> Your new songs seem to be all inner-directed now, inner probing, self-conscious — maybe even a little maudlin or a little cruel on occasion. And it's happening on stage, too. You seem to be relating to a handful of cronies behind the scenes now — rather than to the rest of us out front.[28]

Silber's letter was exemplary of an assumption of ownership over Dylan by elements of the left that was both false and disregarded boundaries. Beyond that, it confused the difference between art and politics, assuming they were always meant to play the same role. All of which missed what Dylan himself was grappling with. This comes through in an exchange with Joan Baez after his last concert with her in March 1965. As Baez recalled:

> [Dylan said] "I heard those kids. I heard them, right? I can't be responsible for those kids' lives." [Baez responded] "Bobby, you rat, you mean you're gonna leave them all with me?" He said, "Hey, hey — take them if you want them. But, man, I can't be responsible." It didn't mean he didn't love them, you know. I think he was just afraid. But it was real. He meant it.[29]

This exchange speaks volumes of the pressure that Dylan — and any artist who spoke to larger issues — was under. What is particularly vexing in the criticism leveled by people such as Silber is that, while Dylan was leaving behind topical songs, the path he was taking would produce art that in many ways was even more radical.

Following *Another Side*, Dylan released *Bringing It All Back Home,* with one side being acoustic music and the other with amplified instruments. Dylan mythology holds that this period ushered in his "going electric," a view which elevates a particular technological change in his music over the more profound substantive one. *Bringing It All Back Home* was unlike anything produced in the pop realm up to then. With songs such as "Gates of Eden," "It's Alright, Ma (I'm Only Bleeding)," "Maggie's Farm," and "Subterranean Homesick Blues," Dylan channeled Beat poetry, surrealism, and humor to offer a sharp critique of the world he was living in. Musically and lyrically, Dylan was drawing from people such as Allen Ginsberg, Woody Guthrie, and Little Richard — tying three of the insurgent elements of the late Fifties into one.

Bringing It All Back Home was followed in August by *Highway 61 Revisited*, a work which all but abandoned acoustic instrumentation. Dylan's shift, along with the appearance of groups like the Byrds, moved the music industry — eager to reap dollar rewards from the change — to promote what they said was the new genre of "folk rock." All of which heightened tensions in the folk community — already consumed in debating issues such as authenticity, Black originators versus white evangelists, urban adopters versus rural originators, etc.[30]

That said, as good an explanation as any of *Highway 61 Revisited* comes through in Dylan's most recognizable song, "Like a Rolling Stone." On one level, it is a largely unsympathetic rant against someone who thought they were special and now find themselves wholly vulnerable. Beyond that simple read, however, is Dylan — who is neither a social-theorist nor left-politician — capturing the spirit of anomie animating the times, where Black people and a sizable section of the youth population no longer knew the "direction home" or what the new norms were, now that the old ones were being tossed aside. This is also sharply drawn in "Ballad of a Thin Man," where the prototypical middle-class everyman, Mr. Jones, walks into a room, totally flummoxed by the perceived strangeness around him, not understanding that *he* is the freak.[31]

With *Bringing It All Back Home* and *Highway 61 Revisited*, Dylan's live performances changed from an all-acoustic set to a hybrid one of acoustic and electric. The pushback from a section of the folk community was immediate. When Dylan performed at the Newport festival that August, amid recording *Highway 61 Revisited*, he was backed by the Paul Butterfield Blues Band, which included guitarist Mike Bloomfield. The set, which opened with "Maggie's Farm," immediately polarized the audience: some applauding, others booing. The song sent Pete Seeger, who was backstage, into a rage. As he recalled, he said, "Damn, if I had an axe, I would cut the cable right now."[32]

While there does appear to have been a problem with the sound system, wherein those closest to the stage, and backstage, were getting overloud amplification, and that Seeger would claim his frustration stemmed from not being able to hear the words because of audio distortion, the bigger issue seems deeper.[33]

In an interview a few years before he died, Seeger told *Democracy Now*'s Amy Goodman that he didn't have an issue with Dylan playing "electrified music," before repeating his explanation of being bothered by the audio distortion. He then offered the faint praise that Dylan was "one of the greatest songwriters of the 20th century," a group he said included Woody Guthrie, Joni Mitchell, Buffy Sainte-Marie, and Malvina Reynolds. Missing in this — and by the time of the interview Seeger had had decades to reflect on the episode — was an acknowledgement that Dylan's performance signaled a radical advance in what was possible in popular music.[34] Unfortunately, the view of Seeger, and others like him, was consequential, including impacting Dylan himself, who would later say of Seeger's reaction, "[Here was] someone whose music I cherish, you know, someone I highly respect, is gonna cut the cables. It was like, oh God, it was like a dagger."[35]

By contrast, Phil Ochs watched the scene with amazement:

I think they were getting a needed dose of musical shock treatment. Dylan as usual was doing the unexpected but was quite responsibly doing what any real artist should, that is, performing the music he personally felt closest to and putting his own judgment before that of his audience [...] The people that thought they were booing Dylan were in reality booing themselves in a most vulgar display of unthinking mob censorship.[36]

While the single "Like a Rolling Stone" did well on the charts, the album as a whole made hardly a ripple in the critical press. San Francisco columnist Ralph Gleason was near alone among US critics to even review it. To his credit, he conveyed that the album was something special. In his review, he presciently pointed out that Dylan's lyrics represent "a merger of poetry with popular music which can have a deep and lasting effect on our entire society." He then offered:

The utter lineliness [sic] and alienation of a young generation born in the shadow of the Bomb and straining to make sense out of life governed, stratified and resting upon assumptions of another age is dramatized in Dylan's songs. This is the New Song, the New Youth and it speaks in images and poetry and its voice is louder than anything we have heard before. [37]

A sharp example of what Gleason is writing about comes through in the album's culminating track, "Desolation Row." The song opens with a reference to "selling postcards of the hanging" — a line easily overlooked if one does not realize the monstrous practice in the US of picture postcards of lynchings. How Dylan came by this is not certain, but an episode from his father's youth in Duluth offers a possible clue. Here is how the press at the time, reported it:

Three Black circus roustabouts, Isaac McGhie, Elias Clayton and Elmer Jackson said to be about 22 years old were accused of raping a 17-year-old white girl were lynched after a mob of 5,000 turned fire hoses on the police and crashed into the jail, breaking the three from their holding cell, then holding a mock trial.

That news report continued describing how "Twice McGhie was jerked into the air to the shouts of the mob, and each time the rope broke. 'God be with them — I am not the right man!' was his last cry as on the third trial he went to his death." The report went on to describe the atmosphere: "General good humor characterized the attitude of the mob at all times."[38]

The story is shocking, but also very revealing of much of the content on Dylan's album, one replete with torturers, guardians of the "cyanide hole," and a promoter ready to sell bleacher seats for those wanting to witness World War III. Dylan may not have been writing topical protest songs any longer, but he was still a blistering social critic.

The way the mainstream responded to *Highway 61 Revisited* was telling. When Grammy nominations were announced for the music of 1965, *Highway 61 Revisited*, neither the album nor any of its songs, was anywhere among the nominees. The only mention of Dylan came in regard to a nomination for the artwork on *Bringing It All Back Home*. It lost.[39]

Indonesia

While 1965 marked a pivot from non-violence toward violent uprisings in the United States, it also marked a full-on assault of counterrevolutionary violence in Indonesia. Under the justification that the Indonesian Communist Party (PKI) was planning a coup — of which the established facts remain elusive — the reactionary military in Indonesia under General Suharto set loose a blood bath, killing anywhere between 500,000 to one million communists and their supporters.[40]

Indonesia was a tack-on Cold War counterinsurgency that was essentially genocidal. And it was backed by the CIA, which supported the killings. As Vincent Bevins writes:

What officials in the [US] embassy and the CIA decided the [Indonesian] Army really did need, however, was information. Working with CIA analysts, embassy political officer Robert Martens prepared lists with the names of thousands of communists and suspected communists, and handed them over to the Indonesian Army, so these people could be murdered and "checked off the list.[41]

In this, there is a confluence between Indonesia and Bob Dylan. In "Desolation Row," Dylan writes of agents and the "superhuman crew" rounding up everyone "who knows more than they do." It is an enigmatic line, though one that haunts — there was an ugliness undergirding the American way of life and Dylan was tuned into it. As the decade lurched forward, millions of others would be as well, and it would forever alter the landscape.

CHAPTER 6
GOD, COUNTRY, AND THE BEATLES (1966)

We're more popular than Jesus now; I don't know which will go first — rock 'n' roll or Christianity.
— John Lennon[1]

We just felt it was so absurd and sacrilegious that something ought to be done to show them they cannot get away with that sort of thing.
— A radio station manager in Alabama, on banning the Beatles[2]

In January 1966, US Army Staff Sergeant Barry Sadler was riding high on the music charts with his (and Robin Moore's) song "Ballad of the Green Berets." A valentine to the singular bravery of the US Army's Special Forces and their trademark headgear, it was an effective bit of military agitprop. Number one on the easy listening charts for five weeks, it was emblematic of where the mainstream culture was at.[3] So it is little surprise that Sadler, appearing on the *Jimmy Dean Show*, when asked about those opposed to the war, responded by saying, "I think it's a small group with a big mouth."[4] While that response was not unexpected, it was nonetheless revealing. Apparently, not *everyone* was singing psalms to the Green Berets.

One of those who was not was himself a Green Beret, US Army Master Sergeant Donald Duncan, who appeared the following month on the cover of *Ramparts*, under the title

"I Quit." Duncan, as the article made clear, had problems with the war being fought in Vietnam. As he would later say, "I liked being a Green Beret. I thought it was good. The problem I had was realizing what I was doing was not good. I was doing it right, but I wasn't doing right."[5]

Unlike Sadler, Duncan was not welcomed by Jimmy Dean or anyone else in the patriotic mainstream. He was also subject to the repressive attention of the FBI, who in 1965 opened a file on him that would run to 231 pages. He was also added to their Security Index and later to its Administrative Index.[6]

This disparity between the two Green Berets perfectly captured the emerging divide in the US. It is also little surprise, then, that Phil Ochs, along with Richard and Mimi Fariña, would wade into the fray. An account of which can be found in the following FBI report:

> A highly confidential source furnished Bringing the Troops Home Now Newsletter (100-445064), dated 3/7/66. This newsletter indicated a Vietnam folk battle erupted between Sgt. Barry "Green Beret" Sadler and Phil Ochs and Dick and Mimi Farina. Following Sadler's rendition of "The Green Beret", a ballad eulogizing the American Special Forces in Vietnam, the Farinas and Ochs dedicated the American militant antiwar songs to Sadler, Barry Goldwater and General Westmoreland.[7]

Barry Sadler may have been given access to the mainstream airwaves, but he was finding resistance on the ground.

The dichotomy between Sadler and Duncan embodied a larger emerging schism in the US about the war in Vietnam, which was becoming the central conflict occupying US society. The country had gone from the relatively modest deployment of 24,000 troops, to the commitment of 184,300 ground forces in 1965, to over 385,000 in 1966, and growing.[8] In turn, this gave rise to tens of thousands openly protesting an ongoing war, organized around a multitude of banners, or no banners at all.

As for artists, unlike the opposition mounted by a group such as the Almanac Singers in the initial phase of World War II — when the Soviet Union and Germany, contrary to US foreign policy aims, signed a non-aggression pact — the musical protest that emerged in the Sixties was not "organized" in a similar way. As such, most artists were not met mainly by an FBI or Justice Department opening files and scheming in the background.[9] Instead, they elicited a response often more insidious than calculating, aimed at bringing things under control, if not stamping them out entirely.

Jefferson Airplane Takes Off

Like many iconic groups of the time, Jefferson Airplane's roots lay in music brought forward in the folk revival, with member Paul Kantner being a student of the Weavers, Marty Balin having been in the folk group the Town Criers, and guitarist Jorma Kaukonen steeped in the roots-blues of Reverend Gary Davis and others.[10] All of this was fusing with the influence of Bob Dylan and the Beatles, who were combining a multitude of styles while writing their own songs. Within all this was the proliferation of the hallucinogenic drug LSD, which, for no small number of cutting-edge artists, served as a creative muse behind some of their most experimental music. In respect to psychedelia, Jefferson Airplane was in the vanguard.

The Airplane, arguably more than other bands, was always in contention against the entrenched forces of the larger system, with their record company, with the rules at venues they played, and with the police.

Jefferson Airplane, 1967
Credit: RCA Victor

From their beginnings, Jefferson Airplane would spar with their record label, RCA. While their first album was nowhere near as controversial as what was to come, RCA pulled the song "Runnin' Round This World," which had already been listed on the album jacket in its initial pressing. RCA took issue with its lyrical reference to "fantastic trips," which in the song meant time spent with a lover. Record executives, however, sensed an LSD reference and pulled it. According to the group's lead vocalist, Marty Balin, the line had nothing to do with drugs. As he explained, "They'd find all this meaning and give it a great deal of importance, but

'Trips' was just a slang word to us, part of the language."[11]
RCA would have been better served, in this instance, by
holding their fire — the challenges the group would later
put in front of them would be far more substantial.

The Beatles in Manila

While efforts to constrain the Airplane were in their infancy,
those leveled at the Beatles, a group in the prime of their
influence, were about to vault to a whole other level. All of
this began with their performance in the Philippines.

When the group landed in Manila in July 1966, they
entered a highly fraught country. The Philippines had,
until 1946, been a US colony. In the 1960s, while nominally
independent, it was a key outpost in US efforts against
global communism. To that end, the US government had
thrown their support behind the regime of newly elected
president Ferdinand Marcos. Their relationship with the
Philippines included hundreds of millions of dollars in
military aid and the stationing of troops in Subic Bay Naval
Base and Clark Air Base — both of which were critical to
the US's efforts in Vietnam.[12]

While Marcos had been democratically elected, his
regime would become a dictatorship, noteworthy for
brutality. As Amnesty International reported, there was
"compelling evidence that a high percentage of both
present and former prisoners," at one especially notorious
jail, had "been subjected to systematic and severe
torture," including "prolonged beatings with fists, kicks
and karate blows, beatings with a variety of contusive
instruments — including rifle butts, heavy wooden clubs
and family-sized soft drink bottles, the pounding of heads
against walls or furniture..."[13]

The Philippines, in other words, was a harshly repressive
country, and would offer a different order of concert from

what the Beatles had encountered up to then. George Harrison would describe the contrast:

> When we got to Manila, a fellow was screaming at us, 'Leave those bags there! Get in the car!' We were being bullied for the first time. It wasn't respectful. Everywhere else — America, Sweden, Germany, wherever — even though there was a mania, there was always a lot of respect because we were famous showbiz personalities. But in Manila it was a very negative vibe from the moment we got off the plane, so we were a bit frightened.[14]

The fear was not misplaced. Unbeknownst to the group, they had been invited to a reception with the country's first lady, Imelda Marcos. However, because of miscommunication, word never made it to the group. As a result, they did not show for the meeting with Marcos and four hundred invited guests, an event that was also being televised. Despite attempts to explain the misunderstanding, the official's outrage was inconsolable.

The group, scheduled to do a matinee and evening show of thirty minutes each, soon confronted open hostility. Tony Barrow, who did press work for the Beatles, reported seeing uniformed security men with large wooden batons beating the knuckles of young spectators who had been watching the show from behind the fences. More ominously, when the group left Rizal Stadium after their evening show, their police escort vanished and the stadium gates were locked. As Barrow recalled, "This left our stationary limousines at the mercy of organized troublemakers, scores I would say rather than dozens, pressing menacingly against our windows, rocking the vehicles to and fro and yelling insults at The Beatles."[15]

After the show, Beatles manager Vic Lewis was "invited" to the police station. Under interrogation, he was challenged, "You represent The Beatles. Why did you not bring them to the palace?" It was not until near daybreak on July 5 that police returned him to the Manila Hotel where the group was based. While all this was happening, the Philippine *Daily Mirror* quoted Manila Airport General Manager, Guillermo Jurado, saying that there would be no special security arrangements for the group. "They will get what they deserve."[16]

That threat was quickly borne out. As Beatles road manager Neil Aspinall recalled, the group and their associates "got pushed about from one corner of the [airport] lounge to another." The entourage, which included Brian Epstein, Vic Lewis, Tony Barrow, Neil Aspinall, Peter Brown, and Mal Evans, tried their best to protect the band members. Someone kicked Epstein, knocking him down and punching him in the face. Evans was kicked in the ribs and was bleeding by the time he reached the plane. Aspinall described the scene as a one-sided attack: "I'm sure nobody got badly hurt, but that was because we didn't fight back. If we had fought back it could have been very bad." George Harrison was more direct, saying, "He tried to kill us, President Marcos."[17]

Catching Hell in the Bible Belt

In the wake of Manila, George Harrison told the press, "We're going to have a couple of weeks to recuperate before we go and get beaten up by the Americans."[18] His comment was not hyperbole.

The problem began with remarks from John Lennon to a reporter in London in March, which were reprinted in the US teen magazine *Datebook* in July. Lennon, as was his style, talked freely about his views on religion:

Christianity will go. It will vanish and shrink. I needn't

argue about that; I'm right and I will be proved right. We're more popular than Jesus now; I don't know which will go first, rock 'n' roll or Christianity.[19]

Lennon's comment reveals someone speculatively sounding off, but hardly slamming the central tenets of Christianity. That did not matter. The remark set loose a firestorm. US radio — still highly influential in the mid-Sixties — picked up on the comment and went to war. Radio station KOB in Albuquerque held a call-in program on the controversy and reported that, of six hundred calls, 65% favored boycotting the group. In Reno, Nevada, KCBN aired an editorial every hour and made plans to burn Beatles albums the following day. Radio WAKY, in Louisville, offered a period of "silent prayer" rather than playing Beatles music.[20] In Birmingham, Tommy Charles, a disc jockey on WAQY, justified the station's ban on playing the group, saying, "We just felt it was so absurd and sacrilegious that something ought to be done to show them they cannot get away with this sort of thing."[21] What exactly the Beatles "were getting away with" — aside from offering an opinion — was not explained. In all, an estimated thirty-five stations in fifteen states said they would no longer play Beatles' records because of the remarks.[22] The Ku Klux Klan, never a group to miss an opportunity to promote white Christian "values," openly picketed the group's gigs.[23]

The controversy was not contained within the United States. The group's music was also banned in South Africa, where the country's broadcast corporation head, Piet Mayer, slammed the group's "arrogance," which he said "had passed the limits of decency" — a comment soaked in hypocrisy, given that country's racist apartheid policy.[24]

In the end, Lennon was forced to apologize, though he did so equivocally, remarking that had he said "television is more popular than Jesus, I might have got away with it."[25]

The *Chicago Defender* drew an interesting parallel to Lennon's remarks. Referring to the incident, they wrote, "Reaction has been widespread, much like [that to] Stokely Carmichael's atomic phrase 'black power'" — a reference to Carmichael's adopting a slogan that was resonating among a large section of Black people.[26] In other words, the *Defender* was drawing a line between the Beatles' perceived slight of something sacred, and Stokely's incendiary slogan, both of which were understood as a challenge to the standing order.

While the Jesus furor was one line of attack on the Beatles, it was not the only one. The media took one final whack at the band via a column by nationally syndicated columnist Jack Anderson. Running the day before their last show in San Francisco, the headline offered, "The Beatles may have finally let their hair down too far," before quoting Harrison and McCartney in what Anderson seemed to think were outrageous remarks:

> I think religion falls flat on its face. All this 'love thy neighbor', but none of them are doing it. How can anybody get themselves into the position of being Pope and accept all the glory and the money and the Mercedes Benz and that; I could never be Pope until I'd sold my rich gates and my posh hat. I couldn't sit there with all that money on me and believe I was religious. Why can't we bring all this out in the open? Why is there all this stuff about blasphemy? If Christianity's as good as they say it is, it should stand up to a bit of discussion.[27]

The piece also pointedly highlighted Harrison's pacifist disposition to the Vietnam War, quoting him saying:

> It's wrong. Anything to do with war is wrong. They're all wrapped up in their Nelsons, and their Churchills and their Montys — always talking about war heroes. Look at all our

yesterdays. How we killed a few more Huns here or there. Makes me sick.[28]

Anderson also took aim at Paul McCartney, who he described as "the baby-faced Beatle." Writing that McCartney "had this to say about America," to quote him saying, "It's a lousy country to be in where anyone who is black is made to seem a dirty nigger." Neither Harrison nor McCartney's comments were inaccurate — though one would not expect McCartney to use the n-word today — but the construction of the column was such as to suggest they had profaned everything near and dear to the United States.[29]

The dominant explanation for why the Beatles quit touring after their show in Candlestick Park on August 29 is that the hoopla had simply become too much. Speaking decades after the fact, McCartney said, "At first, the screaming was exciting. It's like doing autographs, having your photo taken, doing all that. Then, after a while, it got more and more boring."[30] While such is certainly valid, the crush of the crowd, shoddy technology, repetition, and other like factors obviously made touring unattractive. Saying that, none of these were insurmountable, and frankly, all of them are challenges that go with the territory of being a world-class band. Further, they were not the same order of problem as the physical intimidation in the Philippines and the reactionary mobs whipped up over Lennon's Jesus remarks. In that sense, what George Harrison had to say on this gets more to the truth of the matter:

We'd been through every race riot, and every city we went to there was some kind of a jam going on, and police control, and people threatening to do this and that [...] and [us] being confined to a little room or a plane or a car. We all had each other to dilute the stress, and the sense of humor was very important [...] But there was a point where enough was enough.[31]

There was, however, another issue complicating their ability to tour. Even if the group had wanted to come to the US after 1966, the war on drugs — which saw both Lennon and Harrison arrested, in 1968 and 1969, respectively — was going to make that impossible.[32]

Neither Jesus nor Judas

While the Beatles were getting slammed by the right, Bob Dylan was getting hammered by a section of the left and elements of the folk scene who took issue with his musical shift. Prominent in this was Irwin Silber, who launched a more generalized attack on those gravitating to the folk-rock genre. Things came to a certain head when, in January, Robert Shelton published a feature on folk-rock which took Silber's *Sing Out!* to task for its shoddy treatment of artists venturing into the folk-rock milieu. As Shelton wrote, "mostly the *Sing Out!* critics of folk-rock and others have dwelled on its inadequacies rather than its potential and take the naïve point of view that hit-chart popularity is evidence of compromise and poor quality."[33]

Silber's answer came in a *New York Times* piece published, along with responses by Robert Shelton, Nat Hentoff, and Paul Nelson, under the headline, "A Symposium: Is Folk Rock Really 'White Rock?'" In his piece, Silber decried, "what could have been a vital musical integration in keeping with the spirit of the Civil Rights revolution has turned into a Tin Pan Alley gimmick." He also pointedly wrote:

The influence of contemporary rhythm-and-blues, as played by Chuck Berry, Willie Dixon, Muddy Waters, and Sonny Boy Williamson on The Beatles, The Rolling Stones, and, more recently, on such American groups as The Blues Project, The Loving Spoonful, the electronic Bob Dylan and his entourage, The Byrds, and the Paul Butterfield Blues Band, is clear after one comparative listening. But, like its forebears, Folk Rock has been operating, for all meaningful purposes, out of a "white only" bag.[34]

Shelton fired back, noting that Silber "shunts the debate onto another track — the racial issue," leaving unanswered "the questions posed about the role 'Sing Out!' has played in maintaining its disdainful insularity for the folk movement." He continued:

> One can only hope Mr. Silber will find out what the new music is really about. For now, his stolidism seems to be an attempt to set up a "folk academy" by which to measure everything. As with most academies, his could do with the ventilation of fresh air to drive out the doctrinaire. Many of the Folk Rock innovators are more involved with reality than Mr. Silber concedes, it is just another reality than exists in his academy.[35]

While the issue of cultural appropriation was worthy of concern, what was happening was largely not like earlier times. In fact, the opposite was the case. It was an embrace and appreciation of Black culture on the part of young white artists, who were largely keen to break through the Jim Crow strictures that had dominated this realm. Silber's example actually made that point; the Paul Butterfield Band included two prominent Black blues musicians.

Overall, the "white rock" debate was testament to the degree to which "something was happening," and a significant section of the old guard simply did not know how to relate to it, other than by defensively attacking it. In doing so, those who had been allies operated as adversaries.

This adversarial nature was clear on the ground. In the wake of his performance at Newport the previous year, it had become a ritual for a section of the audience to greet Bob Dylan's amplified songs with catcalls and boos. As Dylan described things, "You can't tell when the booing's going to come up [...] It comes up in the weirdest, strangest places, and when it does, it's quite a thing in itself."[36]

The derision was apparently not always ad hoc. As music critic Greil Marcus explained:

> In Britain, the sort of protests that had followed Dylan and the Hawks around the U.S.A. were organized. In the U.K. the Communist Party had long operated a network of Stalinist folk clubs, where what songs could be sung, who could sing what, and in what manner, was strictly controlled.[37]

While Marcus doesn't include a citation for this, the consistency and relentlessness of the disruptions at Dylan's shows belie such incidents being entirely spontaneous.

Bob Dylan was not the first artist that the Old Left did not quite know what to do with. Gordon Friesen — who with his wife, Sis Cunningham, published Dylan's early songs in their *Broadside* newsletter — told Robert Shelton of how the Communist Party treated Dylan's icon, Woody Guthrie. Guthrie had been expelled from his nascent membership for not showing up on a Greenwich Village street corner to sell the *Daily Worker*. As Friesen recalled, the CP "never did understand how to treat artists [...] Woody's role was to write songs, not sell their paper."[38]

Which is not to say Dylan's musical shift was not a stepping away from his overt political songs and turning his back on the left — it was. But, to put it crassly, that was Dylan's business, not theirs. Going beyond musical criticism, attempting to dictate what an artist can or cannot do, as in Silber's "open letter," or by public denunciation, was shameful and out of bounds. That this took place during what Jon Pareles describes as Dylan's "most intemperate, most inspired years, when he burned as brightly as any great artist could," makes it tantamount to criminal.[39]

While that might seem an overstatement, it is a fact that, after performing in the UK, Dylan effectively ended touring until 1974. The popular understanding is that a motorcycle accident in Woodstock was the precipitating event for an extended hiatus. But like the explanation given for the Beatles to stop touring, it largely steps over the impact of the hostility exerted, beginning with the censorship on *The Ed Sullivan Show*, to the *Newsweek* article, to the booing, in the period of 1965–66.

While Dylan stopped performing live, he continued to record, but the songwriting changed. Dylan himself acknowledged as much to CBS's Ed Bradley. Referring to the lyrics of "It's Alright, Ma (I'm Only Bleeding)," Dylan said, "I don't know how I got to write those songs. Those early songs were almost magically written."[40] In the same interview, when asked how he was seen in that period, Dylan replied, "The image of me was certainly not a songwriter or a singer. It was more like some kind of a threat to society in some kind of way."[41]

The Specter of Drugs

While Dylan and the Beatles were under fire in the ways outlined above, they were also targets, along with other musicians, in what would become the war on drugs. By 1966, the minders of US culture were increasingly wary of the experimentation with drugs and began to react in kind. It was an escalation of attention that would not relent for decades.

Writing in the *LA Times*, columnist Mary Campbell attempted to make sense of things, including decoding what she felt were references to drugs appearing in the lyrics of popular music. To that end, she cited Dylan's "Mr. Tambourine Man" — reputedly about "a dope pusher or a drug-induced dream" — and "Rainy Day Women #12 & 35," with its refrain that "everybody must get stoned." While Campbell explained that "stoned" had not long ago been "slang for drunk," it had come to mean being "high on drugs." Similarly, the article pointed out that the Byrds' song "Eight Miles High" was thought to be about being high on LSD. In defense of the new songs, record executive Clive Davis said that "only a small coterie of people" would even be able to get the reference — and regardless, "it doesn't have any influencing factor at all." [42]

Drugs, however, were not wholly the issue, but existed alongside a larger animosity to the emergent culture. Composer André Previn expressed this forthrightly:

> There's an easy way of upgrading pop music to what it was. The disc jockeys could play good music. I think anything heard a lot becomes popular. If they played excerpts from 'Wozzeck' a lot, the kids would whistle it on the way to the ball game. I think it's appalling that the closer the songs are to the idiot level, the more they play them and the better they sell. [43]

Allowing that some pop music was (and is) inane, Previn's comments recall Dylan's Mr. Jones, the middle-class everyman stumbling into a world beyond his grasp. What he was not comprehending is that the culture, like it or not, was being transformed in concert with larger societal changes. As to his suggestion, if the radio was short-sighted enough to play Berg's opera twenty-four hours a day, they would quickly find themselves with no audience whatsoever.

Rising Forces

Some of the music under fire went much further than just sneaking in references to drugs. The Chambers Brothers song "Time Has Come Today," which struggled for attention in 1966 but became a hit in 1968, spoke of one's soul being "psychedelicized." This was a fantastic image — made even more so because it came from a multi-racial band, consisting of the four African-American Chambers brothers and their white drummer.

The same year the Chambers Brothers issued their song, two Merritt College students, Bobby Seale and Huey P. Newton, crafted a ten-point program arguing for the rights of Black people. In turn, they formed the Black Panther Party for Self-Defense (BPP), a group whose initial activity was the monitoring of police, through armed patrols. The BPP would not become a nationwide phenomenon until the spring of the following year, but their formation marked a certain divide in the upsurge that had gripped Black people since the late 1950s.

If, amid all this, the guardians of the status quo were concerned about things getting further out of hand, they were justified — which is not to say they would be able to stop it.

CHAPTER 7
MORE THAN THE SUMMER OF LOVE (1967)

San Francisco (Be Sure to Wear Flowers in Your Hair)
— Song by John Phillips

There was a realization that the powers that be actually looked upon us as important enough to make a big statement and wield the hammer.
— Keith Richards.[1]

On January 2, the United States implemented an initiative in Vietnam called Operation Bolo. The scheme, which used radar jamming and other tricks, deceived the North Vietnamese into thinking that F-105 jets were flying into their territory rather than the actual, much faster F-4s. When the North's MIGs set out to down what they thought were slower jets, they were instead shot down. The *New York Times* would later that year call the Colonel who masterminded the operation "everybody's choice as the hottest pilot in Vietnam."[2] In 1967, the Vietnam War was, or so certain august authorities thought, winnable.

While Operation Bolo seemed to portend a sunny future, the death of three astronauts in a fire while training for a moon launch scheduled for the following month did not. Nor did the ascent in California of Ronald Reagan, sworn in as governor that same month. Reagan would garner national fame for his attacks on campus uprisings, through acerbic verbal assaults and dispatching of the National Guard.

Outside of Vietnam and the US, titanic events were underway in China, where the Great Proletarian Cultural Revolution was taking place. That January was the establishment of "The Shanghai Commune," which overthrew the leadership of the entrenched Communist Party in favor of elements supporting Mao Zedong's efforts to usurp power "from below." The undertaking — as fraught as it would turn out to be — had manifesto-like implications, which would assert themselves globally.[3]

That same month, the Doors released their eponymous masterwork. It was followed that year by iconic albums such as: The Jimi Hendrix Experience's *Are You Experienced*, Cream's *Disraeli Gears,* Jefferson Airplane's *Surrealistic Pillow*, and the Beatles' *Sgt. Pepper's Lonely Hearts Club Band*. In aggregate, it constituted a cultural revolution of another kind.

Today, the clichéd image of 1967 is of one awash with hippies and all things related to peace and love, culminating in what would come to be branded "The Summer of Love." Like most clichés, it holds some elements of truth, but ultimately glides along the surface. Most pointedly, 1967 occupied the same temporal space as the "long hot summer" of riots in Newark and Detroit, the transformation of peaceful protest into confrontational resistance, and an insurgent culture that increasingly found itself living outside the law.

Counterculture and Politics

On January 14, San Francisco's Golden Gate Park was the site of a Human Be-In/Gathering of Tribes. It was an event that sought to join the emerging counterculture with a left-wing politics that was increasingly asserting itself. On the politics/philosophy side, it featured LSD gurus Timothy Leary and Richard Albert (later to become Baba Ram Das), activist-comedian Dick Gregory, and soon to be Yippie, Jerry Rubin. Musically, the one-day event featured the Steve Miller Band, Santana, Quicksilver Messenger Service, and the Grateful Dead — none of whom were yet the marquee names they would become.[4] The event attracted 30,000 people, and the vibe — amid an abundance of top-shelf LSD — was communal. As one attendee described it, "[it was] a huge consciousness raising event which announced to the world that the hip/peace movement was here and growing..."[5] An event of such magnitude, which captured the imagination of a cross section of youth, virtually screamed out for capitalist co-option, which was not long in coming.

In a somewhat similar vein, albeit directly focused on Vietnam, artists under the umbrella of "Angry Arts" — established to oppose the war in Vietnam — presented a series of exhibitions, performances, and concerts beginning in New York. In the Bay Area, the event was held on April 9 and included Quicksilver Messenger Service, Sopwith Camel, Big Brother and the Holding Company, and Country Joe & the Fish.[6] Events in Los Angeles in June and July included "a pyre of burning paintings, plays, poems and passionate essays."[7]

These undertakings gave way to Vietnam Summer, organized by the pacifist Quaker organization, the American Friends Service Committee, which sent volunteers into communities around the country to inform and organize against the war.[8]

Monterey Pop

Many of the artists who had taken part in the Be-In and the Angry Arts events were also showcased two months later in the northern California coastal city of Monterey.

The Monterey Pop Festival, which took place from June

16 to 18, is generally held to be the quintessential event of the "Summer of Love" — and the opening of a certain period of the 1960s that closed two years later with the calamity at Altamont. The mythology surrounding it is in no small part due to the commercialization of the music from the weekend, including the marketing of the film by D.A. Pennebaker. Unfortunately, the mythology obscures the contradictions simmering beneath the surface, many of which stood as counterpoints against the idealized notions about Monterey.

The festival was the product of a collaboration between music producer Lou Adler and John Phillips, the leader of the Mamas and the Papas, who would have a preeminent spot at the concert. As Mat Callahan documents, Monterey was a turning point in which the vibrant music scene that had emerged in the Bay Area was being incorporated into the music business:

> Behind the scenes, managers and record companies began to systematically integrate the bulk of the San Francisco music scene into the corporate machine. The process would take some time to complete and would involve considerable conflict, but it remains the case the Monterey Pop Festival was a turning point.[9]

Watching footage of the event decades later reveals how the festival was antithetical in many ways to the Be-In of only a few months earlier, where people had gathered unconstrained in a large park. By contrast, one sees Monterey as a highly contained environment, amenable to ticket collection and merchandise sales.[10]

As for the music, it cut two ways. The Mamas and the Papas were clearly being promoted both in the concert and later in the film — unfortunately, they had the unwelcome duty of closing the show after Jimi Hendrix's incendiary (literally) performance. Not surprisingly, Cass Elliott — a standout vocalist in the group — was quickly absorbed into the mainstream and by 1968 was performing in Las Vegas, before going on to be a staple on mainstream television.[11]

Despite such appropriation, the bulk of the music existed on what was then the cutting edge. There are standout performances by Hugh Masekela (from apartheid South Africa), Moby Grape, Buffalo Springfield, Simon & Garfunkel, Country Joe & the Fish, the Who, the Grateful Dead, Jefferson Airplane, Ravi Shankar, Jimi Hendrix, Otis Redding, and the Animals.

Beyond the conservatizing moves to monetization, there was also the overhanging specter of the draft. This is seen in the case of Beach Boy Carl Wilson. The group, then at their creative peak, having released their pathbreaking *Pet Sounds* the previous year, had been rumored to appear, but did not. While the exact reasons are still debated, it was the case that Wilson, the group's guitarist, was in the midst of court proceedings for not reporting for military service.[12] Wilson's problems are documented in his FBI file:

On May 1, 1967, CARL DEAN WILSON was arraigned in the United States District Court, Los Angeles, California, and entered a plea of not guilty to the charge of violation of Title 50 Appendix, U.S. Code, Section 462 [the Selective Service Act]. Trial set for June 20, 1967.[13]

As the report makes clear, Wilson's court appearance was to be the day after the concert. Whether that was decisive to the group's decision to play or not is unclear — other theories hold it was a conflict over performance fees or a feeling the group would not fit in. That taken into account, it is hard to imagine the court appearance was not a considerable factor. Either way, their absence from the festival denied them an opportunity of much-needed counterculture legitimacy.

Also missing at Monterey were three of the biggest bands from the British Invasion: the Beatles, the Rolling Stones, and the Kinks. As discussed in the previous chapter, after their besieged tour of 1966, the Beatles had resolved to stop appearing live. While such was not the case with the Rolling Stones, other considerations precluded an appearance.

Rolling Stone Brian Jones was one of the hosts at Monterey. That he was there, but not his band, stemmed from the fact that Mick Jagger and Keith Richards had been arrested on February 12 on drug charges. Richards and Jagger were put on trial in June. They were convicted, receiving a three-month and a twelve-month sentence respectively. It was only because of the intervention of an editorial in the *London Times* calling out the excessive sentences that the conviction would be overturned a month and a half later.[14]

Richards would later reflect on that incident and his remarks get at how contentious the situation was, whether that be in California or London:

> [I]t made us realize that this was a whole different ball game and that was when the fun had stopped. Up until then, it had been as though London existed in a beautiful space where you could do anything you wanted. And then the hammer came down and it was back to reality [...] There was a realization that the powers that be actually looked upon us as important enough to make a big statement and wield the hammer.[15]

While the Stones were confronting one type of obstacle in coming to the US, the Kinks were confronting another.

The Kinks and the AFM

The Kinks had made a splash in the UK and US during the initial wave of the British invasion, but the group saw their career stalled because of their confrontation with the American Federation of Musicians, working with the US government.

As far as politics went, the Kinks tended more toward libertarianism rather than radicalism, but the fact that they came from the UK and were a rock band made them a problem in certain quarters. The group's difficulties stemmed from a series of confrontations during their 1965 US tour. They initially ran into trouble after performing on Dick Clark's *Where the Action Is*. In Ray Davies' telling:

> Some guy who said he worked for the TV company walked up and accused us of being late. Then he started making anti-British comments. Things like, "Just because the Beatles did it, every mop-topped, spotty faced limey juvenile thinks he can come over here and make a career for himself." He called me "A talentless fuck who was in the right place at the right time." The usual schlock.[16]

In response, according to Davies, "I just turned around and hit him about three times. I later found out that he was a union official."[17]

Two days later, more problems emerged when the group declined to perform at the Cow Palace in San Francisco. According to Davies, promoter Betty Kaye had refused to pay the group in cash, which they said was in violation of their contract. As a result of their failure to perform, Kaye submitted a formal complaint to Local 6 of the AFM.[18]

Compounding all this was another incident involving Ray Davies's brother Dave, who refused to sign union documents regarding another live performance, instead telling the union official to "fuck off." To which the official responded, "You're never going to work in America again."[19] All of this would lead the union to come down hard on the group.

Ted Dreber, who had been assistant to former union head Herman Kenan, would tell historian Michael James Roberts that the group had been banned from touring the US for more than four years, based on the regulations of the US Immigration and Naturalization Service.[20] Those years spanned the period from 1966 to 1969, which included Monterey, precluding them from accepting an invitation to perform.[21]

Reflecting on the episode years later, Ray Davies got at the larger issue:

> I even imagined that the powers-that-be, the unions, showbiz insiders, whoever, were so pissed off that the Beatles had taken away so much earning power for American bands that they were looking for any excuse to make an example of someone.[22]

While such is hard to prove, the Kinks, because of their contentious behavior, offered a ready target. However, it should be remembered the union leadership had unsuccessfully tried to ban no less a group than the Beatles. This, coupled with the fact that they were happy to work in concert with governmental authorities to effect this, made it all the more serious.[23]

Phil Ochs in LA

By 1967 Phil Ochs had relocated to Los Angeles, and was exploring music beyond straight-forward topical songs, as seen in 1967's *Pleasures of the Harbor*. He was, however, still heavily engaged in the political vortex. In LA, he undertook an initiative against the Vietnam War, which he dubbed "The War is Over!" This was a call to "celebrate the end of the war," which he described as "a grass roots attempt to create a different reality."[24] Ochs launched the project during a demonstration of ten thousand people who had turned out to protest a June visit by President Lyndon Johnson.

The demonstration, however, was not peaceful. The police were out in force, mobilizing 1,300 cops, who moved violently on the gathering. They also attacked those who assembled to listen to Ochs sing "The War is Over," which he had composed for the event. "As Ochs performed on a flatbed truck, police ordered the crowd to disperse. When people did not move quickly enough, police moved in, "swinging their nightsticks at anyone in their paths."[25] The police violence, shocking as it was, was nothing compared to what came the following month.

Newark and Detroit

As mentioned earlier, the "Summer of Love" was also the "Long Hot Summer" of urban upheavals, where more than 159 civil disturbances took place.[26] The two most extreme episodes occurred in Newark and Detroit, and they were of an order beyond anything ever seen in the United States.

In Newark, what set things off was a rumor on July 12 that a Black cab driver had been killed inside a police precinct — he had not been killed, but had been beaten. What followed was five days of turmoil that ravaged the city. When it ended on July 17, beyond the burned and looted businesses, twenty-six people were dead — twenty-four of whom were residents, along with one firefighter and one police officer. The violence in Newark was beyond that of Watts the previous summer, but what happened in Detroit, less than a week later, was worse.[27]

The spark in Detroit was a police raid on an after-hours

club on July 23, which sparked street violence that lasted until July 28. To regain control, not only was the National Guard deployed, but 4,700 paratroopers from the Army's 18th Airborne Division were put on Detroit's streets. When regular order was finally restored, forty-three people were dead, 342 were injured, and nearly 1,400 buildings had been burned.[28]

Rebellion and Respect

There remains debate as to the underlying causes and character of these risings — some calling them simply riots — or worse, mass criminality — others characterizing them as rebellions.[29] What is clear is that by 1967 such disturbances, while nearing their peak, were also impacting the larger landscape of the Black freedom movement and everything surrounding it — including the culture.

A sharp example of this was Aretha Franklin's version of Otis Redding's "Respect," released that April. At Monterey, Redding introduced his performance by acknowledging, in a collegial way, how Franklin had made the song her own, saying it was "A song that a girl took away from me [...] a good friend of mine."[30] In taking it away, she transformed it from one of a man asking for respect from "his woman," into an anthem of respect on multiple levels, including race and gender.

JA in Bakersfield

Years after the fact, Jefferson Airplane's Grace Slick remarked that, at Monterey, "everything worked."[31] This comment is better understood in the context of how things usually went for the group, a good example being when they performed on September 2, at the Civic Auditorium in the conservative California town of Bakersfield.

At one point during the concert, guitarist Paul Kantner tried to enliven things, telling the audience to "push your chairs back and dance." When the crowd moved to comply, the police — enforcing an ordinance prohibiting dancing for people under sixteen — moved to stop them. What ensued was a back-and-forth confrontation, which lasted till the end of the concert. All this culminated when Kantner said, "What's the matter with you guys out there? Remember, there are only five of them and 5,000 of us." The police begrudgingly backed off, but the venue manager quickly took the stage at the end of the song to announce the concert was over.

As Marty Balin would later recall, "We began to pull that all the time. Sometimes the cops would turn off the electricity. Grace would pick up megaphones and just keep on. Then they'd come out and grab the megaphones."[32] While Balin's remarks suggest this was something of a gimmick, it was one tapping into an underlying spirit of rebellion, one that was escalating.

Drug Arrests

While Jefferson Airplane was sparring with stadium authorities, they would repeatedly contend in a realm where there were no assembled masses they could call up to defend them. According to the group's historian Jeff Tamarkin, bassist Jack Casady was arrested in his hotel room for possession of hashish while the group was in Los Angeles — Tamarkin does not give a date, though it was likely late 1966 or early 1967. In that instance, no charges were leveled, but it was only the beginning of such travails.[33]

As Tamarkin writes, "it was becoming obvious not only to the Airplane but many high-profile rock musicians that their highly publicized high times were becoming of greater interest to law enforcement officials."[34] This came about amid national publicity showered on the Haight section of San Francisco, and the consequent overload in people coming to check out the scene or check out in general. With the mass of people came more toxic drugs and a far more dangerous street life.

Things reached a point where the San Francisco anarchist collective, the Diggers, held a "Death of a Hippie" march on Haight Street that fall, complete with pallbearers. Four days before the parade, a team of narcotics cops raided the Grateful Dead's house at 710 Ashbury, arresting its occupants on drug possession charges. In response, most of the band exited the city, decamping to nearby Marin County.[35]

Also contending with drug charges, this in Southern California, was Buffalo Springfield. In January, the group's bassist, Canadian national Bruce Palmer, had been arrested on drug charges and was deported. While he made his way back to the US, he was again arrested in January 1968, and deported again — forcing him to leave the group permanently.[36]

LSD

At the same time, the government was contending with a drug problem largely of its own creation — lysergic acid diethylamide, or LSD. The drug had found its way into the wider public as a result of experimentation by the US government, which was studying its efficacy in interrogations — which proved fruitless.[37] By the mid-1960s, the legal drug was being popularized by people such as author Ken Kesey and his Merry Pranksters and their acid tests — parties where people freely sampled the drug. For some, its effect — the altered reality — was a window into a different realm of being and consciousness. Among those embracing it early on were groups such as Jefferson

Airplane, the Grateful Dead, and the Beatles — and the line between certain of their experimental musical breakthroughs and the impact of the hallucinogen became fuzzy, to say the least.

While the government had no trouble studying the drug for enhancing their war-fighting capacity, that it would be used by those seeking an alternate state of being was beyond the pale. As a result, by the end of 1966, both New York and California passed laws making LSD use illegal.[38] Following that, in 1968, it was reclassified by the federal government as a Schedule 1 narcotic "with a high potential for abuse, no currently accepted medical use."[39] All of which was laying the basis to escalate repression through the vehicle of a war on drugs.

Joan Baez on the Barricades

The fall of 1967 also marked a qualitative heightening in anti-war resistance. Activists on the West Coast initiated a Stop the Draft Week, which ran from October 16 to 21. Events in Oakland were an uneasy mix of peaceful sit-ins and more militant actions, which in turn encountered an aggressive response from the Oakland Police. One of these was a sit-in at the Army's Oakland Induction Center, where among those arrested was Joan Baez, who was taken into custody along with dozens of others for blocking the entrances to the center.[40]

Baez's year was already one full of controversy. In August, she had been denied use of Washington's Constitutional Hall by the Daughters of the American Revolution, who objected to her opposition to the war. The President General of the group — identifying via her husband's name — Mrs. William H. Sullivan, Jr., proclaimed: "We are directly behind our Government's stand on Vietnam, and we are directly behind our boys who are dying there."

The DAR's opposition would end up as a boon for Baez, who instead of performing in their space gave an outdoor concert at the Washington Monument, which attracted thirty thousandpeople.[41]

While that event turned out advantageous for Baez, the Oakland action was more problematic. At the induction center, she had been arrested with her younger sister, Mimi Fariña. While Joan Baez's FBI file has not been released, Mimi's has, and it strongly suggests both sisters were put on the FBI's radar as a result of their participation in that action. In a memo in Fariña's file, the Bureau cited a recent order instructing that

[A]ll participants in demonstrations and disturbances who are arrested be identified. Background information should be developed on these individuals and the indices of appropriate field offices checked in order that a determination can be made whether further investigation is warranted and if their overall activities would justify including their names on the Security Index.[42]

Put another way, people arrested at such actions were to be considered for a higher degree of federal-law enforcement scrutiny.

In Mimi Fariña's case, matters appear to have started and stopped there — at least according to her file. Whether the same is true of her sister is unclear, though given Joan Baez's tenacious activism, her file is likely more substantial — especially given that she returned to the induction center in December, where she was again arrested, this time along with her mother and the poet Lawrence Ferlinghetti.[43]

This, however, was not the only way government spies were pursuing her. Because Baez had lent her voice to an anti-war group in Japan, she came under the scrutiny of the CIA. This stemmed from her activities in support of four members of the Navy who had deserted — and ended up going to the Soviet Union. The CIA's report on the matter is illustrative on a number of levels:

> The consensus of all available press reports, with no recorded dissent, indicates that the four sailors voluntarily left their ship, went AWOL, and ended up wallowing around Tokyo's hippie-land. Precisely what personal grievances prompted the four to embark on this misadventure is not known. But, up to this point, the four could fairly be categorized as misguided youngsters, gone astray in a foreign land, and due to get slapped back in line with traditional Navy justice when they finally decided to stop the fun and go back to the ship.[44]

The snide tone aside, Baez is referenced in the report for participating in a mass meeting sponsored by the Japanese group Beherien (Peace for Vietnam Committee), held in January in Tokyo to defend the soldiers.[45]

The Pentagon and the Fugs

Back in the US, the anti-war activity of the fall culminated with a march followed by a sit-in at the Pentagon. While the rally held on October 21, which drew around 100,000 people, was of usual type for such things, with speeches and songs — including performances by Peter, Paul and Mary and Phil Ochs — what followed was atypical.

Some fifty thousand people marched from the rally to the Pentagon, where they were met by two thousand District of Columbia police, 1,800 National Guardsmen, and a US military force of three thousand — including an Airborne battalion from Fort Bragg, NC. Pointedly, among the leadership of this force was Lieutenant General John

L. Throckmorton, of the Third Army, who had commanded federal troops during the Detroit riots three months earlier. [46]

The Pentagon, Oct. 21, 1967
Credit: USA Army Photo, NARA

One of the actions at the Pentagon was carried out by the New York band, the Fugs. The group, who took their name from Norman Mailer's term for "fuck" in his novel *The Naked and the Dead,* came out of New York's Lower East Side. One of their first encounters with law enforcement happened in 1966, when the New York Police raided the Peace Eye Bookstore, located on East 10 Street, and arrested its proprietor and member of the Fugs, Ed Sanders. The issue was the publication of Sanders's *Fuck You/A Magazine of the Arts*, which authorities claimed was obscene — though with the help of the ACLU, he was later cleared of those charges.[47]

In keeping with their artistic sensibilities, at one point during the Pentagon demonstration the group conducted a ritual in which they attempted to exorcise the building. As Sanders intoned:

> In the name of the generative power of Priapus, in the name of the totality, we call upon the demons of the Pentagon to rid themselves of the cancerous tumors of the war generals, all the secretaries and soldiers who don't know what they're doing, all the intrigue bureaucracy and hatred, all the spewing.[48]

In parts theater, ritual, satire and protest, the group's action captured the irreverence of the emerging counterculture.

While there was in the Fugs' action a certain humor, overall the demonstration at the Pentagon was quite serious. The protest ended in the early morning hours of October 22, when Military Police beat and arrested those who had chosen to remain.[49]

Targeting Black Radicals and Supporters

The situation among a section of Black people in the US was of escalating concern and invariably came into the purview of the FBI and the CIA. It was in August 1967 that the FBI formally extended its counterintelligence program aimed at Black nationalists and separatists, which they labeled "Black Nationalist-Hate Groups." This was a program which initially had in mind organizations such as the Nation of Islam, the Revolutionary Action Movement, and the Student Non-Violent Coordinating Committee, but soon came to include the Black Panther Party.[50]

A key objective of this initiative, shorthanded as COINTELPRO, was to block support of such groups from wider organizations. In that respect, a memo from the CIA in December 1967 is telling. After noting that they had been accused — wrongly, in their view — of complicity in the killings of Congolese leader Patrice Lumumba and of Malcolm X, they outlined the threat they felt was coming from those advocating Black Power:

> Presently, however, the growing militancy of "black power" disciples — with clear links to both Maoist and Moscow Communist ideologies — and similarly clear threats to counter the Agency's activities, necessitates placing the problem in an entirely new perspective.[51]

The document then listed every significant Black political leader of the time, including Martin Luther King, James Forman, Stokely Carmichael, John Lewis, and Huey Newton, as well as several artists, including Abbey Lincoln, Harry Belafonte, and Malvina Reynolds.

Reynolds, a white woman, was not a particularly well-known artist but had penned several songs that were performed by others, including "Little Boxes," which Pete Seeger had recorded. She was also openly associated with the Old Left. In the CIA's view, she was a "communist folksinger" and a "member of a number of Vietnam protest fronts and organizations as well as activities opposed to HCUA." They also reported that she was part of the Better Berkeley Committee, which the CIA described as "A group formed at Berkeley to counter alleged police harassment in ghetto areas through the use of citizens patrols."[52]

As for Harry Belafonte, he had been a longtime target, particularly for his association and work with Martin Luther King, but he also showed up due to his anti-war work:

> Belafonte was a listed sponsor of the Spring Mobilization Committee to End the War in Vietnam and was one of

those who led a New York City march against the war on 15 April 1967. In 1965, he was indicated to be a cultural advisor to the Republic of Guinea. He was a signatory of an advertisement critical of the U.S. role in Vietnam which appeared earlier this year in the London Times.[53]

They also made note that Belafonte "paid the expenses for eleven SNCC Members who traveled to Guinea."

Belafonte, it should be noted, had the misfortune of having as his financial manager Jay Richard Kennedy from 1955 to 1956, who, after severing his relationship with Belafonte, went on to work as a CIA informant.[54] For that reason, Belafonte shows up in various CIA reports with information from Kennedy that is gossipy and wildly inaccurate. For example, Kennedy wrongly claims "BELAFONTE, of course, is a Communist and undoubtedly Peking controlled." What this claim was based on is unclear, but as was seen in Chapter 1, Belafonte had done a considerable amount of work to disassociate himself from any relations with communists and was ostracized by them because of it.[55]

That said, what is notable in all this is how once an artist went from being organizationally unaffiliated to having some kind of ties with overt political actors or organizations — whether supporting Black freedom or work against the Vietnam War — they became subjects of increased scrutiny by the considerable US intelligence apparatus.

New Haven

While the Doors did not fit the category of political partisans, they were nonetheless drawing heat. Their inaugural release had hit the streets in January, and the group had skyrocketed to stardom with the success of the single "Light My Fire." This garnered them a spot on *The Ed Sullivan Show* on September 17. While rehearsals went well, before the actual appearance one of the show's producers approached the band to tell them the phrase "girl we couldn't get much higher" could not be sung on network TV. At issue was the word "higher" and its perceived reference to drugs. While the band assured the producer they would make a change to avoid the word, in a conference they decided to keep things as they were — and claim a nervous slip led them to do the song as written. As a result, the performance broadcast the original line. It was a mild, almost juvenile rebellion, but it had adult consequences. The group would never again perform on *The Ed Sullivan Show*. It was not the only problem they had that year.[56]

When the Doors took the stage in New Haven on December 11, they immediately noticed a line of police in front of the stage — there, they were told, "for your safety." As the performance moved into an instrumental section of "Back Door Man," singer Jim Morrison shared with the audience that he had been sprayed with mace before coming on stage. The assault occurred when an officer confronted Morrison for making out with an eighteen-year-old student from Southern Connecticut State College. The police had wanted to arrest Morrison then-and-there, but were convinced by the group's manager to let the show go on. However, when Morrison called out the cop from the stage, they decided to arrest him. The lights were turned on and six cops took the stage, taking Morrison into custody. What followed was a scuffle in which thirteen people were arrested, including journalists from the *Village Voice* and *Life* magazine, along with a freelance photographer.

All in all, it was a minor disturbance, with the journalists released on $300 bond and Morrison freed on $1,500. The charges would eventually be dropped. Unfortunately, it was not the last or most serious interaction between the Doors and law enforcement.[57] Things were moving out onto a far more contentious plane.

CHAPTER 8
WHOLE WORLD IN AN UPROAR (1968)

Gentlemen, get the thing straight, once and for all. The policeman isn't there to create disorder; the policeman is there to preserve disorder.
— Chicago Mayor, Richard Daley.[1]

"Il est interdit d'interdire!" (It is forbidden to forbid!)
— Graffiti in Paris, May 1968.[2]

The end of January marked the beginning of the Lunar New Year, known as Tết in Vietnam. To mark the occasion, the North Vietnamese Army, in conjunction with the National Liberation Front in South Vietnam, unleashed an offensive that saw Vietnamese troops make it as far as the grounds of the US embassy in Saigon before finally being repelled.[3]

For the US warmakers, the offensive was staggering. Lyndon Johnson's Secretary of Defense, Clark Clifford, would describe how "the reaction of our military leadership approached panic and their intelligence failure was a critical factor in both the military setbacks suffered in the early phase of the offensive and the backlash in American public opinion."[4] While the Tết offensive was ultimately turned back, it shattered the illusion of United States invincibility.[5]

An Unrelenting Spring

In the eighty-one days between March 16 and June 6, an

onslaught of events took place that would enmesh the United States in a crisis that would haunt it for decades.

On March 16, troops from Charlie Company of the US 23rd (Americal) Infantry Division set loose their fury on the Vietnamese village of Mỹ Lai, murdering 504 old men, women, and children. While news of Mỹ Lai would not become known to the wider American public until the late fall of 1969, when it did, it brought to light in horrifying ways what kind of war the United States had descended into fighting in Vietnam.[6]

At the end of March, US President Johnson — reeling under the abysmal situation in Vietnam — announced he would not seek a second term. His decision threw the US political apparatus into chaos. Johnson's announcement was quickly followed, on April 4, by the assassination of Martin Luther King, Jr. King was killed during a visit to Memphis, where he had come to support a strike by mostly Black sanitation workers. His killing by a white supremacist sniper, James Earl Ray, set off rebellions in near every major city in the United States.

Two weeks later, Black students at Cornell University staged an armed occupation of the college's Willard Straight Hall in response to a cross burning at Wari House, a cooperative for Black women students. While the conflict ended peacefully, the stakes had been raised.[7] A week later, arguably one of the most consequential student strikes of the decade got underway at Columbia University. The spark for the strike, which lasted from April 23 to 30, was Columbia's expansion into the African-American neighborhood of Harlem, but would come to concentrate on the issues of the war in Vietnam, Black power, and even elements of the counterculture.[8] In fact, the Grateful Dead, in an act of solidarity, performed on campus three days after the strike had been broken up by a violent police assault.[9]

While the Dead were playing in the plaza at Columbia,

students in Paris occupied the Sorbonne, joined a month later by workers in a nationwide strike that nearly toppled the De Gaulle Government. Amid all this, the USSR was plotting to undermine reform leader Alexander Dubček's efforts in Czechoslovakia — which would culminate in a Soviet invasion that August, causing severe damage to the USSR's claims of being the epicenter of socialist liberation.

Capping off this whirlwind, presidential candidate Robert F. Kennedy was executed on June 6 by Palestinian extremist Sirhan Bishara Sirhan. Kennedy had seized on the opening of Johnson's withdrawal to run for president as an ostensible "peace" candidate, in opposition to the other anti-war candidate, Eugene McCarthy. His assassination threw the political apparatus into further turmoil — and sharpened the sense that things in the United States were coming undone.[10]

The King Riots

By early 1968, King's doctrine of unity and non-violence was increasingly being left behind by militant elements of the Black freedom movement who were taking up the slogan "Black Power." Further, there were people such as Robert F. Williams, former head of the Monroe, North Carolina NAACP, who had organized a Black Armed Guard under the auspices of the NRA.[11] While Williams, confronting trumped up legal charges after a confrontation with racist whites, would end up in exile, first in Cuba and then China, the Black Panther Party in Oakland would step into the breach, with their calls for armed self-defense.[12]

As a result, when King was assassinated, it served as a pull switch for the widest scale social unrest of the entire period. It was also the bellwether of a new, far more radical situation among all the forces standing in opposition to the various policies and initiatives of the US government.

King's assassination, for many, marked the point of no return, launching them into realms never imagined.

In the ten days following King's murder, nearly two hundred US cities experienced mass violence. The cities that saw the worst were the nation's capital and the nearby city of Baltimore. In Washington, the government dispatched nine thousand troops. A news account of the character of the deployment is astonishing, not only in its numbers, but in how it documents a major military campaign, undertaken *within* the nation's capital:

> Meyer, Va., 700 men; Sixth Armored Cavalry, Fort Meade Md., 2,200; District of Columbia National Guard, 1,300; Marine Corps School Battalion, Quantico, Va., 709; 91st Engineer Battalion, Fort Belvoir, Va.; 700; First Brigade, 82d Airborne Division, Fort Bragg, N. C., 2,000; 716th Transportation Battalion, Fort Eustis, Va. 600; 544th Support and Service Battalion, Fort Lee, Va., 700; and 503d Military Police Battalion, Fort Bragg, N. C., 500.[13]

While the deployment might seem an overreaction, the fact that rioting reached within blocks of the White House and the US Capitol underscores the enormity of the challenge the US government was confronted with. As Peter Levy assessed, "During Holy Week 1968, the United States experienced its greatest wave of social unrest since the Civil War."[14]

Three days after King's assassination, Nina Simone performed a song written by band member Calvin Taylor titled "Why? (The King of Love is Dead)" at the Westbury Music Festival, which was later released as part of Simone's live album, *'Nuff Said!*[15] The song, at once an elegy and an acknowledgement that things had moved into a different realm, where things were "headed for the brink," and that even "if you have to die, it's all right," because at least "you know what freedom is."[16] Simone, like many others, was being propelled in a far more radical direction.

Banning Gordon Lightfoot

The embers of the King riot were still white hot when Gordon Lightfoot attempted to release "Black Day in July," composed in response to the previous year's Detroit riot. With the single set for release in July of 1968, Lightfoot confronted a ban from nearly every station in the United States. The fact that the song broke through the top ten on several charts throughout Canada suggests it could have been a success for Lightfoot in the US as well.

While it is hardly the most radical song of its time, Lightfoot's understanding of it, and his role in the larger tumult, is instructive. This comes through in an interview he conducted with Canadian radio in the wake of the song's banning. As Lightfoot explained:

[T]op 40 stations have a policy, except here in Canada of course, where we've been quite fortunate, but a lot of them don't want to upset their listeners, it's a housewife in the morning, let's give her something that will make her happy, why give her something that's going to make her think?

Beyond that, Lightfoot offered a startling observation on how far things had gotten during the uprising in 1967. Elaborating on events in Detroit, he recalled a friend telling him, "When you see a tank sitting on the main street, with a machine gun going, it sort of wakes you up a little bit."[17] In that context, banning his song, from the authorities' point of view, was the least they could do.

Miriam Makeba

By the mid-Sixties, exiled South African singer Miriam Makeba had established a successful career in the United States, which included a 1965 Grammy for her collaboration with Harry Belafonte and her chart-topping record "Pata Pata" in 1967.[18] Her career would come under attack, however, after her engagement and marriage to Stokely Carmichael (later Kwame Ture), a leader of the Student Non-Violent Coordinating Committee and advocate of the militant position of Black Power.

The fallout began immediately. First, the Bahamian prime minister canceled Makeba's business permit to operate her clothing store, Makeba's Hut, and banned her from the island.[19] More problems ensued. Carmichael told the press in December that "the whole industry is boycotting her. She has cut a new album and they refuse to play it because she married me. They are afraid I will buy guns with the money."[20] The *New York Times* indirectly acknowledged the suppression, writing that Makeba's "musical appearances have declined since her marriage to Carmichael."[21]

The problem for Makeba was not simply that she would marry a Black radical, but that Carmichael was arguably the most reviled one at the time. In the FBI's view, Stokely Carmichael was a potential revolutionary "messiah" who they were determined to stop. As they outlined in their notorious "Black Nationalist Hate Groups" counterintelligence memo, one of the objectives was to

[P]revent the RISE OF A "MESSIAH" who could unify, and electrify, the militant black nationalist movement. Malcolm X might have been such a "messiah;" he is the martyr of the movement today. Martin Luther King, Stokely Carmichael, and Elijah Muhammed all aspire to this position. Elijah Muhammed is less of a threat because of his age. King could be a very real contender for this position should he abandon his supposed "obedience" to "white, liberal doctrines" (nonviolence) and embrace black nationalism. Carmichael has the necessary charisma to be a real threat in this way.[22]

What came with this distinction was a multi-pronged effort to politically neutralize Carmichael.

One of those efforts was a scheme to sully his reputation by publicizing that Makeba and he were spending a good deal of money to buy a house. Apparently, the news media got to this first, which the Bureau nonetheless put in their column as "Tangible results":

WFO [Washington Field Office] was in the process of submitting a recommendation regarding the purchase of a $70,000 house by CARMICHAEL proposing release of this information to appropriate news media for publication upon consummation of the purchase, when news articles regarding this purchase appeared as the Bureau is aware, CARMICHAEL AND MIRIAM MAKEBA thereafter canceled the contract to buy this property, claiming inability to obtain suitable financing. As the Bureau pointed out, it has had an effect on his reputation among some black militants.[23]

By the end of the year, the couple decided to leave the US and repatriate to Guinea, something the FBI documented in detail:

[REDACTED] advised that as of December 11, 1968, half of the furnishings belonging to Carmichael and Makeba had been put on board the boat "African Rainbow" in Baltimore, being handled by the Farrell Lines, Incorporated. He related that prior to departure from Washington, D.C. Carmichael and Makeba purchased a new household refrigerator, two washing machines and a range stove, which they also desired included with the shipment to Conakry.[24]

UNITED STATES DEPARTMENT OF JUSTICE

FEDERAL BUREAU OF INVESTIGATION

In Reply, Please Refer to
File No.

Washington, D. C.   20535
December 11, 1968

ALL INFORMATION CONTAINED
HEREIN IS UNCLASSIFIED
DATE 02-27-2010 BY 60324 UC BAW/DK/TH

STOKELY CARMICHAEL

               Overseas Shipping Company, Incorporated, International Freight Forwarders and Export Packing, 2221 Adams Place, N.E., Washington, D.C., advised on December 11, 1968,   the shipment of household furnishings belonging to Stokely Carmichael and his wife, Miriam Makeba, to Conakry, Guinea. He advised the furnishings, amounting to about twelve thousand pounds, had been removed from their Washington, D.C. residence during mid-November, 1968, preparatory to shipment by boat to Conakry from Baltimore, Maryland, during the early part of December, 1968. Prior to actual shipment, they were stored temporarily in Washington, D.C. at an overseas shipping company warehouse. CARMICHAEL

               advised that as of December 11, 1968, half of the furnishings belonging to Carmichael and Makeba had been put on board the boat "African Rainbow" in Baltimore, being handled by the Farrell Lines, Incorporated. He related that prior to departure from Washington, D.C., Carmichael and Makeba purchased a new household refrigerator, two washing machines and a range stove, which they also desired included with the shipment to Conakry. As of December 11, 1968, all of these ordered appliances had not arrived for shipment. Consequently,   advised when the remainder of the appliances arrive for shipment, they will be included with the other half of the remaining furnishings and taken to New York City. Upon arrival in New York City, they will be loaded onto the "African Rainbow" then due in New York City at about that time. The "African Rainbow" is expected to sail from New York City on December 17, 1968.

105-176973-

FBI report on Miriam Makeba's move to Guinea

That information also made its way into the column by *Washington Post* columnist Jack Anderson: "Carmichael already has shipped all his furniture and belongings, including carpets on the floors of his $70,000 Washington home..."[25] Anderson does not say how he came by the information, but later in the piece, in discussing Carmichael's split with the Black Panther Party, he cites his source as a "confidential Government intelligence report."

All of this was of a piece. Makeba's marriage to Carmichael had dire consequences for her professionally. As Peniel Joseph assessed, it "signaled the end of lucrative television and concert appearances that had placed her on the cusp of international mainstream superstardom."[26]

James Brown — Working Hard for Conciliation

Artists such as Miriam Makeba and Nina Simone unambiguously threw their prestige behind the Black freedom movement. James Brown, by contrast, was more conflicted.

In 1968, James Brown was arguably the most important African-American artist in the United States. As such, there was tremendous pressure on him to take a stand for Black freedom and social justice. How he responded is instructive of the difficult position such artists found themselves in — called on to play a role beyond what many are best suited for. That said, Brown, who was fortunate enough to have a successful career, held to the erroneous notion that anyone could achieve what he had.

Brown had been a major figure since the late 1950s when, as the front man for the Famous Flames, he had a hit with "Please, Please, Please." His career took off in the 1960s with such hits as 1965's "Papa's Got a Brand New Bag" and "I Got You (I Feel Good)," and 1966's "It's A Man's Man's Man's World," a searing blues hymn to male supremacy, albeit with sufficient sentimental condescension toward women. By the middle of the decade, as non-violence gave way to urban uprisings and Black Power, Brown was confronted with singing about more than love, sex, and other romantic tropes. All of which came to a head when Martin Luther King was assassinated.

When King was killed, Brown was active in helping authorities bring things under control. He had a previously scheduled concert in Boston the day after the assassination, and city authorities debated whether to cancel the show in order to prevent unrest or go ahead in order not to inflame the situation further. They decided to go ahead, but also televised the show in hopes of getting people to stay home and watch. Brown, however, took some convincing, his concern being fans lining up for a refund in order to watch the show for free.[27]

Brown appears to have been less conflicted a few days later in Washington, where he called on people to "get off the streets, go home [...] Don't burn." He drove his message home with a pitch for Black capitalism, telling listeners how when he was young, he shined shoes in front of a radio station in August, Georgia. As Brown recalled, "Well now, I own that station. It's mine. I just bought another one in Knoxville, Tennessee. I want five more to make a chain. That's what I call Black Power. It's got some green in it, that's what my soul brothers and sisters [need to] learn."[28]

On the heels of his efforts in Boston and Washington, Brown set off to Vietnam to entertain US troops. Despite whatever good intentions he brought to this, performing in Vietnam in 1968 was a highly charged political statement, putting him in the company of rabid war supporters such as Bob Hope, Martha Raye, and John Wayne. In that respect, it is telling to read Brown's complaints about the tour, which revolve around there not being enough Black artists performing in Vietnam — "All they get are hillbilly shows" — to the sound equipment being substandard.[29] None of these complaints speak to the larger issue of the nature of the war, which was wreaking havoc on the

Vietnamese and the US soldiers sent to fight it — a disproportionate number of whom were poor and/or were people of color.

If there were any doubt where Brown stood on the matter of Vietnam, when he returned to the US, he released the jingoistic "America is My Home," replete with lines proclaiming America is "the best country," and this is "without a doubt."[30]

Such was the backdrop to his breakout "political" hit, "Say it Loud, I'm Black and I'm Proud," released soon after. The song's title and refrain concentrated a bold statement of Black pride — and that is what resonated, making it into an anthem. That said, looking under its hood, the song is soaked in James Brown's "bootstraps" view of realizing the American dream, with repeated lyrics demanding we "get what we deserve," "wanting my share," and "do[ing] things for ourselves."

Brown, driven by a desire to succeed in the US on its own terms, came to regret the song, which — despite its shortcomings — stood as a bold statement of Black affirmation. As he said, "I paid the price for 'Say it Loud.' The white community took it entirely the wrong way, as a kind of aggressive statement to induce fear."[31] All of which may be true, but it misses the positive impact of the song, *and* that it made James Brown far more relevant in the moment than he might otherwise have been.

Country Joe & the Fish

While James Brown sought to keep his distance from radicalism, Country Joe & the Fish embraced it. Their name being exemplary — a concatenation of Joseph Stalin and Mao Zedong's instruction to the Red Army to see themselves as fish in the sea of the people. The group's founders came by this in no small way because of their similar upbringing. According to the group's guitarist, Barry Melton:

> Joe and I had a kind of instant communication. Both of us were "red diaper babies" and had astoundingly similar backgrounds. His dad was from Oklahoma, mine from Texas, and both of our mothers were East Coast Jews. We shared a mutual fondness for Woody Guthrie — Woody and his family had actually been neighbors of mine in early childhood, and my dad was a friend of Woody's and all things Left in folk music.[32]

Country Joe & the Fish, 1967
Credit: Vanguard Records Publicity Photo

The two would tour as a duo performing at universities in the northwest for Students for a Democratic Society.[33] Their biggest song, "I-Feel-Like-I'm-Fixin'-to-Die-Rag" — a satire of the absurdity of fighting the Vietnam War — was first released in 1965, but was re-released on the album *I-Feel-Like-I'm-Fixin'-to-Die* in late 1967. It would become iconic.

While much of the group's music was experimental, with an eye toward psychedelic drugs — *Electric Music for the Mind and Body* was their first release — their third album, *Together*, released in 1968, was pointedly dedicated "To Bobby Hutton — Black Revolutionary 1950–1968." Hutton was an eighteen-year-old Black Panther member killed in a shoot-out with Oakland police two days after the King assassination.[34]

As a result of their radical inclinations, the group found themselves the object of physical assault. When they performed in Chicago, in the days before the Democratic National Convention, members of the group were singled out for attack. The *Washington Post,* which mis-characterized the incident under the headline "Three Yippies Beaten at Hotel" — they were a music group, not Yippies — did correctly report that McDonald, Melton, and bandmate David Cohen were attacked by three men at the Lake Shore Drive hotel for "no apparent reason."[35] Joe McDonald doesn't remember much about the incident, but describes how:

> After our show, I was going into the hotel with David and Barry and there was a guy outside the hotel. We made eye contact. As I was getting into the elevator, he came in and said "I fought in Vietnam for people like you." I was in the elevator, and he hit me in the nose. The elevator closed.[36]

Three of the group's members required treatment at Wesley

Memorial Hospital. Whether the attack was pre-planned is unclear, though three men were reported to have fled the scene together, getting into a car in the hotel's garage. That said, the atmosphere in Chicago in advance of protests planned before the Democratic National Convention was highly charged.

The Festival of Life

In 1968, Jerry Rubin, Abbie Hoffman, Paul Krassner, Stewart Albert, Ed Sanders, and others created an entity — as much a brand as an organization — called Yippie! Throughout the winter and spring of 1968, they had worked on a scheme to mount a protest at the Democratic National Convention, which would take the form of a counterculture statement. They dubbed it "The Festival of Life." The idea of the project was to have a gathering, which would include musicians, as a counter to the "convention of death" of the Democrats.[37] The problem was that this was being conceived in an extremely tense social and political atmosphere.

This was especially true in Chicago, the site of the convention, where riots in the Black community after the King assassination had shaken the city. Things were so charged that at one point, Chicago's powerful mayor, Richard Daley, told the press: "In my opinion, there should have been orders to shoot arsonists to kill, and shoot looters in order that they be detained."[38]

It was in that atmosphere that city authorities did everything they could to keep demonstrators from coming to Chicago. First, they held back on issuing march and rally permits. Second, they undertook a major mobilization of law enforcement, instituting compulsory riot training and putting the 11,900 person police force on mandatory twelve-hour shifts for the duration of the convention. The Illinois governor joined in, putting the National Guard on alert. That was beyond the six thousand troops in Fort Hood, Texas, already prepared, having undertaken advance riot training.

All of which had the desired effect. The anti-war candidate Eugene McCarthy, who had mobilized a section of anti-war youth to support his campaign, encouraged his supporters to stay away from the demonstrations.[39] Along with this, all but one of the acts who had been approached to perform at the Festival of Life in Lincoln Park, including Arlo Guthrie, Country Joe & the Fish, and Judy Collins, decided against coming to Chicago. The only band to perform was MC5, a group aligned with the revolutionary White Panther Party — who modeled themselves on the Black Panther Party — based in Ann Arbor and Detroit.

MC5's experience during the convention was telling of the atmosphere. Their set was hampered because police did not allow a flat-bed truck, which was to serve as their stage, into the park.[40] MC5 singer-guitarist Wayne Kramer described the scene:

> There was no stage, there was no flatbed truck, there was no sound system, there were no porta-toilets, there was no electricity. We had to run an electrical cord from the hot dog stand to power our gear. We played on the ground in the middle of Lincoln Park in Chicago with the crowd all around us sitting on the ground, in the back, standing. I'm going to guess there were maybe 3,000 young people there. And it was very tense. The Chicago police had been very aggressive and very intimidating all day, and even though it was a rock concert and we were the only band to play, it didn't feel like a rock concert. There was a dark cloud over the day because we knew the likelihood of people being hurt was great.[41]

Using the justification that the gathering did not have

permits, the police repeatedly attacked people who stayed past curfew.

Police violence over the course of the Convention was shocking. It included openly beating reporters, who responded by publishing scathing testimony of the police behavior, for example in this *New York Times* report:

> Even elderly bystanders were caught in the police onslaught. At one point the police turned on several dozen persons standing quietly behind police barriers in front of the Conrad Hilton Hotel watching the demonstrators across the street. For no reason that could be immediately determined, the blue-helmeted policemen charged the barriers, crushing the spectators against the windows of the Haymarket Inn, a restaurant in the hotel. Finally, the window gave way, sending screaming middle-aged women and children backward through the broken shards of glass.[42]

Such brutality was eye-opening, not only for reporters, but for their middle-class readers and those watching television coverage. This in turn created a crisis for the authorities, whose power hinged on police violence being seen as appropriate. What people witnessed in Chicago cast serious doubt on police violence being legitimate — and this had consequences that stretched past the days of the DNC.

All this was especially eye-opening for Phil Ochs, who had been in the middle of events. He had been arrested for disorderly conduct along with six other Yippies at a press conference on August 23, where they had debuted the pig they were running for President (which Ochs had paid for), and had performed in Grant Park on August 29. He walked away from the experience shaken.[43]

In the aftermath of the violence, he sat down with Izzy Young to talk about the impact of the incident: "I think it's quite possible the country is so far gone and decayed that there may be no way left to save it, and that the only logical course for the progress of mankind is the destruction of America."[44] Coming from someone who held that the US was a country in need of living up to its dream, and worked tirelessly to make it so, this was an expression of extreme disenchantment.

At the same time the authorities were ratcheting up their attention on Ochs. He was being considered for indictment under US riot laws and was approached by the FBI for an interview:

> During an attempt to interview him on 10/1/68, regarding his participation in demonstrations at the Democratic National Convention held in Chicago, he advised that he would not discuss his activities with Agents. The interview then terminated.[45]

Ochs turning down the FBI was a wise move, given they often used interview approaches as a way to open a dialogue on the way to recruiting informants.

That entry, notably, is included on the Bureau's form FD-305, dealing with their Security Index. The form makes clear Ochs was on their Administrative Index — the name given to the Security Index in the early 1970s — and had been since at least August of 1968.

Arresting Lennon and Censoring the Stones

While political repression intensified, so did social repression — and this was not only in the US. On October 18, John Lennon and Yoko Ono were arrested in London for marijuana possession. It was spearheaded by Norman Pilcher, a UK detective, who had arrested Mick Jagger and Keith Richards for drugs the previous year.

While the arrests by Pilcher have received a good

deal of attention over the years, it tends to focus on his being a ruthless careerist, to the exclusion of his being an instrument in a wider repressive undertaking. In that regard, his own telling is revealing. As Pilcher would later reflect, "The Home Office [akin to the US Department of Homeland Security] were breathing down our necks to move on more of the big names."[46]

Drugs were not the only front where artists were being moved on. In December, the Rolling Stones — fresh from witnessing police beat anti-war demonstrators in London's Grosvenor Square — released *Beggars Banquet,* an album with a populist political bent in songs such as "Factory Girl" and "Salt of the Earth." Most famous in that regard was "Street Fighting Man," which conjured up images of Martha and the Vandellas with its line about "summer's here and the time is right for fighting in the streets, boy." The single was released in August, prompting some Chicago radio stations to refuse to play it, fearing it would further inflame the situation surrounding the Democratic National Convention.[47] The Stones' record company, London/Decca, also took issue with the song. According to Jagger, "They told me that 'Street Fighting Man' was subversive. 'Course it's subversive', we said. It's stupid to think that you can start a revolution with a record. I wish you could!"[48]

RCA also pushed back, successfully, against the album cover, which showed a toilet and a wall covered in graffiti, but they could not fully articulate their issue with the jacket beyond considering it "indecent." According to Jagger, "It's not really any one thing which upsets them — it's the whole concept." Part of the problem was that the graffiti included the phrase "god rolls his own" under the Stones' name, to say nothing of the fact that toilets were simply not to be seen in the 1960s, something the Mamas and Papas discovered when releasing their 1966 debut album, which showed them in a bathtub next to a toilet. That cover moved the record company to first obscure the toilet with text, before editing it out entirely.[49]

Album cover aside, the larger issue was "Street Fighting Man." The song, with its refrain "the time is right for fighting in the streets," was far too close to what was already underway and, as a result, was akin to pouring gasoline on fire.[50] And it appeared in a situation of diminishing middle ground: You were either trying to put the fire out, or you were feeding it.

CHAPTER 9
FIRE IS SWEEPING (1969)

We assembled here tonight in the name of decency, as a revival of decency. We are putting down some of the infiltrators in our society.
— Youth organizer of an Alabama Rally for Decency[1]

Tommy does not advocate overthrowing the government... do you?
— Dick to Tom Smothers[2]

The year 1969 saw two significant — if not obvious — shifts in events. It was the moment the US power structure went into reverse, though not in a linear way, on its commitment in Vietnam. And it was the year that the unprecedented uprisings that had convulsed urban America began to diminish in intensity.[3] While both were tentative, it signaled a different direction. And while there was a good amount of upheaval left, its character would change — with all sides gravitating to more extremes, and those extremes fracturing along the way. This was true for the political authorities, their law enforcement apparatus, and governmental organizations. And it was true for individuals, radical organizations, and within the wider cultural milieu.

The Beatles Dissolve

When the Beatles took to the roof of Abbey Road Studios on the afternoon of January 30 — to perform songs from their album in progress, in what would be their last live performance — little concern was given to logistics and permits. Even though it was "the Beatles," it was still polarizing, in the way many things in 1969 were. The performance quickly led to complaints. A wool merchant with offices next door asserted, "I want this bloody noise stopped. It's an absolute disgrace." Another person on the scene remarked, "This type of music has its place," meaning this was not one of them. Not surprisingly, the police were called.[4]

A similar scene had played out in New York a couple of months earlier with Jefferson Airplane. The group, being filmed by director Jean-Luc Godard, were performing on the roof of the Schuyler Hotel on West 45th Street. In the middle of their second song, a policeman arrived and ordered them to stop. He was soon followed by two others. When the band continued — along with the filming — one of the actors in the project, Rip Torn, along with filmmaker David McMullen, were arrested for harassment, filming without a permit, and amplification. While the charges were eventually reduced to summonses, the filming and music had been stopped cold.[5]

In comparison to the New York incident, the Beatles fared better. When police arrived, the group's assistant, Mal Evans, was able to stall them for ten minutes, before they finally made it up to the roof, where he cut the power on George Harrison's amplifier at the opening of a song. Evans, in fact, had been formally arrested by police as he was taken up to the roof — though Paul McCartney was able to convince police to release him.[6] Later accounts highlight the police restraint, even suggesting, as *Rolling Stone* would later do, that the police "actually cut the band some slack."[7] Perhaps, but if cutting the power on the most popular band of the twentieth century and arresting their assistant during their final live performance ever was indicative of cutting slack, it showed the degree of intolerance in operation for such cultural expressions overall.[8]

Beyond the run-in with police, an undercurrent to the performance was the fact that the band would soon break apart. While an abundance of opinion has been offered on the Beatles' breakup, it mostly circulates around personality clashes within the group. What is less discussed is the impact of events in the world, which were driving members in different directions. Most markedly, John Lennon was inclining toward the left-wing political maelstrom. By contrast, Paul McCartney was largely standing aside. Further, he viewed Lennon's activism negatively. McCartney himself is quite clear on this, as he explains the meaning of his 1971 song "Too Many People":

> "Too Many People" was really a message to John across the airwaves. I did feel like he was, you know, preaching a little bit about what everyone should do, how they should live their lives, and I felt — at the time — that some of it was a bit hypocritical. So, in the song "Too Many People", I started off "Too many people preaching practices". And it was directly aimed at John, but it was about our relationship at that time, and me feeling that I didn't need to be preached at.[9]

McCartney's reaction is exemplary of the political divide more widely among radical and progressive elements, which was manifesting itself forcefully by the end of 1969 — there was less unity, more finger-pointing, and hard schisms.

In hindsight, it seems it could hardly have been otherwise. Not only was there largely a lack of tested and seasoned leadership — organizational or otherwise — to exert the mastery necessary to navigate the tangle of contradictions, but on a more fundamental level, there was an absence of transformative options to take things beyond where they had come. The 1960s had reached incredible heights, but in a fundamental way, there was nowhere else to go. This would impact everyone swept up in the milieu.

The Smothers Brothers

A prime example of the intensity of the polarized situation can be seen in the case of the folk-comedy duo, the Smothers Brothers, and their television show, *The Smothers Brothers Comedy Hour*. The brothers, Tom and Dick, got their start working at the Purple Onion folk music club in San Francisco in 1959.[10] In 1967, they hit gold when CBS Television, desperate to attract an audience that could displace the long-running hit Western *Bonanza*, put them at the head of their own comedy/variety show. The show would become a hit because of its iconoclastic humor and its showcasing of cutting-edge music, both of which would otherwise have had few outlets on prime-time television.

From its inception, the show was enmeshed in controversy, not the least of which was in the music they showcased. Famously, the Who destroyed their instruments and set off a minor explosive on set. Also appearing were Jefferson Airplane, who performed "White Rabbit," their song with unsubtle allusions to mind-expanding drugs. Then there was Buffalo Springfield, who performed "For What It's Worth," ostensibly about the Sunset Strip riots in Los Angeles in 1966, but which came to represent the general contention between youth and the ruling authorities.[11] There were few, if any, other places that a mass audience could hear such artists.

The Smothers Brothers also had as a guest Pete Seeger — breaking the national banning of him that had been in place since the Fifties. Seeger, seeing an opportunity to reach millions, sang his song "Big Muddy," an allegory for

Vietnam. The performance incensed those supporting the war and was a poke in the eye of the political class — who duly noted Seeger's insolence.[12] Were that the high-water mark of the show pushing the envelope, it would have been more than enough for the powers that be. It was not.

In the show's third season, which began in 1968 and ran into 1969, things came to a head. In the fall of that year, Harry Belafonte taped a song called "Don't Stop the Carnival," sung against a photomontage of police violence at the Democratic National Convention. Belafonte's spot was pulled.[13] As the show entered 1969, both sides escalated matters. The brothers, led by Tom, pushed for cutting-edge anti-establishment material, while CBS, which had a new president, was set on shutting the whole thing down. The controversies were relentless.

Things escalated further when Tom Smothers invited comedian David Steinberg back to the show, after an appearance where Steinberg had delivered a mock religious sermonette, much to the chagrin of network executives. Steinberg's second sermonette never aired. They also took issue with an appearance by Joan Baez, who performed "Green, Green Grass of Home," which she dedicated to her husband, David Harris, noting in her introduction that he was in jail for refusing the draft. While her performance was broadcast, her introduction was edited, removing her explanation for why her husband was in prison.

From the beginning, the show had made enemies in high places. Lyndon Johnson had called CBS founder William Paley directly to complain after a skit aired that made fun of him.[14] While Johnson's action did not lead to the show's cancellation, the appointment of a new vice president at CBS, Robert D. Wood, the following year did.

Wood was someone with a track record of stifling dissent. He had earlier been station manager at KNXT in northern California. A sense of his politics can be seen in an editorial he delivered on the Free Speech Movement:

> The pandemonium and chaos created by a group of witless agitators at the University of California campus in Berkeley is making a mockery of the world's greatest educational institutions. KNXT believes it should be dealt with quickly and severely to set an example for all time for those who agitate for the sake of agitation.[15]

For the Smothers Brothers, Wood's ascent was inauspicious. Despite their show having been renewed for a fourth season, the network used a contractual maneuver to cancel it, claiming the brothers were in breach for not supplying advance tapes of an episode. The repercussions were immediate. In the blink of an eye, a mass-media venue for anti-war sentiment, countercultural music, and cutting-edge comedy went dark.

The Doors, the Fugs, and the FBI

The Doors had burst onto the scene in 1967 and had skyrocketed to the top of the charts. However, and this was more so than any other group at the time, their lead singer — eccentric, edgy and prone to cross the line — was relentlessly confronting the blunt edge of law enforcement.

Jim Morrison had been arrested in New Haven in 1967, after police took the stage to shut a concert down. While that episode was resolved with charges being dropped, that was not the case with his Miami arrest, where police claimed — without proof — that he exposed himself. Compounding things, three days after turning himself in to face the Miami charges, Morrison took a flight to Phoenix for an upcoming concert. More trouble ensued. Drinking heavily on the plane with his friend Thomas Baker, he ran afoul of federal authorities. As an FBI report, giving a witness account, documented:

> MORRISON was smoking a small type of cigar while the "No Smoking" sign was on. He stated the stewardesses had to insist that they fasten their safety belts. He stated there was a constant commotion between the two individuals who displayed a very defiant attitude."[16]

The result was federal charges under a newly enacted law against interfering with the flight crew — a law implemented in the wake of several politically charged hijackings. Between the state charges in Miami and the federal charges, Morrison was facing a possible thirteen years in prison.

Along with the FBI's file on Morrison, the agency had another file on the Doors, which includes Bureau reports on the Fugs. A letter in the file notes that a concerned citizen sent the Bureau a copy of the Fugs album *Virgin Fugs*. That album included the songs "The Ten Commandments," credited to Fug member Tuli Kupferberg and "GOD," along with "I Saw the Best Minds of My Generation Rot," credited to Allen Ginsberg and Ed Sanders. Crutchfield's letter also contained a clipping of the Morrison obscenity arrest in Miami. All of this elicited a response from Hoover, who opined that the material "is repulsive to right-thinking people and can have serious effects on our young people."[17] While Hoover's comments can be read as laughable, it should be borne in mind that he was in charge of one of the most powerful agencies of the US government — his opinion had consequences.

The Fugs and Dr. Bettelheim

While Hoover was being appalled, the House of Representatives were holding hearings. In sessions called to investigate campus unrest, one of the witnesses called to give testimony was University of Chicago professor Bruno Bettelheim.

Bettelheim — now understood to be a fraud and a plagiarist — was, in 1969, considered an authority in the field of treating autism in children.[18] As such, he appeared before Congress to offer his insights on youthful rebellion. It was a task he undertook by offering an abundance of opinion, but not much in the way of scientific grounding. For example, he proclaimed — without evidence — that there are "no militants among students of medicine, engineering, and the natural sciences, because they are busy doing things that are important." By contrast, students who engaged in disruptive behavior did so because of a "coddled adolescence." In his learned view, "society keeps the next generation too long dependent in terms of mature responsibility" — except, apparently, those who go into STEM or the Army.[19]

Not surprisingly, Bettelheim's direct testimony also took aim at the counterculture, singling out the Fugs:

If someone advocates urinating on graves as the Fugs did, or if a few girls dress up as witches as they did in Chicago, if they would do so without reference to politics, people would rightly wonder about their sanity; but if they do so as a condemnation of the Vietnam war, or take clothes off while claiming to be demonstrating for some good progressive cause, they have the support of many of the older liberals and enlightened radicals who will inevitably consider it all to be very socially significant.[20]

Beyond the affirming the consequent fallacy — if you dress up as witches to protest, you must be crazy — there was no "urinating" on Senator Joe McCarthy's grave. As Ed Sanders recalled:

> The Fugs and Ginsberg, plus maybe fifty to seventy-five friends, gathered at Senator McCarthy's grave on a chilly winter hillock and performed the Exorcism, which enraged right-wing commentators. I chanted a singsong conjuration of deities and power words, similar to what I had done at the Pentagon Exorcism. With Allen commenting on the Great Red-baiter's homophobia, he led forth with an invocation to bisexual Greek and Indian gods."[21]

Regardless of how problematic this was, Congress lapped it up. Rep. William C. Hathaway of Maine praised the testimony as "probably one of the best statements that has ever been presented to this committee," before adding, without a trace of irony, "it will probably take a long time for us to digest all of it."[22]

Anti-War Music

Given the Fugs' limited influence and their inclination to shock, the attack on them was low-hanging fruit. However, that they were being analyzed in the halls of Congress was no small matter, especially given the cultural resistance underway, which was, by 1969, being brought into the mainstream by an ever-growing number of artists.

In April, a group then called the Chicago Transit Authority (later, simply Chicago) released their eponymous debut. On the final side of the double album was the song cycle "Prologue (August 29, 1968)," "Someday (August 29, 1968)," and "Liberation," all revolving around the protests outside the Chicago Democratic Convention in the summer of 1968 — replete with a recording of the crowd chanting, "The Whole World is Watching."[23]

In Los Angeles, the Flying Burrito Brothers, a band formed by Graham Parsons and Chris Hillman after leaving the Byrds, included a song on their debut, *The Gilded Palace of Sin*, that was one of the more subversive anti-draft songs of the period. "My Uncle" told of a draft-age man fleeing the country to avoid military service and heading to Vancouver, because they don't have the type of law and order that would tend "to drive a good man underground."[24] In a similar vein, Steppenwolf recorded "Draft Resister," which told of someone headed to Sweden to avoid the draft. From the song's point of view, they were doing this "for you and me."[25] In a more populist vein, Creedence Clearwater Revival had a top-ten hit with "Fortunate Son," which decried how the privileged in the US sent those less so off to war to die.[26]

Topping all this off was John Lennon and Yoko Ono's anthem "Give Peace a Chance."[27] The song's pacifist lyrics derived their power from its basic anti-war stand and its sing-along refrain, making it a staple at anti-war demonstrations. That it was done by "the Beatle," John Lennon, meant it could not be ignored, and signaled Lennon's entry into politically overt musical statements.

JA on the Barricades

While these songs were hitting the streets, members of Jefferson Airplane were in the studio recording what would be their most incendiary album. The group, under the leadership of Paul Kantner, had already been weighing in on the political situation with their 1968 release *Crown of Creation* — with its ironic cover portraying the group in the crest of a nuclear mushroom cloud.[28] The press took note:

In their new album The Jefferson Airplane have gone political [...] Grace [Slick] admitted that until recently she had been embarrassed by such activity, and particularly so since she is aware that "anyone who gets up on a stage assumes that he has a certain amount of power, either to please, or to amuse, or to persuade." But the New Political Airplane has come about, she explained, "because when something is on your mind all the time, you've got to talk about it."[29]

If critics thought *Crown of Creation* was political, the follow-up was even more so. It opened with "We Can Be Together," with Jorma Kaukonen's guitar mimicking a bugle charge, its lyrics drawn from an anarchist manifesto which declared "we are all outlaws in the eyes of Amerika."[30] The album closed with the Paul Kantner-Marty Balin song "Volunteers," which musically reprised "We Can Be Together" before lashing into a chorus proclaiming the need for revolution. By way of further provocation, the lead into that song was a musical interlude called "Meadowlands," based on the Soviet folk song "Polyushka Polye" — a staple in the repertoire of the Red Army Choir.

The album was to have been called *Volunteers of Amerika*, using the popular spelling among the left, suggesting fascism in the USA, but that title was shot down by RCA. Also subject to record company intervention was the lyric sheet, where the line in "We Can Be Together" stating, "We steal, cheat, lie, forge, fuck, hide, and deal," was altered, replacing the word "fuck" for the incongruous "fred."[31]

Given their subversive stance, it is little surprise the group came under increased repression, both in their concerts and with drug arrests. Paul Kantner had been arrested in Hawaii for marijuana possession, which he claimed was planted on him.[32] Then, on May 16, Airplane bassist Jack Casady, along with manager Bill Thompson, Casady's brother Chick, Bill Laudner, and two female friends were arrested in a hotel raid in New Orleans for possessing two marijuana joints.[33] A day after the pot arrest, the group was performing in Miami when the power was cut, this after the band continued playing beyond curfew. Kantner cursed out the police, saying "Wait till we burn down *your* society!" He was arrested shortly after.

SDS Falls Apart

A key section of the audience for Jefferson Airplane and other bands like them were students, including those active in the New Left, and the two reinforced one another. Students for a Democratic Society (SDS), the largest and most radical group of the time, sought to energize a "New Left" in the face of the nuclear nightmare of the Cold War. Its early years saw it building social programs, working in concert with SNCC, and doing community work. By decade's end, however, it had evolved into a radical behemoth, claiming 100,000 members. As the FBI would summarize:

> The program of SDS has evolved from civil rights struggles to an anti-Vietnam War stance to an advocacy of a militant anti-imperialist position. China, Vietnam, and Cuba are regarded as the leaders of worldwide struggles against United States imperialism whereas the Soviet Union is held to be revisionist and also imperialist."[34]

Flowing from this assessment was the launching of numerous counter-intelligence operations against the group, with the aim of splitting it apart. That effort had no small amount of success — aided in large part by the sectarianism coursing through the group.[35]

When SDS met for its annual conference in June

1969, it split first two, then three ways. The faction which retained the SDS name was dominated by the faction of the Progressive Labor Party, called the Worker Student Alliance. Another faction, the Revolutionary Youth Movement (RYM), was itself composed of two components, the first of which was the Revolutionary Youth Movement I, which included SDS's national leadership, who would soon become the Weathermen. It was the Weathermen who dominated the media's attention and served as the prototype for the narrative of the futility of white radicalism — this despite their small numbers and modest influence.[36] The other faction, Revolutionary Youth Movement II, consisted of a broad array of radicals, including a sizable Maoist component, with the Revolutionary Union being the largest among them.[37]

The period surrounding the shattering of SDS signaled a demarcation of a kind, both for students and youth of the far-left and those active in the more radical currents of the Black freedom movement — with the considerable number of people active in it having to decide between the embrace of immediate political violence, and the onrush of repression that would call up; or tactics employing a strategic protractedness, which, if not welcomed by the dominant society, would be more tolerable. In this, it should be noted, while those engaged in political violence garnered the overwhelming share of media coverage, the majority of radicals to emerge from the Sixties — despite what popular accounts suggest — embraced a more protracted view of struggle.[38]

Stonewall Riots

Given everything going on in 1969, a police raid on a gay nightspot in New York City, and the resulting violence it set loose, did not make the splash it would have made in a quieter time. It was, however, a signal of the arrival of a movement that would flourish in the Seventies.

In the early morning hours of June 28, New York police raided the Stonewall Inn in Greenwich Village. The *New York Times* described the scene:

> Before order was restored, the cops were targets of thrown coins, cobblestones, and uprooted parking meters, windows were smashed, a police van was nearly overturned and the front of the raided bar, the Stonewall Inn, was firebombed."[39]

The newspaper's coverage of the incident identified two of those arrested as the club's doorman, and Dave Van Ronk, "a folk singer, guitarist and song writer." Van Ronk's participation flowed in part from the fact that he lived in the neighborhood — though his politics would incline him to be where the action was. The FBI, monitoring Van Ronk, took note of the riot, recording his arrest and following the subsequent court proceedings before noting the resolution that he had been "conditionally discharged of the crime."[40]

Woodstock

The Woodstock Music and Arts Festival has been mythologized to such a degree that the actual event exists almost as fiction. For all the talk about embodying the ethos of the counterculture, it was first and foremost a commercial undertaking.[41] As such, the artists who performed at the festival were paid top dollar, film and record rights were agreed beforehand, and a brand would be established that would reap rewards decades after the first song was sung.[42] Yet all this operated in a highly polarized social and political environment, wherein a convocation of "hippies" was unwelcome by a goodly section of the ruling apparatus and its social base.

Woodstock was meant to have been held in the town of Wallkill, NY, about ninety miles north of Manhattan.[43] Preparations, begun in the spring, were well on their way, when three weeks before the concert, a judge, at the request of town authorities, pulled the plug.[44] Festival organizers regrouped and secured a location further south, in the town of White Lake. The eleventh-hour change, however, meant preparations were thrown into crisis. The result was a festival where the stage was still being built, fencing had not been fully erected, and other key logistics had not been tended to. And this happened as hundreds of thousands of people — the festival having tapped into something far beyond the organizer's comprehension — were headed to the location. All of which led the government to respond antagonistically. John Morris, the head of production for the festival, offered a stark account:

[I]t was declared an emergency disaster area. It started out with [Governor Nelson] Rockefeller's people, with the governor's people freaking out at what was going on and wanting to send in the National Guard and remove everyone. Not a very intelligent idea. I took a few hours to talk to them on the phone back and forth [...] They were saying that this was an illegal gathering. They were using exactly the same logic that they used in Attica later [site of the prison uprising in 1971], after Woodstock: This was a confrontation, it was a danger to the community, it was a danger to public health, it was a danger to any damn thing they could think of. They wanted to get rid of it. And they were stupid enough to believe they could mobilize the National Guard and move these kids out.[45]

All of which makes clear that Woodstock, despite the market forces driving it, was anathema to the authorities. Had they felt in a strong enough position to shut it down, they would have.

The antipathy lay in many things, not the least being the music, which was shot through with countercultural mores and left-leaning politics — from Richie Havens's opening of "Freedom," Jimi Hendrix's deconstruction of the "Star-Spangled Banner," Joan Baez's anti-draft remarks about her husband in prison for draft resistance, Joe McDonald's leading the audience in the "Fish Cheer" — spelling out the word FUCK — and Jefferson Airplane's song calling for revolution. Listening to the audio of the event decades later, and watching the film footage, one is struck by the common political assumptions — which director Michael Wadleigh went to pains to include in the film. Everyone was on the same page regarding Black liberation, the Vietnam War, and drugs. Of course, there were likely antagonists in the crowd, but they were a minority.[46]

While Woodstock was at its core a commercial undertaking, since idealized as the seminal Sixties event of "peace and love," that commodification and mystification cannot negate a deeper truth. The basis for Woodstock, and the reason it registered as such a major event, was that it met a felt need of the moment, and in doing so animated and inspired the swirling social and political forces surrounding it.

Summer of Soul

Overlapping Woodstock was a music festival in Harlem called Summer of Soul, which, over its six-week run, drew upwards of 300,000 people. When a film of the event was released in 2021, it was marketed as the "Black Woodstock" — and to the degree the music was a snapshot of the era, that holds; however, in significant other ways, it does not.[47]

Summer of Soul was sponsored by the City of New York and Maxwell House Coffee. As a result, it did not have to deal with pushback from local authorities. Along with this, it did not have to navigate the intricacies of a multiday event. The smooth running was no doubt a result of its underlying, if unspoken, agenda. As concert attendee Darryl Lewis, interviewed in the film, offered, "The goal of the festival may very well have been to keep Black folks from burnin' up the city in 1969."[48] In that respect, Summer of Soul was attempting to meet a different need than that of Woodstock.

That said, the cultural expressions — from the psychedelic blues-rock of the Chambers Brothers, the exhilarating dance music of Sly & the Family Stone, a group that was both mixed in race and gender, the international stamp offered by Hugh Masekela (South Africa) and Mongo Santamaria (Cuba), and the radical Black nationalism of Nina Simone — were miles away from passivity. While the festival may have been aimed at cooling things out, the music was arguing for something else.

Phil Ochs and the Secret Service

Phil Ochs, meantime, had been in the recording studio working on his album *Rehearsal for Retirement*, whose opening song "Pretty Smart on My Part," a fever dream of right-wing delusion, led the FBI, who were listening to his records, to report:

This record was monitored on October 20, 1969 and on side one the first song, entitled "Pretty Smart on My Part," states in song what appears to be: "I can see them coming. They are training in the mountains. They talk Chinese and spread disease. They will hurt me — bring me down. Sometime later when I feel a little better we will assassinate the President and take over the government. We will fry them."[49]

The meaning of the song — ridiculing the paranoia of right-wing fanatics with a tenuous grip on reality — flew by the FBI, who referred the matter to the Secret Service. Going forward, the Bureau would keep the Secret Service in the loop on their efforts against Ochs.

Manson the "Hippie"

While hundreds of thousands were assembled in Woodstock and in Harlem to listen to music, Charles Manson, and members of his cult, were being arrested at the Spahn Movie Ranch in Chatsworth, California, accused of running an auto theft ring. For the moment, police did not know Manson had initiated the brutal murders of Sharon Tate, Abigail Folger, Wojciech Frykowski, Stephen Parent, and, in a separate killing, Leno and Rosemary LaBianca. Through their blundering failure to communicate across jurisdictions, it would be months before they did.[50]

Manson's ties to music have been much remarked on, especially his fixation on the Beatles' *White Album* and his "friendship" with Beach Boy Dennis Wilson, along with the fact that he auditioned for producer Terry Melcher, only to be rejected for a record deal. But Manson as an "artist" is not important here. Rather, he is significant as someone the mainstream culture seized on as a totem, erected in opposition to the communal sensibility, utopian though it was, that had arisen.

On the surface, the Manson "Family," with their long hair, free-spiritedness, and communal lifestyle, appeared to be a composite representative of the counterculture.[51] That the group was responsible for a series of shocking murders, ones that pitted them against the Hollywood liberal elite, was too good an opportunity for assorted editors and news producers to not run with. And run they did, hammering home that Manson and his followers were part of the hippie subculture, with headlines calling them "a nomadic band of hippies," an "Occult band of hippies," an "Outlaw hippie band," etc.[52] In this, Manson himself was cast as a fantastic guru, with a mystic hold over his followers.[53] That they did this, rather than describe Manson and his disciples more accurately as a low-grade criminal gang, led in cult-like fashion by a pimp and a not very cunning outlaw, is telling of either the lack of critical appraisal of the actual content of the Manson "Family" or the hostility by the powers that be toward the youth culture that had emerged out of the turmoil, or some combination thereof.[54]

Unfortunately, some in the radical milieu did not look past the headlines — Weather Underground leader Bernardine Dohrn being a case in point. Dohrn attempted to see something commendable in Manson's actions, telling an assemblage of radicals in Flint, Michigan, most of whom would soon go underground as the Weathermen, "Dig it, first they killed those pigs, then they ate dinner in the same room with them, then they even shoved a fork into a victim's stomach. Wild!" Years later, she claimed her remarks were meant as an "ironic joke," rather than hyper-militant posturing, in line with her and her group's view: "That's what we're about, being crazy motherfuckers and scaring the shit out of Honky America."[55]

Radical posturing aside, the conflation of Manson with the counterculture was also the basis for a larger trope. As Joan Didion wrote, "Many people I know in Los Angeles believe that the Sixties ended abruptly on August 9, 1969, at the exact moment when word of the murders on Cielo

Drive traveled like brushfire through the community, and in a sense this is true."[56] While the Rolling Stones' concert at Altamont would soon come to overshadow Manson's actions as the signal "end of the Sixties" event, it would never fully eliminate it.

While the specter of Manson the murderous hippie was being propagated far and wide, however, something far more horrific was about to make its way into the public consciousness.

Mỹ Lai

In November, the press began publishing a series of articles by investigative journalist Seymour Hersh about what a company of US Army soldiers did to civilians in the Vietnamese village of Mỹ Lai on March 16, 1968. The details were shocking, giving people in the US an unfiltered picture of the worst of what was happening in Vietnam. Hirsch would later publish a long-form account in *Harpers*. The details are stomach-turning:

> reported seeing one woman raped after GIs killed her children. Nguyen Khoa, a peasant, told of a thirteen-year-old girl who was raped before being killed. GIs then attacked Khoa's wife, he said, tearing off her clothes. Before they could rape her, however, Khoa said, their six-year-old son, riddled with bullets, fell, and saturated her with blood. The GIs left her alone.[57]

Unlike the Manson killings, there was no cultural capital to be garnered from promoting the Mỹ Lai story as emblematic of a darkness lingering amid the larger US military in Vietnam. Instead, elements in the media and cultural realm set out to try, if not justify the actions, at least acquit the actors (see Chapter 10).

Vietnamese villagers about to killed
Mỹ Lai, March 16, 1968
Credit: US Army

Protests and Occupation

Hersh's reporting came amid an anti-war movement that was growing exponentially. On November 15, a gathering in Washington, DC, to protest the Vietnam War drew a reported crowd of 250,000 people. According to the *New York Times*, it broke all records: "Until today, the largest outpouring of demonstrators was the gentle civil rights march of 1963, which attracted 200,000." In contrast to the peaceful character of that march, this one held within it a decided edge. For example, after the official protest and rally ended, "a small segment of the crowd, members of radical splinter groups" went to the US Department of Justice, where they "burned United States flags, threw paint bombs and other missiles." The radicals were in turn "repelled by tear gas released by the police.[58]

On the other side of the country, on November 20, eighty native American men, women, and children sailed at night to Alcatraz Island in the San Francisco Bay, to occupy the site in the name of "Indians of All Tribes." At its peak, the occupation would swell to more than six hundred and included a governing council, clinic, kitchen, public relations department, nursery, and grade school. It was also supported by artists, including Creedence Clearwater Revival, who donated $10,000 for the purchase of a boat and other supplies.[59]

In contrast to other political occupations, such as in Berkeley and Columbia, rather than undertake a high-profile confrontation, the Nixon administration, which had jurisdiction over the federal site, decided to let things play out — a tactic made possible by the remoteness of the island. The occupation in turn would last nineteen months.[60]

Fred Hampton and Mark Clark

Alcatraz was a victory for indigenous people and their allies, but events in Chicago a few weeks later would be a harsh blow, especially to the revolutionaries of the Black Panther Party and their supporters.

In the predawn hours of December 4, fourteen Chicago Police officers, claiming they were searching for illegal weapons, forced their way into the first-floor apartment on Chicago's Monroe Street and began shooting. Inside were nine people, in various stages of sleep — all of them members of the Illinois Black Panther Party, including the rising star of the chapter, Fred Hampton. The police claimed they had been fired on, but after a fusillade of more than ninety bullets, the only people shot had been Panthers, with Mark Clark and Hampton killed. A later picture showed grinning cops carrying Hampton's body out of the apartment, in an image that projected "mission accomplished" on the part of the police.[61] This success, however, was not wholly due to their efforts. They had been aided by a floor plan supplied by an FBI informant — a circumstance that would lead to a good deal of negative fallout for the FBI.

The Hampton killing would be a turning point for many in the movement, impelling no small number to greater degrees of radicalism, and some to embrace a doctrine of immediate political violence.

Altamont

News of Hampton and Clark's killing was still dominating the media when the Rolling Stones attempted to resurrect the spirit of Woodstock — three months past, but decades ago in "Sixties" time — via a free concert at the Altamont Speedway in Livermore, California. Given the backdrop of the Hampton and Clark murders, the Manson killings, and revelations of Mỹ Lai, the charged atmosphere at Altamont was less a departure from the general climate than a continuation.

The Stones' tour was the first for the group since 1966 — a circumstance resulting from Mick Jagger and Keith Richards's drug arrests in 1967, and Brian Jones's 1968 conviction for marijuana possession. 1969 was a period of transition for the group. Earlier that year, Jones was kicked out of the band because of his drug problems, and tragically died a month later after consuming a large amount of alcohol and drugs.[62]

The group's plan for northern California had been to stage a free concert in San Francisco's Golden Gate Park as the surprise guests of the Grateful Dead. This was shot down by the city's mayor, Joseph Alioto. As Joel Selvin described, Alioto was an "avowed law-and-order mayor [who] wasn't going to countenance any grooving in the park with the Rolling Stones."[63] In an attempt to keep the free concert plan alive, the group sought permission to perform at Sears Point Raceway, to the north of San Francisco. That effort too was shot down, in this case because of a dispute on who would own rights to any concert film.[64]

Scurrying for a solution, just two days before the concert, the group secured the Altamont Speedway, fifty miles to the east of San Francisco. This was hardly enough time to prepare. That was the context in which the Hell's Angels were recruited as stage security — their presence paid for in exchange for free beer.

The end result was as bad as any sober assessment could have predicted. Among the problems were insufficient facilities, bad drugs circulating, and people beaten by Hell's Angels for getting too close to the stage, for acting out in the crowd, or for touching an Angel's bike — which had been driven through the crowd and parked close to the stage. All the bad energy culminated with the stabbing death of Meredith Hunter, a young Black man who had been repelled by Angels after approaching the stage. When he responded by reaching for the pistol he had on him, a group of Angels beat and fatally stabbed him.

The entire scene was antithetical to the utopian ethic the majority of people were striving for — as illusory as that might have been. Most of the abundant finger-pointing in the concert's aftermath revolved around the particular culpability of individual Rolling Stones — as if they alone, rather than larger systemic (and market!) forces, had preeminent power over these circumstances.[65]

Saying that, Altamont was a far more modest calamity compared to other events that transpired that year.[66] That, however, did not keep it from being put forward by the media and cultural superstructure as a marker of "the end of the Sixties," an analysis that was as much an ideological cudgel — "what fools you are to think that things can be different!" — as an assessment. It was one of a number ideological countermoves that would be leveled as the challenges to the status quo intensified.

CHAPTER 10
FEEL THE FUTURE TREMBLE (1970)

I think today it is as simple as this. They have got to face up to the fact that there is an element in their faculty, there is an element in their student body, that wants, not only the destruction of the University, but the destruction of this system and this way of ours.
— Ronald Reagan.[1]

We are everything they say we are and we are proud of it.
— "Up Against the Wall Motherfuckers," leaflet.[2]

All clichés about "the end of the Sixties" aside, the jump from 1969 to 1970 was relatively seamless, less conclusion than continuation. This was true especially regarding the sustained radicalism of the anti-war movement, which had evolved a strong anti-imperialist, even revolutionary component, as well as the emergence of revolutionary currents among Black radicals and nationalists. Alongside this was the ascent of struggles of a highly militant reformism among Black, Latin, and Asian people, as seen in the San Francisco State and UC Berkeley strikes for Ethnic Studies and the Chicano anti-Vietnam War moratorium. Accompanying this was a full-flowering of second-wave feminism, and the movement for gay and lesbian rights — which had seen their kickoff in the Stonewall Riots the previous summer. These movements would expand and gain larger purchase, coming to define the Seventies and beyond.

All that considered, the first few years of the Seventies

were highly charged — a quaking combination of upsurge, repression, and strengthening counter revolution, rippling into every realm.

The Chicago 8 / 7

Events on the streets of Chicago during the Democratic National Convention did not sit well with the Nixon administration. Given their cry of "law and order," they aimed to send some people to prison — and those people were not police.[3]

As a result, Nixon's Attorney General, John Mitchell, charged Yippies Abbie Hoffman and Jerry Rubin, pacifist David Dellinger, anti-war organizers Tom Hayden, Rennie Davis, Lee Weiner, and John Froines, and Black Panther Chairman Bobby Seale with conspiracy to incite a riot and with a newly enacted federal law that made it a crime to cross state lines to "incite violence."[4] Bobby Seale would have his case severed from the others, but only after the judge in the case had him bound and gagged in the courtroom — this to silence his protestations for not having his attorney Charles Garry present. Separated or not, Seale would be sentenced to forty-eight months for contempt.

Had the Chicago trial only involved political actors, on set government terms, it may well have flown under popular culture radar. However, thanks in part to Abbie Hoffman and Jerry Rubin's political theater, and the insistence by the defense to call some of those who had been invited to perform at the Festival of Life, the trial dominated the media landscape for months.

In attempting to give a sense of the aim of the festival, some of the artists invited, including Phil Ochs, Country Joe McDonald, Judy Collins, and Arlo Guthrie, were called to the stand. Guthrie's testimony was particularly telling in regard to the chilled atmosphere in advance of the protest. As he said in court:

> Abbie and Jerry approached me and asked me if I would come to Chicago to sing the song [his anti-draft song "Alice's Restaurant"]. I said to both of them that I was still concerned about the fact that the permits had not been granted yet, and that I would not attend and that I would do my best to have other people not attend if the permits weren't granted because of the fear of police violence.[5]

During Guthrie's testimony, the government objected, and the judge upheld, to the jury seeing copies of Guthrie's two albums, *Alice's Restaurant* and *Running Down the Road,* and would not let him answer a question about his being the son of Woody Guthrie. They also refused to let him sing "Alice's Restaurant" to the jury.

In similar fashion, Judy Collins testified to her apprehension about attending the event, out of fear of confrontations with the police:

> I said, "Abbie, you must continue to try in every way possible to get those permits, because if we're going to have a celebration, we must do it legally. I don't want to be violent. I'm not going to Chicago to do anything except sing for people in a legal situation."[6]

The specter of violence would, in fact, interrupt her. At the point in her testimony when she attempted to sing "Where Have All the Flowers Gone," as she recalled, "I felt a hand come over my mouth as the court clerk, on the judge's orders, stopped me. It was as if my breath had been taken from me, and I was gagged, silenced. I stood, dazed and frightened."[7]

While the testimony of Guthrie, Collins, and others

raised the profile of the case, it did not impact the verdict. While all the defendants were acquitted of conspiracy to incite a riot, all but John Froines and Lee Weiner were found guilty of crossing state lines to incite to riot. It would take many years to get the convictions overturned.[8]

One result of the trial was that Graham Nash, of Crosby, Stills, Nash & Young, would write the song "Chicago," which recounted Bobby Seale being "bound and gagged' in court.[9] Nash's — who was not known for topical songwriting — recollections of writing the song reveal the intersection of music and politics underway:

> Wavy Gravy [of the Hog Farm commune in Southern California], who was a friend of mine, called me and said that the Chicago defendants needed money. He wanted CSNY to play a benefit concert for them. David and I said we'd go immediately, because we thought what had happened to Bobby Seale was disgusting. You cannot tie a man down in court, and gag him, and call it a fair trial.[10]

Grace and Abbie at Tea

In the aftermath of the trial, Jefferson Airplane's Grace Slick garnered an invitation to a tea by Richard Nixon's daughter, Tricia, for Finch alumni. Slick seized the opportunity:

> So I called Abbie Hoffman and said, "Guess where we're going." I had planned to spike Richard Nixon's tea with acid. But when Abbie and I were on line, a security guard wouldn't let me in. He said, "We checked and you're a security risk."[11]

Nonetheless, they had given it a solid try, with Hoffman reported to be "conservatively dressed and without his beard [*sic* — Hoffman did not have a beard in this period]." However, when Hoffman told White House police he was

Slick's "bodyguard," he was refused entry, being told, "This is strictly for females."[12]

Slick, who had to submit information about her and her escort to the State Department in advance of the event — though she gave Hoffman's name as Leonard Haufman — was never going to attend on her own terms, with Hoffman or not.[13] Regardless, after being rebuffed, Hoffman, who had brought "a black flag emblazoned with a multicolored marijuana leaf," hung it on a gate outside the White House — whereupon it was quickly removed.[14]

Such political theater got some mileage in the media and generated a certain excitement in the counterculture. It also led to the FBI investigating Slick:

> New York is requested to review the records of Finch College and obtain any background information relative to SLICK. New York is also requested to review its indices for any information relative to SLICK as well as contact any sources close to ABBY [sic] HOFFMAN and attempt to determine the relationship between SLICK and HOFFMAN.[15]

The result of the investigation shows up in a sixteen-page FBI release labeled as a "Jefferson Airplane" file. That file, while highly redacted, includes a profile of Slick before she went to Finch:

> While attending Castilleja [high school], Wing [Slick's maiden name] was an impulsive, thoughtless, rather wild, irresponsible young lady and was subjected to disciplinary action during her senior year because of her escapades. There was no evidence of any interest in politics or social issues when she was at Castilleja and was very self-centered and concerned only with herself. She was inclined to make a spectacle of herself."[16]

Whoever the FBI spoke with at the school clearly had issues with Slick, but her disruptive behavior *after* leaving school was being taken far more seriously now that she was a major cultural figure.

Blood, Sweat & Tears in Eastern Europe

A different type of repression was used against the band Blood, Sweat & Tears, who, in 1969 and 1970, had been widely lauded by critics and recognized by the music industry.

At the March 1970 Grammy Awards, the five artists vying for Album of the Year were the Beatles (*Abbey Road*), Johnny Cash (*Johnny Cash at San Quentin*), Crosby, Stills & Nash (*Crosby, Stills & Nash*), the 5th Dimension (*The Age of Aquarius*), and Blood, Sweat & Tears (*Blood, Sweat & Tears*). That *Blood, Sweat & Tears* took the prize was revealing. While the group's album had much to recommend it, it arguably represented the safest option for the artists, engineers, producers, and others who made up the Academy's voting cohort. While none of the albums it was up against were especially radical, *Blood, Sweat & Tears* was the least tainted with a counterculture or anti-authoritarian aesthetic — though the 5th Dimension, aside from covering a song from the counterculture phenomenon *Hair*, ran a close second.

As such, it is less than surprising that, on the heels of that win, the group took off on a tour of the communist countries of Romania, Yugoslavia, and Poland. On their return, *Rolling Stone* ran a feature exposing the State Department's role in the tour. David Clayton Thomas said, "We went over there with the idea of just how much so-called Communist fascism is American propaganda and I found that the propaganda is pretty damn close to the truth." Given the government's aim of bolstering anti-communism, as the magazine noted, "the State Department got its money's worth."[17] That sarcasm was reflective of an assumption that the youth who read *Rolling Stone* had no interest in bands shilling for the US government.

As it turns out, the group did not undertake the tour entirely willingly. Members would later complain they were blackmailed into undertaking this project because Thomas, a Canadian national, had a criminal record and was thus a target for deportation. As guitarist Steve Katz describes it:

> It was very important at that time for the State Department to find a rock band that could represent America abroad, and I don't mean people like the Young Americans, one of the darling Conservative bands of the day. Of course, with the war and all, nobody of significant stature would do it. We certainly weren't jumping on board. This is, until some genius at the State Department leaned on the Justice Department to threaten David with deportation unless we did the State Department a little favor — and if that sounds like extortion, that's exactly what it was. It was either do a tour for the State Department or lose our lead singer.[18]

Katz goes on to reflect, "we should have thought it through a little more, but we stuck with David and signed on for a tour of Eastern Europe."[19] The incident had the effect of making the group a pariah among a key part of their audience, seriously damaging their credibility.

The Uprisings of Spring

Richard Nixon had come into office promising to end the war in Vietnam — a promise he would keep only after invading Cambodia and Laos and inflicting far more suffering on that country and by ratcheting up the level of repression within the US. In turn, the Nixon years would see an intensification of protest and starker manifestations of resistance.

As part of his plan, Nixon accelerated the drawing down of troops deployed in Vietnam. In April, he announced plans to reduce troop strength by 150,000 — a move that significantly reduced the chances of young men being dispatched to Vietnam. On the other hand, he escalated the air war, with reports coming in early May of massive bombing raids carried out against North Vietnam. Then, on April 29, he fatefully ordered US troops to go into Cambodia to attack Vietnamese bases that had been established there.[20]

This move was met with a firestorm of outrage. In the wave of protest on campuses that followed, on May 4, students at Kent State University were confronted by National Guard troops who opened fire. When the shooting stopped, four students lay dead. In the wake of this, Nixon blamed the students:

> This should remind us all once again that when dissent turns to violence it invites tragedy. It is my hope that this tragic and unfortunate incident will strengthen the determination of all the nation's campuses, administrators, faculty and students alike to stand firmly for the right which exists in this country of peaceful dissent and just as strongly against the resort to violence as a means of such expression.[21]

Nixon's response made clear that his administration was going to take a hard line on domestic opposition — a circumstance which served only to raise the level of discontent and pushed things to further extremes.

All of which had cultural ramifications. In the wake of Kent State, Crosby, Stills, Nash & Young's incendiary "Ohio" called out the Kent State killings — "soldiers are cutting us down" — and Nixon explicitly.[22] Similarly, the Steve Miller Band released "Jackson-Kent Blues," which referenced the killing of two Black students at Jackson State in Mississippi, ten days after the Kent incident.[23] The Bay Area band Quicksilver Messenger Service took things a step further. In the song "What About Me" — with images of the Kent State killings — they described feeling the future tremble and foresaw the revolution being "mighty close at hand."[24]

Counter-Revolution

Nixon's stance was emblematic of a shift in how a section of the ruling establishment was responding to the social upheaval. Nixon, who had run for president on a "law and order" campaign, had proclaimed there was a "silent majority" within the US who did not put in with the anti-war and more radical elements within the Black freedom movement. As such, he and those of a similar mindset worked to unleash, through promoting their hard line, a social base to counter those movements.

This was on clear display on May 8, 1970, four days after the Kent State killings, when a demonstration of high school and college students protesting the war's escalation were viciously attacked in lower Manhattan by thousands of construction workers. Author David Kuhn describes one facet of the attack at Wall Street's Federal Hall:

> A man with a duckbill helmet and a tool belt pushed a hippie over a platform edge. The hippie fell, his arms reeling with panic. Students below reached up to catch him. The workman grabbed another hippie by his belt and hurled him into the crowd below.
>
> The trampled girl, who had fallen during the hardhats' first charge, was now "bleeding profusely" from her head.[25]

Kuhn goes on to describe how a tentative police line separating the two groups disappeared, and how the hardhat rioters charge up the steps, beating students along the way.[26]

The attack was not confined to Federal Hall. Workers chased students into nearby Pace University, though it was not the site of a demonstration. Press reports told how "workers smashed windows and beat students in the lobby." One student had to be taken to the hospital "apparently in convulsions." Amid the rampage, workers "threw wooden wedges, pipe joints and rocks through the windows." This in apparent response to an anti-war banner hung on the outside of the building.[27]

One of those at the center of the riot was Peter Brennan, head of the Construction Trades Council of New York — which controlled 200,000 members. While Brennan officially denied any role in organizing the riot, he was quick to defend it. As he said, "Many of them [rioters] are war veterans or have sons or relatives fighting in Vietnam [...] They were fed up with violence by antiwar demonstrators, by those who spat at the American flag and desecrated it."[28] In less than two years, Brennan would be appointed US Secretary of Labor by Richard Nixon.

Enter Merle Haggard

With construction workers beating anti-war youth, country singer Merle Haggard weighed in with songs to promote their reactionary worldview.

Before embarking on a country music career, Haggard had landed in San Quentin on an armed robbery conviction. On his release, he turned to music and had success in the mid-1960s with "Sing Me Back Home" and "Mama Tried."[29] Toward the end of 1969, however, his career would career to the far-right with the release of "Okie from Muskogee," a shot across the bow at the left and the counterculture. The lyrics and melody were plain-spoken and memorable, listing a series of things people in Muskogee, Oklahoma, a prototype for mainstream America, did *not* do — smoking marijuana, dropping acid, and burning draft cards. The song would dominate the airwaves for the next year. Haggard followed "Okie" with the even more virulent "Fightin' Side of Me," an open threat to anyone who did not show ample fealty to the United States.

Haggard was but one artist offering up such fare. A profile of a "wave" of patriotic music in the *Wall Street Journal* made clear the aims of such songs and the social base they were aimed at:

> "Okie from Muskogee" and songs like it appeal to the truck-drivers, ranch hands, farmers, factory workers, hardhats and others who work hard, support their local police, honor their flag — and who now are reacting sharply against the drug culture, the New Left, the hippie movement and other real or imagined threats to what they believe in and hold dear.[30]

As the article pointed out, Haggard's hit was being heard at the same time country singer Bobby Bare released "God Bless America Again," and Guy Drake recorded "Welfare Cadillac" — whose lyrics constituted a dog-whistle racist screed.[31]

Haggard's songs, however, stood out for their artistic quality, for which he was duly rewarded. At the 1970 Country Music Awards, he garnered five wins, including top male vocalist and record of the year. An article in the *LA Times* reporting on his achievement referred to him as "country music's newest superstar."[32]

The recognition showered on Haggard was not simply a matter of acknowledging songs with popular appeal.

Rather, it was emblematic of the rising level of aggression by the ruling authorities who sought to energize a reactionary base to counter an upsurge that had far outstripped the bounds of their tolerance.

Paranoia Strikes Deep

The unprecedented upheaval was unnerving to the rulers of the United States. As such, it was of a piece with a larger apprehension circulating in the country — the word "paranoia" being the operative term. Ronald Reagan offered a conspiratorial assessment of the situation. "Is this just the ferment of youth? Are these young people just showing their idealism? Or is it possible that there is a plot involved?" Answering his own question, he offered, "our young people, many, many of them, have been indoctrinated in thousands of social science courses not to find it the way it is, but to believe it the way it isn't [...] regarding our system."[33] On the one hand, this reads as a real attempt to understand something that had got beyond someone like Reagan's limited imagination. On the other, it was a view that fed a repressive disposition that saw threats everywhere.

Reagan's paranoia was one thing, but the paranoia of a wide section of youth was something else entirely. David Crosby, in the Crosby, Stills, Nash & Young song "Almost Cut My Hair," captured the uneasiness with the metaphor of paranoia being akin to "looking in a mirror and seeing a police car."[34] Crosby's lyric was exemplary of the constant danger of running afoul of the authorities, especially with their myriad drug laws.

Hammering home the dangers lurking in the drug culture was Vice President Spiro Agnew, who by 1970 had become the point person in the reactionary counteroffensive: "I do not suggest for one moment that there is a conspiracy among some songwriters, entertainers, and movie producers to subvert the unsuspecting listener. In my opinion, there isn't any." Instead, for Agnew, the problem was normalizing anti-social behavior:

> Listen to these: "The Acid Queen," [the Who] "Eight Miles High," [the Byrds] "I Couldn't Get High," [the Fugs] "Don't Step on the Grass, Sam," [Steppenwolf] and "Stoned Woman" [Ten Years After]. These songs present the use of drugs in such an attractive light for the impressionable, that "turning on" becomes the natural and even the approved thing to do.[35]

Behind all the scaremongering and sensationalism was a conscious policy of seizing on the drug culture to criminalize the section of the population seen as the biggest threat to domestic security. In 1970, Richard Nixon had declared, "there is no higher priority in this Administration than attacking the addiction problem." Two years later, he would ramp things up, calling for "total war." While couching this in terms of concern over the harm caused by drugs, there was a deeper aim.[36] In a rare moment of candor, Nixon's domestic security advisor, John Ehrlichman, toward the end of his life, laid it all out:

> The Nixon campaign in 1968, and the Nixon White House after that, had two enemies: the antiwar left and black people. You understand what I'm saying? We knew we couldn't make it illegal to be either against the war or black, but by getting the public to associate the hippies with marijuana and blacks with heroin, and then criminalizing both heavily, we could disrupt those communities. We could arrest their leaders, raid their homes, break up their meetings, and vilify them night after night on the evening news. Did we know we were lying about the drugs? Of course we did.[37]

Ehrlichman's comments do not delve into the nuance of the administration's program, which included promoting methadone — itself an addictive opiate — and concern about heroin addiction among returning Vietnam veterans. It does, however, further explain how the specter of drug use was used to promote a moral panic, which in turned reinforced repression on every level — including among federal, state, and local law enforcement. Nuance aside, Ehrlichman's statement is stunning, validating the darkest suspicions of those who had been targeted.[38]

And it was not just the anti-war left and Black people who were in the crosshairs. Also singled out, beyond a large section of the youth population who were experimenting with various drugs, were the cultural icons of the day. By 1970, key rock musicians were finding themselves arrested for drugs — a lot.

One of the more famous arrests was a raid on the Grateful Dead. As *Rolling Stone* reported, the group had performed on January 31 at the Warehouse in New Orleans. After the concert, they returned to their hotel to discover "their room had already been searched and the narcs were just sitting around waiting for them." Nineteen people were caught in the raid and were booked for possession "of some combination of marijuana, LSD, barbiturates, amphetamines, or other dangerous non-narcotic drugs." Drug laws in Louisiana were harsh, with mere possession holding a possible sentence of five to fifteen years in prison.[39] The event would be memorialized in the band's song "Truckin'" — with its refrain "they just won't let you be." Little more than two months later, police raided another post-concert hotel room. This time, the target was Jefferson Airplane. Specifically, Marty Balin and two others were arrested in Bloomington, Minnesota.[40]

Such would become a pattern over the next few years. Joe Cocker and six members of his band were arrested in 1972 after a concert in Australia, when police claim to have discovered marijuana and heroin in their hotel rooms. The group was then given four hours to leave the country. In another incident that year, all six members of Sly & the Family Stone were arrested in Hollywood after police searched their tour bus and found two pounds of marijuana and two vials of cocaine. The following year, the Grateful Dead's Jerry Garcia would again be arrested for drug possession, after being stopped for speeding by the New Jersey State police. Also in 1973, Grateful Dead bassist Phil Lesh was arrested after Marin County authorities searched his home and found small traces of marijuana, LSD, and hashish. The charges were dropped a month later when the DA admitted the warrant was "probably illegal."[41]

Capitalizing on Loss

It was against the backdrop of an intensifying war on drugs that, in September, the transformative guitarist Jimi Hendrix died in London of an overdose of barbiturates. Less than a month later, Janis Joplin died of a heroin overdose.[42] While the specifics of both deaths varied — barbiturates and heroin being quite different — the media used it as a "teaching moment" on the danger of hard drugs.

A piece in London's *Globe and Mail* was instructive in that respect: "In her dress and free-wheeling ways, perhaps her death by drugs, directly or indirectly, will have a different effect. Perhaps rock and its fans will now take another, more cautious, inward look."[43] In a more aggressive vein, Mike Curb, head of MGM records, offered this opinion: "I credit hard drug-record acts with starting hundreds and hundreds of new young drug users." As a result, he claimed his company was going to stop using "18 unnamed rock groups" because of their "glorifying and promoting the use of hard drugs."[44] All this synced well with other efforts, such as the Nixon administration's war on drugs, to clamp down on social unrest.

Joplin and Hendrix's deaths meant different things to different people. For those who cherished their music, it was a tragic loss — lives cut short with so much left to be done. For others, they served as emblems of how far out of hand things had become. That polarization would heighten further over the course of the next several years, diminishing, to a degree, without ever disappearing.

CHAPTER 11
THE SIXTIES END (1971–1972)

We have changed America, and America has changed the world.
— Richard Nixon, 1972[1]

Your flag decal won't get you into heaven anymore.
— John Prine[2]

In the late summer of 1972, Jefferson Airplane took the stage at the Rubber Bowl in Akron, Ohio, for an evening concert. The crowd of twenty thousand or so were assembled in the stands, having been told to stay off the stadium's grass that the University of Akron had recently reseeded. Meantime, hundreds more sat on the hills outside the stadium, trying to catch the show for free.

All in all, things appeared to be proceeding well, though Commander Cody and his Lost Planet Airmen, who opened the show, created a stir when they encouraged the crowd to come down onto the field and dance in front of the stage. Still, so far so good. But as darkness fell, a few of those sitting on the hill, for reasons unclear, started throwing rocks at the scores of police who had been dispatched as security for the concert. Things went from there. A lieutenant on the scene, John Cunningham, described how police were largely operating in the dark, and that the cops "were getting pummeled with rocks and bottles and stones and whatever else they could throw." At least twenty of the police were hit. In response, they countered with tear gas, before rushing the accused stone-throwers. What followed was a prolonged battle. According to Cunningham, "In some cases, we darn near fought all night long [...] It was like a war." Thomas Derrig, on his way into the show when things started to break, described how

> Before you know it, just all hell broke out [...] It was a small war zone, let me tell you. There was cops and teen-agers just going at it everywhere. Fist fighting, throwing rocks, anything that people could get their hands on to throw.[3]

Meantime, the tear gas had wafted into the stadium and was breathed in by concertgoers and musicians alike. When news of the fighting outside filtered backstage, the band and crew were drawn into the fray. Bass player Jack Casady's brother, Chick, got involved when he saw a cop wrestling with a fan; the police smashed him in the nose and then arrested him for assaulting an officer. When Grace Slick confronted the cops about their attack on Casady, a scuffle ensued and they arrested her. Paul Kantner, trying to intervene, was first maced and then arrested.[4]

The scene at the Jefferson Airplane concert was at once the most extreme the group had encountered and a demarcation pointing toward an ending. The years 1971 to 1972 saw a considerable amount of tumult, including the largest action against the Vietnam War, the entrance on the political stage of anti-war veterans, and an escalation in episodes of political violence. Those years also, however, ushered in the actual "end of the Sixties," with the drawdown of troops in Vietnam, the relative abatement of urban unrest, the US's rapprochement with communist China, and cultural elements that arose to counter the radical ones that had asserted themselves. There were not only the beginnings of retreat, but a strengthening "counterrevolutionary" current — sometimes insidious, other times openly hostile — that denoted a social polarization between those asserting a certain kind of "America" and those with alternate visions, all of which presaged a lasting divide.

Stalking Miriam Makeba

On March 8, 1971, a group of peace activists broke into a small FBI office in Media, Pennsylvania, and walked off with a trove of secret FBI records. The group, calling itself the Citizens' Commission to Investigate the FBI, in turn sent copies to the news media, who reported, with some astonishment, that the United States was systematically spying on and carrying out underhanded disruption tactics aimed at Black activists, anti-war figures, and others the FBI deemed threats to the national security of the US.[5]

It would take some time before the full importance of the events in Pennsylvania was realized — including fighting in the courts for the release of further clarifying records — but as a fuller picture emerged, the effect, for a large section of the American public, was jarring.[6]

The fallout from the Media break-in would eventually lead to the curtailment of FBI domestic operations, but that was several years in the future. For the first years of the Seventies, however, the Bureau was operating more or less at full steam. This is shown in the FBI's continued attention to the South African singer Miriam Makeba.

When Makeba toured the US in 1971, the Bureau followed her closely, including garnering information from informants who attended her concerts. Thus, we learn that, "On November 2, 1971, a source who has furnished reliable information in the past" reported that Makeba had performed at the Soldiers and Sailors Memorial Hall,

Pittsburgh, with Hugh Masekela and the Bob Johnson Dancers, a local group.[7] The reason for the monitoring was not that Makeba was thought to have done anything or was about to do something. Rather, the attention was a result of her marriage to Kwame Ture (Stokely Carmichael).

Miriam Makeba, 1969
Credit: Rob Mieremet — National Archives (Netherlands)

While the concert report was somewhat neutral, later entries were less so, taking pleasure in her perceived difficulties. Such was the case in her performance in Baltimore on November 5, which they reported as a "complete flop with only about 100 persons in attendance." Similarly, they report that, at a show in Washington, DC, two days later, "MAKEBA gave away at least 300 tickets in Washington, D.C. just to get a large crowd."[8]

Stokely Carmichael in Alabama, 1966
Credit: Birmingham Public Library Archives

Ticket sales aside, the Bureau was keen to discern any overt political statements taking place during her performances:

Makeba, in introducing several of her songs, alluded to her difficulties with the South African government and her denial of a passport by that government. She thanked other black African governments which had granted her citizenship and issued her passports in order that she might continue her travel and musical activities.[9]

Unintentionally, that report is evidence of just how hard the South African and US governments were making things for Makeba.

Had her relationship been with a lesser activist, it is not likely she would have merited as much attention. However,

Carmichael was a "Key Black Extremist" — meaning the attention would be unrelenting. In the FBI's view:

> Stokely Carmichael's prominence as a black extremist, his consistent advocacy of violent revolution in this country and his efforts to persuade black Americans to dedicate themselves to Pan-Africanism and to aiding African revolutionaries make it essential that coverage of him be as thorough and as penetrating as possible...[10]

Things had escalated for the couple around the time of Martin Luther King's assassination, a period that also corresponded with Carmichael's affiliation with the Black Panther Party. As Makeba recalled, "The FBI, which has been following Stokely everywhere he goes for a long time, now begins to follow me, too." She tells of being constantly followed, to the point that she and her husband refer to their minders as "babysitters." But the humor does not negate the stress it caused. "It is nerve-wracking, and it is something I never would have expected in America. This is really nasty treatment from a country that is supposed to be free.[11]

Makeba, unlike Carmichael, was not a radical activist. That said, she was clear on her sympathies. As she told a Swedish magazine in early 1970, in response to a question about her relationship to Black Power and the Black Panthers, she made clear she was not part of the organization. She also asserted that:

> I am no longer afraid of the word, 'violence.' I don't know why we blacks are not allowed to use that word. Show me a country that has not used violence to get where it is today. I would be very happy if you could. In that respect, Sweden is no better than any other country. But blacks are supposed to be like Jesus Christ. We always have to be 'nice.' And we

have been. But in many of us good nature has gone so far that it has become stupidity."[12]

Her militant Pan-African spirit comes through even more clearly when asked, "Would you like to see the blacks in your native South Africa come to power by means of violence?" Without flinching, she answered, "I wouldn't just like to see it happen, I want it to happen! Because South Africa is mine. It belongs to the blacks. All Africa belongs to us blacks."[13]

It is little surprise, then, that not only was she being stalked by the FBI but also the IRS, who claimed the couple owed $48,000 in back taxes.[14] From surveilling her concerts, to trailing Carmichael as a key activist, to micro-auditing their taxes, the couple was being hit from multiple sides.

The BPP and the Soledad Brothers

The efforts against Carmichael — which made Makeba a target — were reflective of the extremes to which things had gotten to in the Black liberation movement. In Carmichael's case, it meant repatriating to Conakry. In the case of the Black Panthers, it meant a near unimaginable pressure.

By early 1971, the Black Panther Party, after having grown exponentially between 1968 and 1970, was in disarray. The group's leader, Huey Newton, freed from jail after a nationwide campaign, was now at the center of a split between a faction led by Eldridge Cleaver, which inclined toward political violence as an immediate strategy, and his own reformist "survival pending revolution" strategy.

Those tensions undergirded an event attended by six thousand people to commemorate Newton's birthday and an "Intercommunal Day of Solidarity for Bobby Seale, Ericka Huggins, Angela Davis, and Ruchell McGee" — all of whom were entangled in legal battles. Despite their problems, the

Panthers had garnered a good deal of support, and, as such, performances that day not only included their own musical group, the Lumpen, but also the Grateful Dead.

The Dead had always been vocal in proclaiming their status as "not being political." In the words of Dead guitarist Jerry Garcia, "We don't deal with things on the basis of content, the idea of philosophy or any of that shit, mostly its personalities — people."[15] Nonetheless, they found themselves in all manner of political situations, from the Human Be-In of 1967, to the Columbia Strike of 1969, to the Panther benefit in 1972.[16]

As for the BPP, Newton, who by then had taken to calling himself the Supreme Servant of the People, would lead the group's consolidation in Oakland, focusing on their Breakfast for Children and health care programs. At the same time, they developed a secret criminal component that would take hold as the decade went on, leading to a corrosion of the good will and support they had garnered in their early years.[17]

Developments within the Panthers were consistent with a wider level of disarray. Not only were they struggling to keep Bobby Seale and Erika Huggins out of prison — the two were accused of having a role in the killing of an alleged informant within the group, charges that would later be dropped after a mistrial — the group was also working in a coalition to free the revolutionary prisoner George Jackson, who, with Fleeta Drumgo and John Clutchette, were known as the Soledad Brothers, and were accused of killing a Soledad prison guard.[18]

Along with this would be the matter of Angela Davis, who was implicated in the Soledad case by virtue of her ties with George Jackson's seventeen-year-old brother, Jonathan. Unfortunately for Davis, a gun she had purchased had been used in a failed attempt by Jonathan Jackson to free the Soledad Brothers in a scheme that August, which involved taking a judge, district attorney, and three jurors hostage at a courthouse in Marin County, where three prisoners, Ruchell McGee, William Christmas, and James McClain, were in court for trial. The effort was a violent disaster, leaving the young Jackson, Judge Harold Haley, and two of the prisoners — Christmas and McClain — dead. For her part, Angela Davis was targeted by federal authorities, with the FBI adding her to the most wanted list. She was eventually caught and put on trial along with Magee. She was acquitted in June 1972.[19]

Davis's case nonetheless became a cause célèbre, leading the Rolling Stones to record the well-intentioned but problematic "Sweet Black Angel," (one line referencing "ten little niggers" sitting on the wall), which appeared on *Exile on Main St.*. Similarly, John Lennon and Yoko Ono recorded "Angela" — a weaker song in comparison — for their record *Sometime in New York City*.

Compounding the tragedy surrounding Jonathan Jackson's death, a year later, George Jackson himself, in a desperate escape attempt from San Quentin, would be killed along with three guards and two prisoners. That incident, too, saw a significant artistic statement, this time from Bob Dylan, who recorded the song "George Jackson," a single which adhered to the un-nuanced movement summation of the time — casting Jackson as an unambiguous victim and hero — rather than the far more tragic and awful episode it was.[20]

Attica

Such incidents would reach a crescendo in September 1971 with the Attica prison uprising, where over three thousand prisoners took control of the facility and issued demands ranging from better food to an end to political and racial persecution. This was met, after a five-day standoff, by the

New York State police who, set loose by Governor Nelson Rockefeller, entered the prison, killing thirty-nine inmates and ten of the hostages.[21]

Attica, among other things, lead to a crisis for the status quo, a certain de-legitimation of state violence in the eyes of many, especially after New York officials were shown to have lied about the slaughter at the prison. This quickly found its way into popular culture, as seen in the film *Dog Day Afternoon*, where Al Pacino's character is able to incite the crowd against the police by simply striking up the chant "Attica, Attica!" Before Pacino though, John Lennon and Yoko Ono featured the song "Attica State" on their 1972 album *Sometime in New York City*. While the lyrics are didactic, resulting in a song with more statement than power, that it came from Lennon meant it would not be ignored. A more commanding statement on the uprising, however, came from jazz saxophonist Archie Shepp, whose 1972 album was titled *Attica Blues*, which, along with two tracks dedicated to the prison uprising, also included an homage to George Jackson.[22]

Vietnam Veterans and the Culmination of Anti-War Protests

The year 1971 also saw within the anti-war movement a larger presence of veterans and active military members. That was the backdrop to actors Jane Fonda and Donald Sutherland launching the FTA Show (Fuck the Army). The undertaking was effectively an anti-Bob Hope revue, in contrast to the pro-war comedian's USO shows for active-duty military members. As such, it drew on prominent cultural figures. The first FTA show, held at Fort Bragg, NC, included Fonda, Sutherland, actor Peter Boyle, Barbara Dane, comedian Dick Gregory, and the improvisational comedy group the Committee.[23] As it continued, including touring the Far East, it would include comedian Paul Mooney, singers Len Chandler, Holly Near, and others.

The FTA Show grew out of a burgeoning anti-war movement within the military itself, crystallizing in the organization Vietnam Veterans Against the War. In early 1971, VVAW held hearings it called the Winter Soldier Investigation in Detroit, where 150 veterans testified about the real nature of the war being fought in Vietnam.[24] There too, the effort garnered the support of prominent cultural figures, in this case the financial support of Fonda, Sutherland, Joan Baez, David Crosby, and Graham Nash.[25]

The hearings themselves were both shocking and revelatory. One of those who appeared was Marine Sergeant Scott Camil, who testified, "Anybody that was dead was considered a VC. If you killed someone, they said, 'How do you know he's a VC?' and the general reply would be, 'He's dead,' and that was sufficient." Camil went on to describe how GIs raped the women, justifying it as "searching."[26] His testimony, on the heels of news of the Mỹ Lai massacre, was further evidence of what was actually happening in Southeast Asia.

Camil's testimony resonated with Graham Nash, who would write the song "Oh Camil (Winter Soldier)," which offered a blistering counter to anyone who thought there was honor in the war the US was fighting.[27] The album it was released on, *Wild Tales*, also included "Prison Song," about how marijuana laws were sending people to serve arduous prison sentences. The album was unwelcomed in certain quarters. Nash would later remark that "I have it on very good authority that *Wild Tales* was buried [...] No promotion."[28]

Beyond the Winter Soldier testimony was a high-profile gathering on April 17–20 of more than one thousand Vietnam veterans, organized by Vietnam Veterans Against the War, to come to Washington to protest the war. Their gathering culminated in a ceremony where they threw their medals onto the steps of the US Capitol. As the group's newspaper would later recall, "The sentiments of the vets were expressed best by one veteran who tossed his medals away and stated: 'If we have to fight again, it will be to take these steps.'"[29] These were images that made the news throughout the country, offering a picture of a type of anti-war opposition most were unaware of.[30]

A few days after the VVAW demonstration, on April 24, over a half million people marched on Washington to protest the war — the largest such demonstration ever. At the rally, Peter, Paul and Mary reprised their version of "Blowin' in the Wind" from the 1963 March on Washington, but the most enthusiastic response came when Country Joe sang the no-holds-barred anti-war song "I-Feel-Like-I'm-Fixin'-to-Die-Rag."[31]

The march was followed by an effort to shut down Washington, DC, in an act of mass civil disobedience. The tens of thousands who had stayed in the city after the earlier demonstration were met with unprecedented repression, including the largest mass arrest in US history, with the number of arrestees approaching thirteen thousand. So many people had been arrested that city authorities had no room in their jails and were forced to requisition a practice field near Robert F. Kennedy stadium to hold the mass of arrestees.[32]

As impressive as the demonstrations in Washington that spring were, they coincided with moves by the Nixon administration toward extricating the US from Vietnam. While over 150,000 troops remained in Vietnam that spring, by the following year the number would be under 25,000 and shrinking fast, signaling, for all intents and purposes, the end of the war, and along with it the protests against it.[33]

Phil Ochs in South America

For his part, Phil Ochs was not doing especially well in 1971, suffering from undiagnosed manic depression. Nonetheless, he continued a level of political activism, traveling to Europe with Jerry Rubin and Stew Albert, who were attempting to popularize the Yippies in Europe.[34]

After the European trip, Rubin and Ochs headed to Chile, where the socialist government of Salvador Allende had come into office. While there, he was able to meet and perform with Víctor Jara and get exposed to the Chilean left. After Chile, he and his companion, David Ifshin, traveled to Uruguay, where they were invited to speak at a political rally. Unbeknownst to the pair, the gathering was illegal. When the police arrived to break it up, the two were arrested and would go from being jailed in Montevideo to being removed from the country and sent to Argentina, where they were put in a jail in Buenos Aires. In Buenos Aires, Ifshin was beaten, before he and Ochs were then deported to Bolivia. On the advice of prisoners they had encountered along the way, Ochs created a scene at the airport in order to avoid being detained, and possibly disappeared. Their effort was a success, and they were able to fly to Peru before heading back to the US.[35]

Ochs's experience in Latin America, especially Chile, would lead him to organize a benefit in the aftermath of the US-supported coup in Chile in 1973. The event would include Dave Van Ronk, Bob Dylan, Pete Seeger, Arlo Guthrie, Víctor Jara's widow, Joan, and others. It would be the last major political undertaking for Ochs. He would take his own life in 1975.[36]

Morrison Exits

While the efforts against Phil Ochs represented a conscious effort by governmental authorities at suppression because of his political associations, the measures against Jim Morrison had a more complicated character. In his case, the repression he confronted stemmed not only from his often-reckless behavior, but also elements of a reactionary counteroffensive — today referred to by the ambiguous term "culture wars" — which were essentially being field-tested in the 1960s.

The Doors, 1968
Credit: Agency for the Performing Arts, Publicity Photo

Morrison had been sentenced to six months of hard labor in Miami's notorious Raiford Penitentiary in October 1970 for the indecent exposure conviction in Florida. He was in the process of appealing in March 1971 when the group finished recording *L.A. Woman.* Then, to the surprise of his bandmates, he announced he was going to Paris.[37] Three months later, Morrison was reported dead from natural causes, though it is speculated he actually died of a heroin overdose.[38]

Unlike Hendrix and Joplin from the previous year, Morrison's particular path was marked in no small measure by his legal problems, stemming from his pushing the envelope of performance art in Miami and "acting out" on an airplane. Band mate Ray Manzarek would later say that Morrison likely would have been able to avoid prison, but that it nonetheless "weighed on Jim's psyche."[39] Given all the effort the authorities had leveled at Morrison, Manzarek's view seems optimistic.[40]

Winding Down

After the demonstrations in the spring of 1971, the anti-war movement was largely in decline, as were the uprisings of Black people and the organizations, such as the SNCC and the BPP, that they gave rise to. Most people and groups — aside from small cells set on political violence — were stepping back, trying to consolidate, or fighting to keep their people out of prison. While the move toward retreat was not obvious in the moment — the surface still showed a good deal of ferment — things were moving in another direction.

This was clear to the discerning eye when John Lennon and Yoko Ono — who for a brief moment were wholly immersed in the radical left — co-hosted the *Mike Douglas Show* for a full week in February 1972. In their role as co-hosts, the couple was allowed to invite their own guests, which they did, asking people such as Joan Baez, Jerry Rubin, and Bobby Seale to appear.

Seale's appearance was especially striking in signaling

the shift underway. The man who had become iconic for his defiance in Judge Julius Hoffman's court during the Chicago conspiracy trial was not talking revolutionary politics but instead pitching the Black Panthers' "survival programs," such as their sickle cell anemia testing project, their clothing project, and their free breakfast for children program.[41] While the Panthers were still enmeshed in controversy, things had changed.

By August 1972, Lennon himself was stepping away from radical politics, having broken with the activists he had been working with. As the FBI reported:

> [Lennon] has fallen out of the favor of activist JERRY RUBIN, STEWART ALBERT, and RENNIE DAVIS, due to subject's lack of interest in committing himself to involvement in anti-war and New Left activities.[42]

As a result, the New York FBI office put his case "in a pending inactive status."[43] Despite stepping back from activism, however, Lennon's troubles with the US government were hardly over, as he would then confront deportation because of his previous drug arrests — though he would ultimately prevail, after years of court battles, and obtain a Green Card.[44]

Most retrospective reflections today focus on Lennon's political behavior in the early Seventies as a phase soon passed through, however, it misses just how impactful it was at the time. While many artists took political stands, some more controversial and career-threatening — there was no band in the 1960s bigger than the Beatles. In that respect, while hard to quantify, it is easy to underestimate the role Lennon played in legitimating — and, yes, he alienated some as well — radical sentiments to a massive fan base.

Macabre Ballads

While the US war in Vietnam was being drawn down, the controversies around it were not. By 1971, the consensus that had made Barry Sadler's "Ballad of the Green Beret" a hit had disappeared — along with *The Ed Sullivan Show*, which had showcased it.[45] In a far more polarized atmosphere, songs that heralded the singular bravery of soldiers gave way to something else.

In March 1971, Plantation Records released the "Battle Hymn of Lt. Calley," by a group calling itself C Company featuring Terry Nelson.[46] Released amid the trial of Lt. William Calley for killing twenty-two civilians at Mỹ Lai, it was set to the tune of the "Battle Hymn of the Republic" and presented a revisionist version of the massacre — "we responded to their rifle fire with everything we had!" It also offered a defense of Calley, arguing that he was simply doing his duty as a soldier. Calley himself had made the same argument during his trial, saying, "The soldier's job is to carry out any orders given to the best of your ability."[47]

Calley's position was bolstered by a Harris Poll, which posed the question, "If you were a soldier in Viet Nam and were ordered by your superior officers to shoot old men, women, and children suspected of aiding the enemy, would you follow the orders and shoot them, or would you be more right to refuse to shoot them?" Astonishingly, 43% of the respondents said they would kill the civilians.[48]

While the "Battle Hymn of Lt. Calley" would end up selling a million copies, it was not universally welcome. Country artist Tex Ritter saw his record company, Capitol, scotch the idea for a cover version of the song. Similarly, the US Army banned its playing on Armed Forces Radio. The reasons they cited were that Calley's case was still working its way through the courts and "it might offend Vietnamese who listened to the station."[49] None of which could obscure the fact that there was a sizable audience in the US for a song extolling mass murder.

Resurrecting the Past

The defense of Calley concentrated a certain unapologetic view of what the US had done in Vietnam that went far beyond the actions of any individual. While the social base of this would not, because of the larger social divide, become a majority opinion, there were other elements in the culture that worked to bring about a polarization which, if not nullifying the Sixties upsurge, might at least take the edge off. These involved works promoting a reactionary notion of "looking back" — to the 1940s, 1950s, early 1960s, and even back to the dawn of the first millennium, where the upheaval of the Sixties was unheard of. This was displayed in two 1971 films that cast a halcyon view of the past, the *Last Picture Show* and *Summer of '42*, which were followed by the Broadway show *Grease* (1972) and *American Graffiti* (1973) — the latter using the once incendiary "Rock Around the Clock" as a nostalgic evocation of a less contentious time. All of this presaged a wave of Fifties nostalgia that took hold as the Seventies unfolded.[50]

Given this, it should then be little surprise that Christianity too got in on the act. The rumblings of this could be seen as far back as 1969 in popular music, with Norman Greenbaum's top forty hit "Spirit in the Sky" — its refrain being "you know you have a friend in Jesus." In a similar vein, the Byrds (in 1969) and the Doobie Brothers (in 1972) had success with the song "Jesus is Just Alright" — an equally unabashed Christian song, albeit with a rock beat.

All of these might have been dismissed as anomalies — perhaps even irony — had it not been for the fact that there emerged in the late 1960s a sub-culture of "hip" Christianity, whose adherents came to be called, not a little derogatorily, Jesus Freaks — a mixed bag of neo-Christians with various interpretations of religious canon.

While some saw this as a challenge to conventional religion, others saw an opportunity to bring a number of those living outside the dominant social conventions back into the fold. As theologian Dr. Carl A Henry told the *LA Times*, "A whole generation is up for grabs. The way we respond to the counterculture may be a criterion of the effectiveness of our evangelical witness in the remainder of the 20th century."[51]

Reinforcing such calls were developments in the cultural realm beyond the songs named above. In the spring of 1971, the play *Godspell* — based on the New Testament book of Matthew — premiered off-Broadway. In the view of theater critic Clive Barnes, the show exuded "naïve but fey frivolity," before adding a suggestion, "Young churchmen looking for ways to fill their empty pews might well find hope at this seemingly hip Christian message, with its perfectly contemporary and perfectly vulgar concept of peace and goodwill to all men."[52] *Godspell* was followed by the "rock-opera" of composer Andrew Lloyd Webber and lyricist Tim Rice — another "hip" neo-Christian confection. Notably, Lloyd Webber was pretty straightforward about his intentions, crass as they were: "When you're just sitting around and nobody knows who you are, you look for something that will bring you attention."

As if on cue, some religious forces took issue with the production. According to the *New York Times*, the show's detractors "regarded the strutting, mincing, twitching, grinding, souped-up 'Superstar' as theatrical sacrilege." From another angle, the Jewish Committee and the Anti-Defamation League of the B'nai B'rith accused the production of anti-Semitism, portraying Jews as Christ killers. Lloyd Webber pushed back on that, claiming the priests in the production were "establishment people not Jewish people." The attacks kept no one away from the show who had wanted to see it, and instead lent it a legitimacy among the more alienated it might otherwise not have garnered.[53]

On the whole, the dressing up of traditional religion into "cool" garb signaled a larger move to integrate elements of the rebellious culture into the mainstream — a process that continues today.

By the end of 1972, the period of upsurge was coming to an end. The Paris Peace Accords would be signed the following January, presaging the full-on retreat of the US from Vietnam. Richard Nixon, who had tried and failed to conclude that war in favor of a US victory, would soon be under full-on siege for his role in the break-in at Democratic Party Headquarters at the Watergate complex. The FBI, too, was coming under increasing scrutiny as revelation after revelation of its secret break-ins, surveillance, and counterintelligence measures came to light, and would soon see its domestic mandate constrained — at least for a time.

Musically, the vibrancy of the counterculture was being co-opted with the ascendance of "arena rock," the further commodification of all types of popular music, and the numbing presence of drugs.

Things were coming to an end, but that did not nullify the space that had been opened. The period between 1955 and 1972 concentrated decades of experience and transformation. Myriad genies had been set loose, never again to be contained.

CONCLUSION
YESTERDAY AND TODAY

I do not suggest for one moment that there is a conspiracy among some songwriters, entertainers, and movie producers to subvert the unsuspecting listener. In my opinion, there isn't any. But the cumulative impact of some of their work advances the wrong cause.
— Spiro T. Agnew[1]

The artist is first and foremost the reflection of his times, and his ability to stay a few steps ahead of the rest of the society is his contribution to his society.
— Phil Ochs[2]

Between 1955 and 1972, the United States, the most powerful country in the world, attempted to navigate a thicket of contradictions globally and domestically to maintain an advance into what they hoped would be an "American Century." Not only did this fail, leading to, among other things, their biggest ever military defeat, it created circumstances where, at moments, it seemed "the government itself might come apart at its seams."[3] While that did not happen, the ferocity of the challenges set loose led to unprecedented measures to hold the line to maintain the ruling status quo. This was true in foreign interventions, in domestic political repression, and in attacks in the cultural arena.

Unlike other realms, one hears little of systemic forces operating against an insurgent culture. Instead, there is a circumscribed focus on things such as individual agency, artistic missteps, decontextualized notions of genius, and the recklessness of individuals. While such elements play their part, often times a critical one, all of this operates within a social framework that has a standing necessity to fight for its own interests, and frustrate those that would "advance the wrong cause."

Which is not to suggest a grand conspiracy. Things were more complicated than that. In that respect, the quote from Spiro Agnew above — as honest a statement as one might hope for — says as much. This was societal pushback to a music giving aid and comfort to the adversary, at a moment when the power structure was confronting unprecedented challenges. As such, it had to be countered. All of which resulted in the music and the artists producing it contending with both conscious and reflexive reaction. Regardless of the specific tack, the effect was the same: a generalized brake — or worse — on artists trying to bring forward pathbreaking music.

That so much was produced in spite of this is testament to the power of the upsurge and the tenacity of the artists operating within it. That said, it was no easy road, and there were consequences. From the premature exit of the touring stage of the Beatles and Bob Dylan — who contended with opposition from both the right and the left — to the FBI pursuit of Dave Van Ronk, Phil Ochs, and Miriam Makeba, the withheld visas of the Kinks, John Lennon, George Harrison, Mick Jagger, and Keith Richards, the censorship and suppression of Buffy Sainte-Marie, Johnny Cash, and Gordon Lightfoot, the energy-draining weight of drug arrests — often multiple times — of Jefferson Airplane, the Grateful Dead, Sly & the Family Stone, and Buffalo Springfield, the denial of permits of the use of private and municipal space, from Woodstock to Altamont, the prospect of prison for Jim Morrison — this, and quite a bit else, had a chilling effect. And here it need be noted that there arose ways in the Sixties of targeting unwelcome cultural forms that foreshadow contemporary reactionary moves, branded culture wars. While the FBI is a clear and recognizable villain, many of these artists confronted antagonists in different garb. As Paul Simon noted in his song "Adios Hermanos" — about the vilification of Puerto Rican youth — the newspapers and TV would kill you if they could, though the media was hardly the only other adversarial element.

As I noted in my previous book, *The Folk Singers and the Bureau*, one can only imagine what could have been produced had such not been the case, and while that is ultimately an exercise in "what might have been," to not recognize there was loss is to not appreciate history properly and be in a position to draw appropriate lessons.[4]

All of this, it need be noted, was playing out in an extraordinary time, when the Cold War was at both its most dangerous and in the midst of a monumental transition.[5] That was a critical driver in setting the framework — impacting everything from the Black freedom movement to the anti-war movement, the rising of a radical New Left to the rebellion against the dominant culture.[6] Such was the backdrop on which this unprecedented music was able to assert itself — impossible things were then possible.

Which brings us to our current moment, where not only do the best dreams and aspirations of the Sixties seem a million miles out of reach, so too does the possibility of a liberatory future — or even the possibility of any future at all. There is no simple platitude to quench that longing, but some historical perspective is worth bearing in mind.

In 1962, Bob Dylan wrote "Song to Woody," an homage to his idol, Woody Guthrie. In it, he reflected on the state of the world, writing that it looked like it was dying, though "it's hardly been born." It was a dire assessment, if one grounded in perilous circumstances. We now know that, as dangerous as the situation was, the world did not end, and indeed, things both terrible and wonderful lay ahead. All of which can serve as a useful grounding. While we cannot see into *our* future, one no less fraught than that of sixty years ago, it is, for better or worse, wide open. Who can say what wonders, musical and otherwise, await?

APPENDIX: FBI FILES

Notes on FBI Files

With the onset of COVID-19 in March 2020, obtaining records from the FBI and the National Archives became increasingly difficult, leading to longer and longer waiting times. As a result, the release dates of a number files requested were put far into the future. Despite that, through earlier releases, a considerable number of files were obtained. Below is a chart of those records, cited in the book, as well as those that remain pending.

Note on FBI file Code

The first three numbers in the FBI code represents the FBI's "Offense Code." The relevant codes for the files listed in the chart are as follows:

25 – Selective Service Act
61 – Treason
62 – Miscellaneous
63 – Not listed (possibly miscellaneous)
94 – Research Matters
100 – Domestic Security
105 – Foreign Counterintelligence
145 – Interstate Transportation of Obscene Matter
164 – Crime Aboard Aircraft
176 – Anti-riot laws

Artist/Entity	FBI File Number/Notes	Pages
Armstrong, Louis	N/A	28
Cole, Nat	100-379380	40
Cooke, Sam	File Destroyed	0
Darling, Erik (The Weavers)	100-HQ-437047	21
Fugs	145-0-1770	8
Ellington, Duke	100-HQ-434443	35
Farina, Mimi & Richard	100-59875	13
Freed, Alan	63-5721-1	16
Fugs	145-4031 Interstate Transfer of Obscene Matter	8
Ginsberg, Allen	105-63483 (Foreign CI—Cuba)	90
Gleason, Ralph	100-SF-54295—100 pages	Awaiting
Havens, Richie	Files Destroyed—October 27, 1978 & May 7, 1997.[7]	0
Heron, Gil Scot	N/A Also files are held at NARA as 91-AX-3713, unreleased.	25
Hoffman, Abbie	100-449923 Section 7	159
Lewis, Fulton (Journalist)	62-0 (Miscellaneous—Non-Subversive)	106
Mailer, Norman	100-370923 (SM-C)	166
Masekela, Hugh	Awaiting	TBD
Makeba, Miriam	105-HQ-176973 (Foreign CI)	302
Morrison, Jim	164-1004	95

Ochs, Phil	**Sections of HQ file obtained for this book courtesy of Woody Guthrie Center (195)**	195
	100-HQ-441378 — w/NARA 300 pages- unreleased	
	176-HQ-44 — w/NARA 400 pages- unreleased	
	100-NY-15200 — FBI says files transferred to NARA NARA says not transferred – missing	
Presley, Elvis	62/63 3064 -X (Misc./Non-Subversive)	205
Reagon, Cordell (Freedom Singers)	Awaiting	TBD
Reynolds, Malvina	100-HQ-19446 (2000 pages) 100-LA-4692 (800 pages) 61-SF-242 (2500 pages)	Awaiting
Rotolo, Suze	100-HQ-435482	175
Seeger, Pete	100-HQ-200845	1761
Stanley, August Owsley	100-HQ-457671	3
Shelton, Robert	100-HQ-419947 (Awaiting)—500 Pages	Awaiting
Jefferson Airplane	No code—From FBI Vault	16
Steiner, Jacqueline	100-HQ-352930 (Awaiting) 100-BS-20765, 100-NY-88449 100-BS-30	TBD

Sullivan, Ed	94-HQ-4 SUB 1295 150 Pages (Awaiting)	Awaiting
Van Ronk, Dave	100-HQ-440146 100-NY-136446	582
Weavers	100-NY-140720 v. 1	3
Wilson, Carl	25-551714	80
		3964

BIBLIOGRAPHY

Armstrong, Gregory. *The Dragon Has Come*. New York: Harper Row, 1974.

Arrighi, Giovanni. *The Long Twentieth Century: Money Power and the Origins of Our Times*. New York: Verso, 1994.

Arrighi, Giovanni. *Adam Smith in Beijing: Lineages of the 21st Century*. New York: Verso, 2007.

Belafonte, Harry, and Michael Schnayerson. *Harry Belafonte, My Song: A Memoir*. New York: Knopf, 2011.

Bevins, Vincent. *The Jakarta Method: Washington's Anti-Communist Crusade & the Mass Murder Campaign That Shaped the World*. New York: Hachette, 2020.

Bianculli, David. *Dangerously Funny: The Uncensored Story of The Smothers Brothers Comedy Hour*. New York: Touchstone, Simon & Schuster, 2009.

Callahan, Mat. *The Explosion of Deferred Dreams: Musical Renaissance and Social Revolution in San Francisco, 1965–1975*. Oakland: PM Press, 2017.

Carson, Clayborne. *In Struggle: SNCC and the Black Awakening of the 1960s*. Cambridge: Harvard University Press, 1995.

Clifford, Clark with Richard Holbrooke. *Counsel to the President: A Memoir*, New York: Random House, 1991.

Cohen, Ronald D. *Rainbow Quest: The Folk Music Revival and American Society*. Amherst, MA: University of Massachusetts Press, 2002.

Cohen, Ronald D and Rachel Clare Donaldson. *Roots of the Revival: American and British Folk Music in the 1950s*. Urbana, Chicago & Springfield: University of Illinois Press. 2014.

Cohodas, Nadine. *Princess Noir: The Tumultuous Reign of Nina Simone*. Chapel Hill, NC: University of North Carolina Press, 2010.

Collins, Judy. *Sweet Judy Blue Eyes: My Life in Music*. New York: Three Rivers Press. 2012.

Cott, Robert. *Bob Dylan: The Essential Interviews*. New York: Simon & Schuster, 2017 ed.

Coyne, John R. Jr. *The Impudent Snobs: Agnew vs. the Intellectual Establishment*. New Rochelle: Arlington House, 1972.

D'Ambrosio, Antonio. *A Heartbeat and a Guitar: Johnny Cash and the Making of Bitter Tears*. New York: Nation Books, 2009.

Davis, Mike and Jon Wiener, *Set the Night on Fire: L.A. in the Sixties*, New York: Verso, 2020.

Davies, Ray. *X-Ray: The Unauthorized Autobiography of Ray Davies*. New York: Overlook Press, 1995.

Dobbs, Michael. *One Minute to Midnight: Kennedy, Khrushchev, and Castro on the Brink of Nuclear War.* New York: Penguin Random House, 2009.

Doggett, Peter. *Crosby, Stills, Nash & Young*. New York, London, Toronto Sydney, New Delhi: Atria Books, 2019.

Doggett, Peter. *There's a Riot Going On: Revolutionaries, Rock Stars and the Rise and Fall of '60s Counter-Cultures.* Edinburgh: Canon Gate, 2007.

Donner, Frank. *Age of Surveillance: The Aims and Methods of America's Intelligence System*, New York: Vintage, 1981.

Donner, Frank. *Protectors of the Privilege: Red Squads and Police Repression in Urban America*. Berkeley: University of California Press, 1992.

Durden-Smith, Jo. *Who Killed George Jackson*, New York: Knopf, 1976.

Dylan, Bob. *Chronicles*. New York: Simon and Schuster, 2005.

Ehrlichman, John. *Witness to Power: The Nixon Years*, New York: Simon & Schuster, 1982.

Einarson, John, with Ian Tyson & Sylvia Tyson. *Four Strong Winds: Ian & Sylvia*, Toronto: McClelland & Stewart, 2011.

Evans, Karl. *The Messenger: The Rise and Fall of Elijah Muhammad*. New York: Vintage Books, 1999.

Farber, David, R. *Chicago '68*. Chicago & London: University of Chicago Press, 1994.

Farber, David, R. *Age of Great American Dreams: America in the 1960s*, Hill & Wang, 1994.

Farber, David. *The Sixties from Memory to History*, Chapel Hill & London: The University of North Carolina Press, 1994.

Fisher, Mark. *Capitalist Realism*. London: Zero Books, 2009.

Friedman, Jonathan C. *The Routledge History of Social Protest in Popular Music*, New York: Routledge, 2013.

Garabedian, Steven P. *A Sound History: Lawrence Gellert, Black Musical Protest, and White Denial*. Amherst: University of Massachusetts Press, 2020.

Garrow, David. *The F.B.I. and Martin Luther King, Jr*. New York: Penguin, 1986.

Gitlin, Todd. *The Sixties: Years of Hope, Days of Rage*. New York: Bantam, 1993.

Gosse, Van. *Rethinking the New Left: An Interpretative History*. New York: Palgrave McMillan, 2005.

Gould, Jonathan. *Can't Buy Me Love: The Beatles, Britain, and America*. New York: Three Rivers Press, 2008.

Guinn, Jeff. Manson. *The Life and Times of Charles Manson*. New York: Simon and Schuster, 2013.

Guralnick, Peter. *Dream Boogie: The Triumph of Sam Cooke*. New York: Back Bay Books, 2006.

Haas, Jeffrey. *The Assassination of Fred Hampton: How the FBI and Chicago Police Murdered a Black Panther*. Chicago: Lawrence Hill Books, 2011.

Hajdu, David. *Positively 4th Street: The Lives and Times of Joan Baez, Bob Dylan, Mimi Baez*. New York: Bloomsbury, 2002.

Halberstam, David. *The Fifties*. New York: Villard, 1993.

Hinton, Elizabeth. *America on Fire: The Untold History of Police Violence and Black Rebellion Since the 1960s*. New York: Liveright, 2021.

Hobsbawm, Eric. *Age of Extremes: A History of the World 1914–1991*. New York: Vintage, 1996.

Hoffman, Abbie. *Woodstock Nation: A Talk Rock Album*. New York: Pocket Books 1971.

Hoffman, Abbie. *Revolution for the Hell of It*. New York: Dial Press, 1969.

Hollings Haus, Wade. *Philosophizing Rock Performance: Dylan, Hendrix, Bowie*. Toronto and Plymouth: Scarecrow Press, 2013.

Isserman, Maurice and Michael Kazin. *America Divided: The Civil War of the Sixties*. New York: Oxford University Press, 2000.

Jarnow, Jesse, *Wasn't That a Time, the Weavers, the Blacklist and the Battle for the Soul of America*. Boston: DeCapo Press, 2018.

Joseph, Peniel E. *Stokely: A Life*. New York: Basic CIVITAS, 2014.

Katz, Steve. *Blood, Sweat, and My Rock 'n' Roll Years: Is Steve Katz a Rock Star*. Lanham, MD: Lyons Press, 2015.

Kerouac, Jack. *On the Road*. New York: Penguin. 2000.

Kramer, Michael J. *The Republic of Rock: Music and Citizenship in the Sixties*, New York: Oxford University Press, 2013.

Kuhn, David Paul. *The Hardhat Riot: Nixon, New York City, and the Dawn of the White Working-Class Revolution*. New York, London: Oxford University Press, 2020.

Kutschke, Beate and Barley Norton (eds.). *Music and Protest in 1968*, Cambridge: Cambridge University Press, 2013.

Liberatore, Paul. *The Road to Hell: The True Story of George Jackson, Stephen Bingham and the San Quentin Massacre*, New York: Atlantic Monthly Press, 1996.

Leonard, Aaron J. *The Folk Singers and the Bureau: The FBI, the Folk Artists and the Suppression of the Communist Party USA, 1939–1957*. London: Repeater Books, 2020.

Leonard, Aaron J., and Conor A. Gallagher. *Heavy Radicals: The FBI's Secret War on America's Maoists*. London: Zero Books, 2015.

Levin, John F. and Earl Silbar. *You Say You Want a Revolution: SDS, PL, and Adventures in Building a Worker-Student Alliance*. San Francisco: 1741 Press, 2019.

Levine, Mark. *The Trial of the Chicago 7 Transcript*. New York: Simon and Schuster, 2020.

Levy, Peter, B. *The Great Uprising: Race Riots in Urban America During the 1960s*. Cambridge: Cambridge University Press, 2018.

Li, Danhui and Yafeng Xia. *Mao and the Sino-Soviet Split: 1957–1973.* Lanham, MD: Lexington, 2020.

Li, Mingjiang. *Mao and the Sino-Soviet Split, 1959–1973. Mao's China and the Sino-Soviet Split: Ideological Dilemma,* London, and New York: Routledge, 2012.

Lüthi, Lorenz. *The Sino-Soviet Split: Cold War in the Communist World.* Princeton: Princeton University Press, 2008.

Lynskey, Dorian. *33 Revolutions Per Minute: A History of Protest Songs, From Billie Holiday to Green Day.* New York: Ecco Books, 2011.

Lytle, Mark Hamilton. *America's Uncivil Wars: The Sixties Era from Elvis to the Fall of Richard Nixon,* New York, Oxford: Oxford University Press, 2006.

Mailer, Norman. *Advertisements for Myself,* New York: J.P. Putnam, 1959.

Mailer, Norman, *Armies of the Night: History as a Novel, The Novel as History.* New York: Plume (reprint) 1995.

Mailer, Norman. *Miami and the Siege of Chicago: An Informal History of the Republican and Democratic Conventions of 1968.* New York: Random House, 2016 ed.

Makeba, Miriam and James Hall. *Makeba: My Story,* New York and Scarborough, Ontario: New American Library, 1987.

Makower, Joel. *Woodstock The Oral History 40th Anniversary Edition.* Albany: State University of New York Press, 2009.

Manzarek, Ray. *Light My Fire: My Life With the Doors.* New York: Putnam, 1998.

Marqusee, Mike. *Wicked Messenger: Bob Dylan and the 1960s.* New York: Seven Stories Press, 2005.

Marcus, Greil. *Bob Dylan: Writings 1968–2010.* New York: Public Affairs, 2010.

Marcus, Greil. *Like a Rolling Stone: Bob Dylan at the Crossroads.* New York: Public Affairs, 2006.

Marcus, Greil. *The Old, Weird America: The World of Bob Dylan's Basement Tapes.* London: Picador, 2011.

McMillian, John. *Smoking Typewriters: The Sixties Underground Press and the Rise of Alternative Media in America.* New York: Oxford University Press, 2011.

McDonald, Ian. *Revolution in the Head: The Beatles Records and the Sixties.* Chicago: Chicago Review Press, 3rd Ed., 2007.

Medsger, Betty. *The Burglary: The Discover of J. Edgar Hoover's FBI.* New York: Vintage, 2014.

Noebel, David A., *Rhythm, Riots and Revolution.* Tulsa: Christian Crusade Publications, 1966.

O'Neill, Tom. *Chaos: Charles Manson, the CIA, and the Secret History of the Sixties.* New York: Little Brown, 2019.

Petrus, Stephen, and Ronald D. Cohen. *Folk City: New York and the American Folk Music Revival.* New York: Oxford University Press, 2015.

Plohky, Serhii, *Nuclear Folly: A History of the Cuban Missile Crisis.* New York: W.W. Norton, 2021.

Richardson, Peter. *No Simple Highway: A Cultural History of the Grateful Dead*, New York: St. Martin's Press, 2014

Roberts, Lawrence. *May Day 1971: A White House at War, a Revolt in the Streets, and the Untold History of America's Biggest Mass Arrest.* Boston: Mariner Books, 2020.

Roberts, Michael James. *Tell Tchaikovsky the News Rock 'n' Roll, the Labor Question, and the Musicians' Union, 1942–1968.* Durham, NC: Duke University Press, 2014.

Rosenfeld, Seth. *Subversives: The FBI's War on Student Radicals, and Reagan's Rise to Power* New York: Picador, 2013.

Rotolo, Suze. *A Freewheelin' Time: A Memoir of Greenwich Village in the Sixties.* New York: Broadway Books, 2008.

Rubin, Jerry. *Do It! Scenarios of the Revolution.* New York: Simon & Schuster, 1970.

Sale, Kirkpatrick. *SDS.* New York: Vintage, 1974.

Sanders, Ed. *Fug You: An Informal History of the Peace Eye Bookstore, the Fuck You Press, the Fugs, and Counterculture in the Lower East Side.* Boston: DeCapo Press, 2011.

Santoro, Gene. *Myself When I am Real, The Life and Music of Charles, Mingus*. New York: Oxford University Press, 2000.

Saunders, Frances Stonor. *The Cultural Cold War: the CIA and the Cultural Cold War*. New York: The New Press, 2001.

Schumacher, Michael. *There But for Fortune: The Life of Phil Ochs*: Minneapolis, University of Minnesota Press ed., 2019.

Selvin, Joel. *Altamont: The Rolling Stones, the Hells Angels and the Inside Story of Rock's Darkest Day*. New York: Dey St, 2016.

Selvin, Joel. *The Summer of Love: The Inside Story of LSD, Rock & Roll, Free Love, and High Times in the Wild West*. New York: Plume, 1994.

Simone, Nina. *I Put a Spell on You*. Boston: De Capo Press, 1991, 2nd ed., 2003.

Shelton, Robert. *No Direction Home: The Life and Music of Bob Dylan*. Revised & Updated Edition. Milwaukee: Backbeat Books, 2011.

Slick, Grace with Andrea Cagan. *Somebody to Love?: A Rock-and-Roll Memoir*. New York: Warner Books, 1998.

Smith, Judith E. *Becoming Belafonte: Black Artist, Public Radical*. Austin: University of Texas Press, 2014.

Stein, David Lewis. *Living the Revolution: The Yippies in Chicago*. Indianapolis, New York: Bobbs-Merrill Company, 1969.

Stonechild, Blair. *Buffy Sainte-Marie: It's My Way*. Markham, Ontario, Fifth House Books, 2012.

Strain, Christopher B. *The Long Sixties: America 1956–1973*. Chichester, UK: Wiley Blackwell, 2017.

Tamarkin, Jeff. *Got A Revolution! The Turbulent Flight of Jefferson Airplane*. New York: Atria Books, 2003.

Thompson, Heather. *Blood in the Water: The Attica Prison Uprising of 1971 and its Legacy*. New York: Pantheon, 2016.

Unterberger, Richie. *Eight Miles High: Folk-Rock's Flight from Haight-Ashbury to Woodstock*. Lanham, MD: Backbeat Books, 2003.

Van Ronk, Dave, and Elijah Wald. *Mayor of MacDougal Street*. Cambridge MA: DaCapo Press, 2013.

Varon, Jeremy Peter. *Bringing the War Home: The Weather Underground, the Red Army Faction, and Revolutionary Violence in the Sixties and Seventies,* Berkeley: University of California Press, 2004.

Vincent, Ricky. *Party Music: The Inside Story of the Black Panther's Band and How Black Power Transformed Soul Music.* Chicago: Lawrence Hill Books, 2013.

Von Bothmer, Bernard. *Framing the Sixties: The Use and Abuse of a Decade from Ronald Reagan to George W. Bush.* Amherst: University of Massachusetts Press, 2007.

Von Eschen, Penny, *Satchmo Blows Up the World: Jazz Ambassadors Play the Cold War*, Cambridge: Harvard University Press, 2006.

Wald, Elijah. *Dylan Goes Electric: Newport, Seeger, Dylan, and the Night That Split the Sixties,* New York: Dey Street Books, 2016.

Weissman, Dick. *Talkin' 'Bout a Revolution: Music and Social Change in America.* Lanham MD: Backbeat Books, 2010.

Weissman, Dick. *Which Side Are You On? An Inside History of the Folk Music Revival in America.* New York: Continuum, 2006.

Wiener, Jon. *Gimme Some Truth: The John Lennon FBI Files*, Berkeley: University of California Press, 1999.

Williams, Jakobi. *From the Bullet to the Ballot: The Illinois Chapter of the Black Panther Party and Racial Coalition Politics in Chicago.* Chapel Hill: University of North Carolina Press, 2013.

Young, Izzy, Scott Barretta (ed.) *The Conscience of the Folk Revival: The Writings of Israel "Izzy" Young.* Lanham, MD: Scarecrow Press, 2013.

SELECT DISCOGRAPHY

Animals, The. *The Animals*. MGM, 1964. CD.

Animals, The. *Animal Tracks*. MGM, 1965. CD.

Baez, Joan. *Joan Baez*. Vanguard, 1960. Vinyl.

Baez, Joan. *Joan Baez, 2*. Vanguard, 1962. Vinyl.

Beatles. *Rubber Soul*. Capitol, 1965. Vinyl.

Beatles. *Revolver*. Capitol, 1966. Vinyl.

Belafonte, Harry. *Calypso*. 1956. RCA Victor, CD.

Berry, Chuck. *Chuck Berry is on Top*. Chess, 1959. CD.

Blood, Sweat & Tears. *Blood, Sweat & Tears*. Columbia, 1968. CD.

Brown, James. *Please, Please, Please*. King, 1959. CD.

Brown, James. *Say It Loud — I'm Black and I'm Proud*. King, 1968. CD.

Byrds. *Mr. Tambourine Man*. Columbia, 1965. Vinyl.

Byrds. *Turn! Turn! Turn!* Columbia, 1966. Vinyl.

Byrds. *Fifth Dimension*. Columbia, 1966. CD.

Chad Mitchell Trio. *Reflecting*. Mercury, 1964. Vinyl.

Chambers Brothers. *The Time Has Come*. Columbia, 1967. Vinyl.

Chicago Transit Authority. *Chicago Transit Authority*. Columbia, 1969. Vinyl.

Collins, Judy. *Wildflowers*. Elektra, 1967, CD.

Cooke, Sam. *Live at the Copacabana*. RCA, 1964, CD.

Country Joe & the Fish. *I-Feel-Like-I'm-Fixin'-to-Die*. Vanguard, 1967

Country Joe & the Fish. *Together*. Vanguard, 1968. Vinyl.

Creedence Clearwater Revival. *Willy and the Poor Boys*. Fantasy, 1969. Vinyl.

Crosby, Stills, Nash & Young. *Four Way Street*. Atlantic, 1971. Vinyl.

Dane, Barbara. *Barbara Dane and the Chambers Brothers*. Folkways, 1966, CD.

Dane, Barbara. *I Hate the Capitalist System*. Paredon, 1973.

Doors, The. *The Doors*. Elektra, 1967, CD.

Doors, The. *Waiting for the Sun*. Elektra, 1968, CD.

Doors, The. *The Soft Parade*. Elektra, 1968, CD.

Dylan, Bob. *The Freewheelin' Bob Dylan*. Columbia Records 1963. Vinyl.

Dylan, Bob. *The Times They Are A-Changin'.* Columbia Records 1963. Vinyl.

Dylan, Bob. *Another Side of Bob Dylan*. Columbia Record s 1963. Vinyl.

Dylan, Bob. *Bringing It All Back Home Bob Dylan*. Columbia Record s 1963. Vinyl.

Dylan, Bob. *Highway 61 Revisited*. Columbia Records 1965. Vinyl.

Dylan, Bob. "George Jackson." Single, Columbia 1971. Single-45.

Flying Burrito Brothers. *The Gilded Palace of Sin*. A&M, 1969. Vinyl.

Franklin, Aretha. *I Never Loved a Man*. Atlantic, 1967. CD.

Fugs, The. *The Fugs*. 1966. ESP-Disk. CD.

Gateway Singers. *Live at Stanford*. 1957, Folk Era Records, 1957. CD.

Gaye, Marvin. *What's Going On?* Tamla, 1971. CD.

Grateful Dead. *Live Dead! Warner Bros.* 1969. Vinyl.

Grateful Dead. *American Beauty*, Warner Bros. 1970. Vinyl.

Guthrie, Arlo. *Alice's Restaurant*. Reprise 1967. Vinyl.

Haggard, Merle. *Okie from Muskogee (Recorded "Live" in Muskogee, Oklahoma)*. Capitol,   1969. Vinyl.

Haggard, Merle. *The Fightin' Side of Me*. Capitol, 1970. Vinyl.

Havens, Richie. *Mixed Bag*. Verve, 1966. Vinyl

Hester, Carolyn. *Carolyn Hester*. Tradition Records, 1961. CD.

Hendrix, Jimi. *Electric Ladyland*. 1968, Reprise. Vinyl.

Hendrix, Jimi, and Otis Redding. *Historic Performances Recorded at the Monterey International Pop Festival*. Reprise, 1970. Vinyl.

Heron, Gil Scott. *Pieces of Man*. Sony 1995. CD.

Holly, Buddy. *Buddy Holly*. Coral, 1958, CD.

Jefferson Airplane. *Crown of Creation*. RCA, 1969. Vinyl.

Jefferson Airplane. *Volunteers*. RCA, 1969. Vinyl.

Kantner, Paul and Grace Slick. *Sunfighter*. Grunt, 1971. Vinyl.

Kantner, Paul. *Blows Against the Empire*. RCA, 1970. Vinyl.

Kingston Trio. *The Kingston Trio*. Capitol, 1958. CD.

Kingston Trio. *At Large*. Capitol, 1959. CD.

Kinks. *Kinks*. Reprise, 1964. CD.

Kinks. *Kinkdom*. Reprise, 1965, Rhino Reissue. CD.

Lennon, John. *Imagine*. Apple, 1971. Vinyl.

Lennon, John. *Sometime in New York City*. 1972. Vinyl.

Lightfoot, Gordon. *Did She Mention My Name*? United Artists, 1968, CD.

Little Richard. *Here's Little Richard*. Specialty, 1956. CD.

Makeba, Miriam. *Pata Pata*. Reprise, 1967. CD.

McDonald, Country Joe. *Real Live Country Joe*. Vanguard, 1973. CD.

MC5. *Kick Out the Jams*. Elektra, 1969, CD.

Nash, Graham. *Songs for Beginners*. Atlantic, 1971. CD.

Nash, Graham. *Wild Tales*. Atlantic, 1973, CD.

Nelson, Terry. "Battle Hymn of Lt. Calley." (single) Plantation, 1971.

Newport Folk Festival. *Newport Broadside*. Vanguard, 1964. Vinyl.

Nyro, Laura. *Christmas and the Beads of Sweat*. 1970 Columbia/ Sony. CD.

Ochs, Phil. *All the News That's Fit to Sing*. Elektra, 1964. CD.

Ochs, Phil. *I Ain't Marching Anymore*. Elektra, 1965. CD.

Ochs, Phil. *Phil Ochs in Concert*. Elektra, 1966. Vinyl.

Ochs, Phil. *Rehearsals for Retirement*. A&M, 1969. CD.

Odetta. *At the Gates of Horn*. Tradition Records, 1957. CD.

Paxton, Tom. *Ramblin' Boy*. Elektra, 1964. CD.

Paxton, Tom. *Ain't That News*. Elektra, 1965. CD.

Payne, Freda. "Bring the Boys Home," (single) Invictus, 1971. CD.

Peter, Paul and Mary. *Peter, Paul and Mary*. Warner Brothers, 1962. CD.

Peter, Paul and Mary. *In the Wind*. Warner Brothers, 1963. CD.

Presley, Elvis. *Elvis Presley*. RCA, 1956. CD.

Prine, John. *John Prine*. Atlantic, 1971. CD.

Quicksilver Messenger Service. *What About Me*. Capitol, 1970. CD.

Reynolds, Malvina. *The Truth*. Columbia 1967. CD.

Roach, Max. *We Insist! Max Roach's Freedom Now Suite*. Candid, 1960. CD.

Rolling Stones. *Beggars Banquet*. London 1968. Vinyl.

Rolling Stones. *Let It Bleed*. London, 1969. Vinyl.

Rolling Stones. *Exile on Main St*. Rolling Stones Records, 1972. Vinyl.

Sadler, Barry. *Ballad of the Green Beret*. RCA, 1966. CD.

Sainte-Marie, Buffy. *She Used to Want to be a Ballerina*. Vanguard Records, 1971. CD.

Sainte-Marie, Buffy. *The Best of Buffy Saint Marie*. Vanguard Records, 1970. CD.

Seeger, Pete. *The Rainbow Quest*. Folkways, 1960. CD.

Seeger, Pete. *Waist Deep in the Big Muddy and Other Loves Songs*. 1967, Columbia. Vinyl.

Shepp, Archie. *Attica Blues*. Impulse, 1972. CD.

Shepp, Archive. *Fire Music*. Impulse! Records, 1965. CD.

Simone, Nina. *Nina Simone in Concert*. Philips, 1965. CD.

Simone, Nina. *Black Gold*. RCA, 1970. CD.

Staple Singers. *Be Altitude: Respect Yourself*. Stax, 1972. CD.

Sly & the Family Stone. *Stand*. Epic, 1969. CD.

Smothers Brothers. *The Two Sides of the Smothers Brothers*. Mercury, 1962. Vinyl.

Steppenwolf. *Monster*. ABC Dunhill, 1969. Vinyl.

Steve Miller Band. *Number 5*. Capitol, 1970. Vinyl.

Van Ronk, Dave. *Folksinger*. Prestige, 1962. MP3.

Various Artists. *The Best of Broadside 1962–1988*. Smithsonian Folkways, 2000. CD

Various Artists. *The Monterey International Pop Festival*. Rhino Records, 2006. CD.

Various Artists: *Next Stop Is Vietnam 1961–2008*. Bear Family Records. CD Box Set.

Various Artists. *Woodstock, Original Soundtrack*. Cotillion, 1970. Vinyl.

Webber, Andrew Lloyd, Tim Rice. *Jesus Christ Superstar*, Decca, 1970. Vinyl.

SELECT FILMOGRAPHY

Bowser, Kenneth, director. *Phil Ochs: There but for Fortune*. First Run Features, 2010.

Brooks, Richard, director. *Blackboard Jungle*. MGM, 1955.

Brown, Jim, director. *The Weavers — Wasn't That A Time*. United Artists Classics, 1982.

Brown, Jim, director. *Pete Seeger: The Power of Song*. PBS: American Masters, 2007.

Cohen, Joel and Ethan, directors. *Inside Llewyn Davis*. CBS Films, 2013.

Czarnetzki, David, director. *Lady You Shot Me: Life and Death of Sam Cooke*. Vision, 2017.

Duane, Kelly, director. *ReMastered: The Two Killings of Sam Cooke*. Netflix, 2019

Garbus, Liz, director. *What Happened, Miss Simone?* Netflix, 2015.

Heffron, Richard T., director. *Fillmore: The Last Days*. Twentieth Century Fox, 1972.

Hopper, Dennis, director. *Easy Rider*. Columbia, 1969.

Jackson, Peter, director. *The Beatles: Get Back*. Disney, 2021.

King, Shaka, director. *Judas and the Black Messiah*. Warner Brothers, 2021.

Lerner, Murray, director. *Festival*. Peppercorn-Wormser, 1967.

Lester, Richard, director. *A Hard Day's Night*. United Artists, 1964.

Lester, Richard, director. *Help!* United Artists, 1965.

Maysles, David & Albert, directors. *Gimme Shelter*. Twentieth Century Fox, 1970.

Morris, Errol, director. *The Fog of War*. Sony, 2003.

Pennebaker, D.A., director. *Bob Dylan: Don't Look Back*. Leacock-Pennebaker, 1967.

Pennebaker, D.A., director. *Monterey Pop*. Leacock-Pennebaker, 1968.

Scorsese, Martin, director. *No Direction Home: Bob Dylan*. Paramount, 2005.

Sears, Fred F. director. *Rock Around the Clock*. Columbia Pictures, 1956.

Slater, Andrew, director. *Echo in the Canyon*. Greenwich, Entertainment, 2018.

Sorkin, Aaron, director. *The Trial of the Chicago 7*. Netflix, 2020.

Taylor, Tate, director. *Get on Up: The James Brown Story*. Universal Pictures, 2014.

Wadleigh, Michael, director. *Woodstock*. Warner Bros, 1970.

NOTES

Introduction

1   Lyndon B. Johnson, Great Society Speech, May 22, 1964, Teaching American History website. Accessed August 7, 2020. https://teachingamericanhistory.org/library/document/great-society-speech/

2   Mao Zedong, "Two Birds: A Dialogue — To the tune of *Nien Nu Chiao*," Autumn 1965. Marxist.org, accessed August 7, 2020. https://www.marxists.org/reference/archive/mao/selected-works/poems/poems36.htm

3   Shirley Halperin, "Drummer says Jim Morrison never exposed himself," December 2, 2010, *Reuters* online, accessed August 7, 2020. https://www.reuters.com/article/us-jimmorrison-idUSTRE6B20CF20101203. The Living Theater themselves were target of unwanted government scrutiny as seen in poet Allen Ginsberg's FBI file. Specifically, there is reference to a letter Ginsberg sent to the Manhattan District Attorney Robert Morgenthau in 1963: "In this letter GINSBERG protests the Government's prosecution of an income tax case against the Living Theater, JULIAN BECK and JUDITH MOLINA [*sic*] [...] He said he felt it would be his duty to go all out to start screaming through these media [he has ties to] if he judges that the Government policy decision in the LIVING THEATER matter ultimately, amounts to political and/or cultural confusion." NY Field Office Memo, 4/26/1965, Ginsberg FBI file, 35.

4   John Burks, "Jim Morrison's Indecency Arrest," *Rolling Stone*, April 5, 1969.

5   Louis Wolfson, "Jim Morrison: The Doors," Florida Moving Image Archive, Miami Dade College. Site accessed, August 7, 2020. https://www.mdc.edu/archives/wolfson-archives/wolfson_archives_search.aspx

6   Ibid.

7   John Van Gieson, "30,000 Rally for Decency," *The Washington Post*, Mar 24, 1969.

8   Richard Nixon, "Letter to a Student Concerning the Miami Teen-Age Rally for Decency." The American Presidency Project. Site accessed August 7, 2020. https://www.presidency.ucsb. edu/documents/letter-student-concerning-the-miami-teen-age-rally-for-decency

9   Gieson, "30,000 Rally for…"

10   "Youths Rally for Decency in Alabama." *Chicago Tribune*, Apr 17, 1969, and "138 Hurt, 142 Arrested at Rally for Decency," *The Baltimore Sun*, April 27, 1969.

11   Dorian Lynskey, *33 Revolutions Per Minute: A History of Protest Songs, From Billie Holiday to Green Day*, New York: Ecco Books, 2011, 159.

Chapter 1: Eisenhower's Grave Diggers (1955–1960)

1   The Kitchen Debate — transcript 24 July 1959 Vice President Richard Nixon and Soviet Premier Nikita Khrushchev, watergate.info, accessed April 11, 2022. https://watergate. info/1959/06/24/kitchen-debate-nixon-khrushchev.html

2   Jack Kerouac, *On the Road*, New York: Penguin. 2000, 68.

3   Allen Ginsberg, "Howl," Poets.org, accessed, October 11, 2020. https://poets.org/poem/howl-parts-i-ii

4   James Sederberg, "The Howl Obscenity Trial," Foundsf website, accessed, August 8, 2020. http://www.foundsf.org/index. php?title=The_Howl_Obscenity_Trial "Instigating the Howl Trial — March 25, 1957," March 25, 2017, AllenGinsberg.org, accessed August 8, 2020. https://allenginsberg.org/2017/03/ instigating-howl-trial-march-25-1957/; Alan Chandler, "Howl and the Obscenity Trial," *Tablet Magazine*, accessed October 11, 2021. https://www.tabletmag.com/sections/news/ articles/howl-and-the-obscenity-trial

5   SAC, WFO, to Director FBI, 12/31/1964. Allen Ginsberg FBI
    file, 5. Accessed from the FBI Vault, October 14, 2020. https://
    vault.fbi.gov/irwin-allen-ginsberg

6   Herb Caen, "On the Town," *San Francisco Chronicle*, April 10
    and 27, June 4 and 27, 1958.

7   John Fordham, "Jazz audiences are always on the Road,"
    The Guardian, August 7, 2008, accessed November 28, 2021.
    https://www.theguardian.com/music/musicblog/2008/
    aug/07/foreditorsjazzontheroad

8   Nat King Cole, FBI file. https://archive.org/details/
    NatKingColeFBI/page/n17/mode/2up

9   "Nat 'King' Cole attacked on stage," April 12, 1956, *The
    Guardian* posted, April 12, 2018, site accessed, November
    29, 2021. https://www.theguardian.com/world/2018/apr/12/
    nat-king-cole-attacked-on-stage-archive-1956

10 "An Evening at the White House with Duke Ellington," April
    29, 1969. Richard Nixon Foundation, posted, April 27, 2016,
    accessed January 4, 2021. https://1www.youtube.com/
    watch?v=jW9PdAY8_D0; Terry Teachout, "The Duke and
    the Reds: Courted but never compromised," *Commentary*,
    February 2013, accessed November 28, 2021. https://www.
    commentary.org/articles/terry-teachout/the-duke-and-the-
    reds/; Edward Kennedy (Duke) Ellington, FBI file, FBI Vault,
    accessed November 28, 2021 https://vault.fbi.gov/Edward%20
    Kennedy%20%28Duke%29%20Ellington/Edward%20
    Kennedy%20%28Duke%29%20Ellington%20Part%201%20
    of%201.pdf/view

11 Louis Armstrong, FBI file, released per FOIA request of
    The Black Vault, accessed, Nov 28, 2021. https://ia801205.
    us.archive.org/14/items/LouisArmstrongFBI/larmstrong.pdf;
    Jason Burke, "Louis Armstrong and the spy: how the CIA used
    him as a 'trojan horse' in Congo," *The Guardian*, September 12,
    2021, accessed November 28, 2021. https://www.theguardian.
    com/music/2021/sep/12/louis-armstrong-and-the-spy-how-
    the-cia-used-him-as-a-trojan-horse-in-congo

12   Penny Von Eschen, *Satchmo Blows Up the World: Jazz Ambassadors Play the Cold War*, Cambridge: Harvard University Press, 2006, 58, 59, & 67. Frances Stonor Saunders, *The Cultural Cold War: the CIA and the Cultural Cold War*, New York: The New Press, 2001, 245

13   Ed Vulliami, "'Rockers and spies' — how the CIA used culture to shred the iron curtain," *The Guardian,* May 3, 2020, accessed Nov 28, 2021. https://www.theguardian.com/us-news/2020/may/03/rockers-and-spies-how-the-cia-used-culture-to-shred-the-iron-curtain

14   Sonny Rollins, *Freedom Suite,* 1958, Craft Records, 2020, vinyl reissue.

15   Max Roach, *We Insist! Max Roach's Freedom Now Suite*, Candid, 1960, CD.

16   Gene Santoro, *Myself When I am Real, The Life and Music of Charles, Mingus*, New York: Oxford University Press, 2000, 203. Jonathan C. Friedman, *The Routledge History of Social Protest in Popular Music,* New York: Routledge, 2013, 111–112.

17   "Jazz: The Devils Music," WGBH, Culture Shock website, accessed December 16, 2021. https://www.pbs.org/wgbh/cultureshock/beyond/jazz.html; Nat Hentoff, "The Devil's Music," *Washington Post*, August 23, 1985.

18   Letter to Hoover, May 16, 1956. Hoover reply, May 22, 1956. Presley FBI file, Section 1, 34–36. For Bureau's Presley file see "FBI Vault." https://vault.fbi.gov/Elvis%20Presley%20

19   Ibid.

20   Eric Zolov, *Refried Elvis: The Rise of the Mexican Counterculture*. Berkeley: University of California Press, 1999, 42.

21   From: Legat, Mexico, To: Director FBI, March 11, 1957. Presley file Section 4, 22–24.

22   Rock and Roll Hall of Fame website, Freed Induction, 1986. Site accessed, October 11, 2020. https://www.rockhall.com/inductees/alan-freed

23   "Rock 'N Roll Banned in Boston After Alan Freed Causes 'Riot,'" New England Historical Society website, accessed

October 11, 2020. https://www.newenglandhistoricalsociety. com/rock-n-roll-banned-boston-after-alan-freed-causes-riot/

24 "Freed is Indicted Over Rock 'n' Roll: Faces Charges in Boston on Fracas After Show" *New York Times*, May 9, 1958 and "Freed Denies Charges," *New York Times*, May 17, 1958.

25 "This Day in History May 2, 1960: Dick Clark Survives the Payola Scandal," History.com, accessed January 19, 2022. https://www.history.com/this-day-in-history/dick-clark-survives-the-payola-scandal

26 Lydia Hutchinson, "Alan Freed and the Radio Payola Scandal," *Performing Songwriter*, August 20, 2015, accessed January 19, 2022. https://performingsongwriter.com/alan-freed-payola-scandal/

27 Michael James Roberts, *Tell Tchaikovsky the News Rock 'n' Roll, the Labor Question, and the Musicians' Union, 1942–1968*. Durham, NC: Duke University Press, 2014, 152 & 158.

28 Ben Fong-Torres, "Alan Freed, Biography," AlanFreed.com, accessed January 11, 2022. http://www.alanfreed.com/wp/biography/

29 Bernard Weinraub, "The Man Who Knew It Wasn't Only Rock 'n' Roll," *New York Times*, October 14, 1999.

30 M.A. Jones to Mr. DeLoach. Subject: DISC JOCKEY "PAYOLA" SCANDAL: ALAN FREED, NEW YORK "ROCK & ROLL" PROMOTER 12/2/59. Alan Freed's FBI file. While Freed's file consists of a cover memo and several press clippings documenting his travails, it also includes a *Newsweek* article titled "Music and the Mob," from March 17, 1986.

31 Val Adams, "Alan Freed Loses 2d Broadcast Job," *New York Times*, Nov 24, 1959.

32 "Alan Freed, Disk Jockey, Dead: Popularized Rock 'n' Roll Music," *New York Times*, January 21, 1965.

33 "Rioters at Princeton," *New York Times*, May 19, 1955, "Blackboard Jungle Banned in Memphis," *San Bernardino Sun*, March 31, 1955 and "Obituary: Lloyd Binford," *Chicago Tribune*, August, 28, 1956.

34 "August 26, 1955: Blackboard Jungle Removed as U.S. Entry in Venice Film Festival," Today in Civil Liberties History, website accessed January 11, 2022. http://todayinclh. com/?event=blackboard-jungle-removed-as-u-s-entry-in-venice-film-festival

35 P. Ronan Thomas, "British Rattled by Rock 'N' Roll," *New York Times*, Sep 12, 1956.

36 "Rock 'N' Roll Banned: Admiral Acts After Enlisted Men Riot at Newport," *New York Times*, September 20, 1956.

37 Thomas, "British Rattled…"

38 "Belgian Town Bans U.S. Film," *New York Times*, December 17, 1956.

39 "Cuba Bans Rock 'n' Roll: Use on TV Shows Halted by Communications Minister," *New York Times*, Feb 14, 1957.

40 "Iran Outlaws Rock 'n' Roll." *New York Times*, Jul 30, 1957.

41 Thomas, "British Rattled…"

42 "While Elvis Presley Served," November 11, 2015, Graceland. com, accessed January 12, 2022. https://www.graceland.com/blog/posts/while-elvis-presley-served

43 Bosley Crowther, "Screen: Elvis — A Reformed Wriggler: Presley Drops Swivel for 'G.I. Blues' Role He Is Clean-Cut Type in Show at Victoria," *New York Times,* November 5, 1960.

44 1984 Interview with Little Richard, "On his conversion from Rock to Religion during the 1957 Australian Tour," YouTube post, May 11, 2020. Site accessed November 14, 2021. https://www.youtube.com/watch?v=GC_9bmCjT60

45 "This Day in History, December 23, 1959. Chuck Berry is arrested on Mann Act charges in St. Louis, Missouri," History. com, accessed September 26, 2020. https://www.history.com/this-day-in-history/chuck-berry-is-arrested-on-mann-act-charges-in-st-louis-missouri

46 Contrary to mythology, Elvis's torso was not wholly obscured in his first appearance on *The Ed Sullivan Show*. Rather, cameras moved to a close up, at a point after he started dancing. The overall character of his movements, however,

are still quite clear. Christine Gibson, "Elvis on The Ed Sullivan Show: The Real Story," Elvis Presley Music website, accessed 10/31/2020 https://www.elvispresleymusic.com.au/pictures/1956-september-9-ed-sullivan-show.html

47 Reese Cleghorne, "From Grand Ole Opry to U.S. Senate? High Noon for Tex Ritter?" *New York Times*, July 12, 1970.

48 See, for example, "Songs at New China Rally: From Kentucky Mountain Ballads to Chinese People's Songs," *Daily Worker*, June 14, 1949.

49 Silber quote in, "Weavers Issue Folk-Song Folio," *Sing Out!* March 1952, taken from Jesse Jarnow, Jesse, *Wasn't That a Time, the Weavers, the Blacklist and the Battle for the Soul of America*. Boston: DeCapo Press, 2018, 119. Also see Aaron J Leonard, *The Folk Singers and the Bureau*. London: Repeater Books, 181–182.

50 Janice C Simpson, "Hugh Hefner: Civil Rights Activist?" *The Root*, July 30, 2020, accessed October 25, 2020. https://www.theroot.com/hugh-hefner-civil-rights-activist-1790880423

51 Steven L. Hamilton. Special Access and FOIA Program, to Aaron J. Leonard, March 18, 2020.

52 Barbara Dane telephone interview with Aaron Leonard, June 1, 2021. Also, Ben Fong-Torres, "A Life of the Blues." SF Gate website, July 22, 2007, accessed December 16, 2021. https://www.sfgate.com/entertainment/radiowaves/article/A-LIFE-OF-THE-BLUES-2579855.php

53 Burl Ives's Testimony, "Subversive Infiltration of Radio, Television, and the Entertainment Industry," March 20, 26, April 23, and May 20, 1952. Part 2, United States Government Printing Office, Washington: 1952, 208–221.

54 "Communist Activities Among Youth Group," Testimony of Harvey Marshall Matusow. HUAC Hearings, February 6 and 7, 1952, 3286.

55 SAC New York to Director FBI, Pete Seeger, SM-C, 2/15/57. Seeger FBI file Section 3, 161.

56 Leonard, *Folk Singers and the Bureau*, 145–146.

57 Belafonte Tracks website, accessed, October 25, 2020. http://
    www.belafontetracks.ca/television_1.htm; Judith E. Smith.
    Becoming Belafonte: Black Artist, Public Radical, Austin:
    University of Texas Press, 2014, 86.

58 Ed Sullivan, "Little Old New York," *New York Daily News*, Jun.
    21, 1950.

59 Smith, *Becoming Belafonte*, 116.

60 Ibid., 101–102.

61 Henry Louis Gates, "Belafonte's Balancing Act," *The New
    Yorker*, August 18, 1996.

62 Peter Dreier and Jim Vrable, "The Kingston Trio and the
    Red Scare," *The Nation* October 14, 2008 and Katherine Q.
    Seelye, "Jacqueline Steiner, 94, Lyricist Who Left Charlie on
    the M.T.A., Dies," *New York Times*, February 5, 2019. Also,
    Leonard, *Folk Singers and the Bureau*, 221–222 and Note, 300.

63 Ibid.

64 Robert Shelton, "Folk Music on the Hit Parade," *New York
    Times*, July 12, 1959.

65 Brian Blair, "A folk legend plays on: Carolyn Hester, daughters
    set for Columbus concert," *The Republic*, September 17,
    2019, accessed, September 3, 2021. http://www.therepublic.
    com/2019/09/19/a_folk_legend_plays_on_carolyn_hester_
    daughters_set_for_columbus_concert/

66 Ronald D Cohen and Rachel Clare Donaldson, *Roots of the
    Revival: American and British Folk Music in the 1950s.* Urbana,
    Chicago & Springfield: University of Illinois Press. 2014,119.

Chapter 2: The Great Folk Scare (1961–1963)

1   Stephen Petrus and Ronald D. Cohen, *Folk City: New York and
    the American Folk Music Revival,* New York: Oxford University
    Press, 2015, 122.

2   *Sing Out!* Volume 18, No. 1, March-April 1968, 37, in *The
    Conscience of the Folk Revival: The Writings of Israel "Izzy" Young*,
    Scott Barretta, ed. Lanham, MD: Scarecrow Press, 2013, 152.

3   "Seeger Explains Stand at Inquiry," *New York Times,* March 15, 1961.

4   See, for example: Alan Brinkley, "The Legacy of John F. Kennedy," *The Atlantic*, September 19, 2013, accessed November 15, 2021. https://www.theatlantic.com/magazine/archive/2013/08/the-legacy-of-john-f-kennedy/309499/; Brent Budowsky, "JFK Reached Greatness," *The Hill*, December 8, 2009, accessed November 15, 2021. https://thehill.com/opinion/columnists/brent-budowsky/71033-jfk-reached-greatness; Robert Shrum, "The enduring greatness of JFK," *The Week*, January 19, 2011, accessed November 15, 2021. https://theweek.com/articles/487947/enduring-greatness-jfk.

5   Jason Steinhauer, "A Historical Perspective on the Cuba-U.S. Relationship," Library of Congress, December 19, 2014, accessed January 25, 2022. https://blogs.loc.gov/kluge/2014/12/historical-perspectivecuba-u-s-relationship; Tony Perrottet, "When Fidel Castro Charmed the United States," *Smithsonian Magazine*, January 24, 2019, accessed January 25, 2022. https://www.smithsonianmag.com/history/when-fidel-castro-charmed-united-states-180971277/

6   "Bay of Pigs," John F. Kennedy Presidential Library, accessed August 24, 2021. https://www.jfklibrary.org/learn/about-jfk/jfk-in-history/the-bay-of-pigs

7   See Michael Dobbs, *One Minute to Midnight: Kennedy, Khrushchev, and Castro on the Brink of Nuclear War*. New York: Penguin Random House, 2009, and Errol Morris, *The Fog of War: Eleven Lessons from the Life of Robert McNamara*, Sony Pictures, 2003. Also "General Curtis Emerson LeMay U.S. Air Force, Biography Display," accessed November 11, 2020. https://www.af.mil/About-Us/Biographies/Display/Article/106462/general-curtis-emerson-lemay/ Also see, Serhii Plohky. *Nuclear Folly: A History of the Cuban Missile Crisis*. New York: W.W. Norton, 2021, especially page 30, where he discusses how the US maintained nuclear superiority at the point of the crisis — despite claims of a missile gap favoring the Soviets.

8   "The Great Debate: Documents of the Sino-Soviet Split,"
    Marxists.org website, accessed August 24, 2021. https://www.
    marxists.org/history/international/comintern/sino-soviet-
    split/index.htm

9   "Great Polemic — Letters between Communist Party
    of the Soviet Union and Communist Party of China,"
    Perspective Monde website, accessed October 4, 2021.
    https://perspective.usherbrooke.ca/bilan/servlet/
    BMDictionnaire?iddictionnaire=1651

10 *Communist Activities in the Buffalo, N.Y. Area.* Hearings
    Before the Committee on Un-American Activities, House of
    Representatives, Eighty-Eighth Congress, Second Session.
    April 29 and 30, 1964. US Government Printing Office,
    1964, 1517.

11 U.S. House of Representatives, Committee on Internal
    Security. *America's Maoists — The Revolutionary Union, The
    Venceremos Organization.* Report by the Committee on Internal
    Security, House of Representatives, Ninety-Second Congress,
    Second Session. U.S.A. Congress. Washington: US Government
    Printing Office, 1972, ix.

12 "Greensboro Sit-In," *HISTORY.com*, accessed November
    15, 2021. https://www.history.com/topics/black-history/the-
    greensboro-sit-in.

13 Clayborne Carson, *In Struggle: SNCC and the Black Awakening
    of the 1960s.* Cambridge: Harvard University Press, 1995. 209–
    211. Also, Aaron J Leonard and Conor A. Gallagher, *A Threat of
    the First Magnitude.* London: Repeater Books, 2018, Chapter 7:
    The Never-Ending Campaign Against James Forman.

14 "Port Huron Statement," The Sixties Project, accessed
    November 13, 2020. http://www2.iath.virginia.edu/Sixties/
    HTML_docs/Resources/Primary/Manifestos/SDS_Port_
    Huron.html.

15 See David R. Farber. *Chicago '68.* Chicago & London: University
    of Chicago Press, 1988, 62–63. Carson, *In Struggle*, 105–106.

16 The phrase is often attributed to Dave Van Ronk, who

popularize it, however Elijah Wald — co-author of Van Ronk's memoir — references it as coming from Phillips: "The 'Great Folk Scare' as folksinger and humorist Utah Phillips has dubbed it." Elijah Wald, *Josh White: Society Blues*. Amherst: University of Massachusetts, 2000, 258. Also Douglas Brinkley reviewing Van Ronk's memoir writes, "Utah Phillips called the 'Great Folk Scare' of the 1960s." Douglas Brinkley, "A Legendary Village Voice." *The Boston Globe*, July 24, 2005, accessed January 2, 2021 http://archive.boston.com/ae/books/articles/2005/07/24/a_legendary_village_voice/.

17 J. Pat Brown, "FBI's Campaign to Discredit HUAC Protests as Communist Agitation Faced Internal Pressures," *MuckRock*, August 8, 2018, accessed, January 2, 2021. https://www.muckrock.com/news/archives/2018/aug/08/fbi-huac-protests/.

18 Seth Rosenfeld. *Subversives: The FBI's War on Student Radicals, and Reagan's Rise to Power* New York: Picador, 2013, 87.

19 James Baldwin. *Another Country,* New York: Vintage, 1962, 1992 ed., 28.

20 Stephen Petrus and Ronald D. Cohen, *Folk City: New York and the American Folk Music Revival,* New York: Oxford University Press, 2015, 159.

21 Ibid, 123.

22 Ibid, 126.

23 Ibid, 128.

24 Paul Hoffman, "Folk Singers Riot in Washington Sq," *New York Times*, April 20, 1961.

25 Petrus and Cohen, *Folk City,* 130.

26 Ibid., 143–144.

27 "FBI, Estimated Communist Party Membership," As of March 31, 1962 the FBI put membership at 5,164, Three years later, in 1965, in a document titled, "Comparative Estimated Numbers by Field Division," they put the group's membership at 3,665.

28 Seeger was cited with contempt in 1956 for his refusal to

answer questions and subsequently indicted in 1957, before coming to trial in early 1961. "Seeger Explain Stand at Inquiry." *New York Times,* March 15, 1961.

29 Seeger Testimony: *Investigation of Communist Activities, New York Area — Part VII* (Entertainment) HUAC, August 17 and 18, 1955, Washington, USGPO, 1955, 2449–2450.

30 "When Pete Seeger Faced Down the House Un-American Activities Committee," *Slate*, January 28, 2014, accessed January 24, 2022. http://www.slate.com/blogs/browbeat/2014/01/28/pete_seeger_huac_transcript_full_text_of_anti_communist_hearing_courtesy.html.

31 Philip Benjamin, "Seeger Convicted of U.S. Contempt," *New York Times* Mar 30, 1961.

32 Edward Ranzal, "Seeger Gets Year in Contempt Case," *New York Times.* April 5, 1961.

33 "WQED Cancels Folk Singer: Accused of Commie Ties," *Post-Gazette and Sun Pittsburg.* April 14, 1962.

34 United States of America, Appellee, v. Peter Seeger, Defendant appellant, 303 F.2d 478 (2d Cir. 1962) U.S. Court of Appeals for the Second Circuit - 303 F.2d 478 (2d Cir. 1962) Argued April 9, 1962, Decided May 18, 1962. http://law.justia.com/cases/ federal/appellate-courts/F2/303/478/458148/

35 Ibid.

36 Jack Gould, "TV: 'Hootenanny' Debut," *New York Times* April 8, 1963.

37 Elijah Wald, *Dylan Goes Electric: Newport, Seeger, Dylan, and the Night That Split the Sixties,* New York: Dey Street Books, 2016, 104.

38 "Seeger Bars Oath for TV 'Hootenanny,'" *New York Times*, September 6, 1963.

39 Report of Robert E. Bowe, Title: Pete Seeger, April 13, 1964, Seeger HQ File, Section 6, 166.

40 "Trio, Drake Patron Battle, Over Anti-Racist Song," *Chicago Daily Defender,* June 13, 1963.

41 SAC New York to SAC Albany, 6/5/58. Re: Dave Van Ronk,

Young Socialist League IS-ISL. Dave Van Ronk FBI file, Section 1, 29.

42 Supv. Thornton M. Wood to SAC New York, Subject David Van Ronk, SM-SWP, 8/22/63. Van Ronk FBI file, Sec. 2, 4–9.

43 Supv. 45 to SAC New York. Re: David Ritz Van Ronk, SM-Workers League, June 25, 1973. Van Ronk FBI file Sec. 3, 195.

44 Dave Van Ronk and Elijah Wald. *Mayor of MacDougal Street.* Cambridge MA: DaCapo Press 2013, 176–178., 59.

45 SAC New York to SAC Washington Field Office, Re: David Ritz Van Ronk aka David Van Ronken. SM-SWP, 2/15/63. Van Ronk FBI file, Section 1, 127.

46 H.J. Lynch, Acting Chief, Intelligence Division, US Coast Guard, to J Edgar Hoover, Coast Guard, 7/11/63. Van Ronk FBI file, Sec. 1, 32.

47 SAC Chicago, to Director FBI, Re: David Ritz Van Ronk. SM-SWP, 8/2/63. Van Ronk file, Section 1, 35. Also see, Aaron J Leonard "Newly Unearthed FBI File Exposes Targeting of Folk Singer Dave Van Ronk," *Truthout*, July 8, 2018. Accessed October 5, 2021. https://truthout.org/articles/newly-unearthed-fbi-file-exposes-targeting-of-folk-singer-dave-van-ronk/

48 Van Ronk and Wald, *Mayor of MacDougal Street,* 168.

49 Seeger had in fact performed the song at the 1949 Peekskill, Paul Robeson concert — which turned into a reactionary riot — which took place during the trial. Aaron J Leonard. *The Folk Singers and the Bureau.* London: Repeater Books, 2020, 129 & 132.

50 Chart history, Trini Lopez. Billboard online accessed August 29, 2021. https://www.billboard.com/music/trini-lopez/chart-history/HSI/song/575687

Chapter 3: The Unwelcome Arrival of Bob Dylan (1963–1964)

1 Val Adams, "Satire on Birch Society Barred from Ed Sullivan's TV Show," *New York Times* May 14, 1963.

2   Jack A. Smith, "A World of His Own," *National Guardian*. August 22, 1963.

3   Robert Shelton, *No Direction Home*, Milwaukee: Back Beat Books, 2011, 87.

4   Robert Shelton, "Bob Dylan: A Distinctive Folk Song Stylist," *New York Times*, September 29, 1961.

5   *Strategy and Tactics of World Communism (Communist Activity in New York):* Subcommittee to Investigate the Administration of the Internal Security Act and Other Internal Security Laws of the Committee on the Judiciary United States Senate, January 4, 5, 6, 1956. Part 17, Washington: USGPO, 1956. 1721–1728. See also John Pareles, "Robert Shelton," Obituary, *New York Times*, December 15, 1995. The FBI responded to an FOIA request on Shelton stating that no records were found, a subsequent request under Shelton's birth name, Robert Shapiro, is pending as of publication. Michael G. Seidel to Aaron J. Leonard, August 2, 2020.

6   John Einarson with Ian Tyson & Sylvia Tyson, *Four Strong Winds: Ian & Sylvia*, Toronto: McClelland & Stewart, 2011, 102.

7   Martin Scorsese. *Bob Dylan: No Direction Home, A Martin Scorsese Picture*. Paramount, DVD, 1:52.

8   Einarson, *Ian & Sylvia*, 97.

9   Suze Rotolo, *A Freewheelin' Time*. New York: Broadway Books, 2008, 239–240. Also see, "FBI Tracking of Bob Dylan and Suze Rotolo Foreshadowed Future Abuses," Aaron J. Leonard, *Truthout*, September 1, 2019, site accessed October 5, 2021. https://truthout.org/articles/fbi-tracking-of-bob-dylan-and-suze-rotolo-foreshadowed-future-abuses/

10   Andy Greene, "Suze Rotolo, Bob Dylan's Muse and Girlfriend, Dead At 67," *Rolling Stone*, February 27, 2011.

11   SAC New York, to Director, FBI, July 20, 1964. Subject: Susan Elizabeth Rotolo, IS C. FBI Rotolo file Section 1, 16–17.

12   SA Martin A. Crowe to SAC New York, Subject: Dave Ritz Van Ronk, 2/19/63. Van Ronk NY FBI file, Section 1, 129.

13 SA REDACTED to SAC, Hazard Miners Aid Committee, IS-C, 12/23/63, Phil Ochs FBI HQ File, author page 2.

14 Val Adams, "Satire on Birch Society Barred from Ed Sullivan's TV Show," *New York Times* May 14, 1963.

15 "Bob Dylan on The Ed Sullivan Show," *The Ed Sullivan Show* website, Wednesday, November 24th, 2010. Site accessed August 23, 2021. https://www.edsullivan.com/bob-dylan-on-the-ed-sullivan-show/

16 Adams, "Satire on Birch..."

17 Along with "Talkin' John Birch Paranoid Blues," the original *Freewheelin'* included "Let Me Die in My Footsteps," "Rocks and Gravel," and "Gamblin' Willie's Dead Man's Hand." These songs were replaced by the newly recorded songs, "Girl From the North Country," "Masters of War," "Talking World War III Blues," and "Bob Dylan's Dream," Shelton, *No Direction Home*, 116.

18 Bob Dylan, *Bob Dylan the Bootleg Series Volume 1–3, Rare and Unreleased: 1961–1991*, Sony Records, 1991 and Andy Greene, How Bob Dylan Took Flight, *Rolling Stone*, April 2, 2013.

19 Clayborne Carson, *In Struggle: SNCC and the Black Awakening of the 1960s*, Cambridge, Harvard University Press, 1995, 56–65, also Rowland Scherman, "Dylan In Pictures: Newport 1963," NPR website, July 31, accessed August 23, 2021. https://www.npr.org/sections/allsongs/2009/07/dylan_in_pictures_newport_1963.html

20 Andy Greene, "Flashback: Bob Dylan Performs at the 1963 March on Washington," *Rolling Stone*, June 9, 2020.

21 "I Am My Words," *Newsweek*, November 4, 1963. Notably, *Life* also exhibited a fixation on Dylan's appearance *and* perceived lack of hygiene. In a profile in its April 10, 1964, issue, under the headline, "Bob Dylan is sloppy, steamed up, and successful." The article also described how, "Dylan scorns clothes, baths, and razors."

22 "Oscar Brand with Bob Dylan 1961," YouTube accessed August 23, 2021. https://www.youtube.com/watch?v=EKdDYM_MY-

w&t=100s

23 Robert Shelton, "Freedom Songs' Sweep North," *New York Times,* July 6, 1963.

24 Ibid. *Newsweek*, November 1963.

25 Shelton, *No Direction Home...*, 138.

26 "Bob Dylan: 'You Can Boo but Booing's Got Nothing to Do With It', Bill Of Rights Dinner — 1963," *Speakola*, April 4, 2016, accessed October 6, 2021. https://speakola.com/arts/bob-dylan-tom-paine-acceptance-1963. Philip Luce, who Dylan references in the speech, would become a staunch anti-communist. For more see, "Interview with Philip A, Luce: Ex-Communist," *Plain Truth*, May 1969, 17–22.

27 FBI, Re: Susan Elizabeth Rotolo, December 30, 1964. Suze Rotolo FBI file, Section 1, 85.

28 M.A. Jones to Cartha Deloach, October 15, 1963. Fulton Lewis FBI file.

29 Report by SA Henry Naehle, Re: Emergency Civil Liberties Committee, 6/8/1964 MaryFarrell.org, accessed January 24, 2022. https://www.maryferrell.org/showDoc.html?docId=173572#relPageId=7&search=%22Bob_Dylan%22

30 SA James P. Halleron to SAC New York, 1/6/1964, MaryFarrell.org, accessed January 24, 2022. https://www.maryferrell.org/showDoc.html?docId=2495#relPageId=4&search=%22Bobby_Dyllon%22

Chapter 4: Mississippi, Harlem, Havana... Goddam! (1964)

1 George Wallace, Inaugural Speech as Governor, 1963, "Wallace Quote," *PBS: American Experience*, site accessed October 6, 2021. https://www.pbs.org/wgbh/americanexperience/features/wallace-quotes/

2 *Nina, A Historical Perspective*, documentary produced by Peter Rodis, 1970, 15:05. https://www.dailymotion.com/video/x14hgds

3 Homer Bigart, "St. Augustine Mob Attacks Negroes," *New York Times*, Jun 26, 1964.

4   Ibid.

5   "Negroes Defy Ban, Clash with Police," *Los Angeles Times*, June 10, 1964.

6   Mahatma Gandhi, Selected and Introduced by Ronald Duncan, *Selected Writings of Mahatma Gandhi*, London: Faber and Faber Limited, 2005, 88, 95. It should also be noted that Gandhi was a racist for much of his life — privileging Indians over Black South Africans during his twenty-one years living in the apartheid state, as well as holding highly repressive views on sexuality. Ọbádélé Kambon, "Ram Guha is wrong. Gandhi went from a racist young man to a racist middle-aged man," *The Print*, December 24, 2018, accessed, August 9, 2021. https://theprint.in/opinion/ramachandra-guha-is-wrong-a-middle-aged-gandhi-was-racist-and-no-mahatma/168222/; Lauren Frayer, "Gandhi Is Deeply Revered, But His Attitudes on Race and Sex Are Under Scrutiny," *NPR Morning Edition*, October 2, 2019, accessed August 9, 2021. https://www.npr.org/2019/10/02/766083651/gandhi-is-deeply-revered-but-his-attitudes-on-race-and-sex-are-under-scrutiny.

7   Martin Luther King, "Pilgrimage to Nonviolence," April 13, 1960. Stanford: Martin Luther King, Jr. Research and Education Institute, accessed January 20, 2022. https://kinginstitute.stanford.edu/king-papers/documents/pilgrimage-nonviolence

8   Barbara Dane. *Barbara Dane and the Chambers Brothers.* Liner notes, Folkways Records, 1966. Liner notes found at Folkways Record website, accessed October 6, 2021. https://folkways.si.edu/barbara-dane-and-the-chambers-brothers/american-folk-struggle-protest/music/album/smithsonian

9   Carl Nolte, "S.F. Sit-in Helped Start Revolution 50 Years Ago." *SF Gate*, February 28, 2014.

10 Barbara Dane, liner notes, *Barbara Dane and the Chambers Brothers*, Folkways Records, 1966, vinyl and Nolte, "S.F. Palace Hotel sit-in..."

11 Jack Whatley, "Revisit A Sprawling Letter from Bob Dylan

About Money, Fame and Love From 1964," *Far Out Magazine*, June 6, 2020, accessed November 28, 2020. https://faroutmagazine.co.uk/bob-dylan-letter-to-broadside-rotolo-money-fame-love/. Tom Paxton, it should be noted, went straight for the throat of the FBI in his song, "Daily News," offering the line that J Edgar Hoover being the man of the hour and "All he needs is a little more power."

12 Forrest Wickman, "'BEATLEMANIA!' Is Born," *Slate*, Oct 24, 2013, site accessed October 6, 2021. https://slate.com/culture/2013/10/beatlemania-origin-50-years-ago-the-beatles-played-london-palladium-and-the-term-beatlemania-was-born.html

13 *Red Skelton Hour*, August 5, 1964, posted on YouTube. https://www.youtube.com/watch?v=j1Wf9uqCDGs

14 Jack Gould, "It's the Beatles (Yeah, Yeah, Yeah): Paar Presents British Singers on Film,"
New York Times. Jan 4, 1964.

15 Jack Gould, "Quartet Continues to Agitate the Faithful," *New York Times*. Feb 10, 1964.

16 William, F. Buckley, "The Beatles: They're Not Just Awful, but They Are Much More," *Los Angeles Times*, September 9, 1964.

17 Wald, *Dylan Goes Electric*, 184.

18 Roger Catlin, "The Incomparable Legacy of Lead Belly," Smithsonian.com. February 23, 2015. Accessed May 4, 2019. https://www.smithsonianmag.com/smithsonian-institution/incomparable-legacy-of-lead-belly-180954390/

19 Kenneth Womack, "The Beatles in Jacksonville, 1964: Inside the Fab Four's Historic Stand Against Segregation," *Salon*, June 27, 2020, site accessed October 7, 2021. https://www.salon.com/2020/06/27/the-beatles-in-jacksonville-1964-inside-the-fab-fours-historic-stand-against-segregation/.

20 American Federation of Musicians, website accessed October 7, 2021. https://www.afm.org/about/about-afm/

21 Michael James Roberts, "A Working-Class Hero Is Something to Be: The American Musicians' Union's Attempt to Ban the Beatles,

1964," *Popular Music*, Cambridge University Press, January 2010, Vol. 29, No. 1, pp. 1–16. https://www.jstor.org/stable/40541475

22 "New Blasts Rock 2 Mississippi Sites: Violence Erupts in Vicinity of Freedom Houses," *New York Times*, Aug 16, 1964.

23 Claude Sittons, "Mississippi Is Gripped by Fear of Violence in Civil Rights Drive," *New York Times*. May 30, 1964.

24 "Bodies of Chaney, Goodman, and Schwerner Discovered," SNCC Digital Gateway, accessed December 6, 2020. https://snccdigital.org/events/bodies-chaney-goodman-schwerner-discovered/.

25 Nadine Cohodas, *Princess Noir: The Tumultuous Reign of Nina Simone,* Chapel Hill, NC: University of North Carolina Press, 2010, 157.

26 Liz Fields, "The story behind Nina Simone's protest song, 'Mississippi Goddam,'" PBS, *American Masters*, website accessed October 7, 2021. https://www.pbs.org/wnet/americanmasters/the-story-behind-nina-simones-protest-song-mississippi-goddam/16651/; Elodie Maillot, "1964: Nina Simone sings 'Mississippi Goddam," *PAM* (Pan African Music Magazine), February 21, 2020, site accessed October 7, 2021. https://pan-african-music.com/en/1964-nina-simone-sings-mississippi-goddam/

27 James G. Hershberg, "New Russian Evidence on Soviet-Cuban Relations, 1960–61: When Nikita Met Fidel, the Bay of Pigs, and Assassination Plotting," February 2019. https://www.wilsoncenter.org/publication/new-russian-evidence-soviet-cuban-relations-1960-61-when-nikita-met-fidel-the-bay-pigs

28 Susan Elisabeth Rotolo. Security Matter C, 8/4/64 Rotolo FBI file, Section 1, 27–28.

29 "Phil Ochs — Talking Cuban Crisis," Genius lyrics website, accessed November 29, 2020. https://genius.com/Phil-ochs-talking-cuban-crisis-lyrics.

30 In the aftermath of the Kennedy assassination the Fair Play for Cuba Committee would dissolve. As the FBI documented,

The December 27, 1963, edition of *The New York World Telegram and Sun* newspaper stated that the pro-Castro FPCC was seeking to go out of business and that its prime activity during its lifetime had been sponsorship of pro-Castro street rallies and mass picket lines, and the direction of an active propaganda mill highlighting illegal travel to Cuba campaigns. Its comparatively brief span of life was attributed to mounting anti-Castro American public opinion, the 1962 Congressional hearings which disclosed FPCC financing by Castro's United Nations Delegation, and ultimately the bad publicity which the FPCC received from disclosures on its behalf by suspected Presidential assassin LEE H. OSWALD.

SAC, Washington Field to SAC, San Francisco, Subject: Institute of Policy Studies IS, 4/5/72. Memo is contained in Robert Fitch FBI file, 416.

31 Karl Dallas, "Phil Ochs: America's Fieriest Songwriter," *Melody Maker,* September 17, 1966.

32 FBI report from Michael Schumacher, *There But for Fortune: The Life of Phil Ochs*: Minneapolis, University of Minnesota Press ed. 2019, 75.

33 Phil Ochs, "Power and the Glory," Genius lyrics accessed, May 5, 2022. https://www.lyrics.com/lyric/30385673/Phil+Ochs/Power+and+the+Glory

34 Lynskey, *33 1/3 Revolutions*, 81. Curtis Mayfield website, accessed December 29, 2021. https://www.curtismayfield.com/civil-rights.html; Jonathan C. Friedman, The Routledge History of Social Protest in Popular Music, New York, NY, Routledge, 2013, 112.

35 Rollo Roming, "Dancing in the Street': Detroit's Radical Anthem," *The New Yorker*, July 22, 2013. https://www.newyorker.com/books/page-turner/dancing-in-the-street-detroits-radical-anthem

36 Theodore Jones, "Negro Boy Killed; 300 Harass Police," *New York Times.* Jul 17, 1964.

37 Spencer Stultz, "The Harlem Race Riot of 1964," Black Past, December 4, 2017, accessed August 14, 2021. https://www.blackpast.org/african-american-history/harlem-race-riot-1964/

38 "Malcolm X Lays Harlem Riot To 'Scare Tactics' of Police," *New York Times,* Jul 21, 1964.

39 Stultz, "The Harlem Race Riot Of 1964."

40 For Maoist background of PLP see, Socialist Workers Party, "PL Breaks with Maoism," *The Militant*, September 24, 1971, accessed October 7, 2021 https://www.marxists.org/history/erol/1960-1970/militant-pl-china-1.pdf

41 Richard JH Johnston, "Epton Convicted on Riot Charges," *New York Times*, Dec 21, 1965 and Douglas Martin, "William Epton, 70, Is Dead; Tested Free-Speech Limits," *New York Times*, February 3, 2002.

42 For more see Aaron J. Leonard and Conor A. Gallagher. *Heavy Radicals: The FBI's Secret War on America's Maoists.* London: Zero Books, 2015 and Leonard and Gallagher, *A Threat of the First Magnitude*, especially Chapter 7, The Never-Ending Campaign Against James Forman.

43 Fred Powledge, "Fighting the System: Negro Violence Viewed as a Reaction to Frustrations of Ghetto Wastelands," *New York Times*, August 6, 1964.

44 Joseph Lelyveld, "Police Break Up Antiwar Rally," *New York Times*, Aug 9, 1964.

45 Seth Rosenfeld, *Subversives: The FBI's War on Student Radicals, and Reagan's Rise to Power.* New York: Picador. 2013, 153–154.

46 "Unforgettable Change: 1960s: Free Speech Movement & The New American Left," Picture This, accessed December 15, 2021. http://picturethis.museumca.org/pictures/jack-weinberg-being-interviewed-inside-police-car-was-taking-him-away-after-his-arrest-viol; Weinberg famously coined the phrase "Don't Trust Anyone Over 30," which was actually a rebuke to a reporter's question about communist manipulation. "Don't Trust Anyone Over Thirty: Unless It's

Jack Weinberg," *Berkeley Daily Planet,* April 6, 2000, accessed December 15, 2021. https://www.berkeleydailyplanet.com/issue/2000-04-06/article/759

47 "Words of freedom: video made from Mario Savio's 1964 'Machine Speech,'" *Berkeley News* website accessed October 7, 2021. https://news.berkeley.edu/2014/09/30/words-of-freedom-video-made-from-mario-savios-1964-machine-speech/

48 "Cal Students' Sit-In is Now Police Lock-In," *Chicago Tribune,* Dec 3, 1964, and "Visual History: Free Speech Movement, 1964 | Berkeley FSM," Accessed November 2, 2020. https://fsm.berkeley.edu/free-speech-movement-timeline/.

49 Editorial, Robert D. Wood, Vice President, CBS Television Stations and General Manager, KNXT. Subject: The Chaos at Berkeley, Friday, December 4, and Sunday, December 6, 1964, Online Archive of California, accessed November 17, 2021. https://oac.cdlib.org/ark:/13030/kt8d5nb337/?brand=oac4

50 "Former CBS-TV Network President Robert Wood Dies At 61," *AP NEWS,* accessed December 4, 2020. https://apnews.com/article/baaa1c3e40785943fa0bae1bbe1efe75.

51 "Sam Cooke | Billboard," *Billboard,* accessed December 7, 2020. https://www.billboard.com/music/sam-cooke.; "Nina Simone | Billboard," *Billboard,* accessed December 7, 2020. https://www.billboard.com/music/nina-simone/chart-history.

52 For a concise overview of Cooke's life and career see the Duane Kelly documentary *ReMastered: The Two Killings of Sam Cooke,* Netflix, 2019.

53 All Things Considered, "Sam Cooke's Swan Song of Protest," *NPR,* December 16, 2007, accessed November 17, 2021. https://www.npr.org/templates/story/story.php?storyId=17267529.

54 "Negro Band Leader Held in Shreveport," *New York Times,* Oct 9, 1963. See also Peter Guralnick *Dream Boogie: The Triumph of Sam Cooke,* New York: Little Brown, 2005, 526.

55 "Singer Sam Cooke Slain, Woman Motel Owner," *Boston Globe,* Dec 12, 1964, and "The Mysterious Death of Sam Cooke," A.S. "Doc" Young, *Chicago Daily Defender,* Dec 29, 1964.

56 Jordan Runtagh, "Regina King's new film *One Night in Miami* raises questions about the soul legend's 1964 murder in a Los Angeles motel," *People*, accessed, Nov 17, 2021. https://people.com/movies/why-mystery-still-shrouds-singer-sam-cookes-shooting-death-nearly-60-years-later/

57 Ben Crandell, "Revisiting The Time Cassius Clay, Malcolm X, Sam Cooke and Jim Brown Spent 'One Night In Miami,'" *Sun-Sentinel.Com*, January 1, 1970, accessed Nov 17, 2021. https://www.sun-sentinel.com/entertainment/theater-and-arts/sf-one-night-in-miami-cassius-clay-play-miami-new-drama-20181017-story.html.

58 Duane Kelly, *ReMastered: The Two Killings of Sam Cooke*, Netflix, 2019, 51:16.

59 "Records which may have been responsive to your request were destroyed." David Hardy, FBI to Aaron J. Leonard, June 29, 2016. A subsequent appeal upheld the initial response. Sean R. O'Neill, Chief, Administrative Appeals Staff to Aaron J. Leonard, September 2, 2016.

60 See David Cantwell, "The Unlikely Story of 'A Change Is Gonna Come,'" *The New Yorker*, March 17, 2015 and Guralnick, *Dream Boogie*, 512.

Chapter 5: Ready to Go Anywhere (1965)

1 Emile Durkheim. *Selected Writings: Anomie and the Moral Structure of Society,* Cambridge, UK, Cambridge University Press, 1972, 177.

2 Bob Dylan Interview with Nora Ephron & Susan Edmiston, 1965. https://www.interferenza.net/bcs/interw/65-aug.htm

3 Peter Kihss, "G.I.'s Advance in Santo Domingo," *New York Times,* May 2, 1965.

4 Arthur Krock, "The Larger Stake in Santo Domingo," *New York Times,* May 2, 1965.

5 Harvey Taylor, "A Singing Radical Sits for a Closeup," *Detroit Free Press,* October 10, 1965.

6   Christopher Wm. Newman, "Letter to the Editor," *Baltimore Sun*, February 26, 1965.

7   Marjorie Hunter, "March's Sponsors Deny Aiding Reds," *New York Times*. Nov 29, 1965.

8   Buffy Sainte-Marie website, accessed August 16, 2021. https:// buffysainte-marie.com/

9   "It's More Dangerous to Be an American Indian Under 18 Than to Be In Viet Nam," Buffy Sainte-Marie, *KRLA Beat,* October 7, 1967.

10 Elio Iannacci, "The Interview: Polaris 2015 Winner Buffy Sainte-Marie," *Macleans,* May 5, 2015, December 31, 2020. https://www.macleans.ca/culture/arts/the-interview-songwriter-and-activist-buffy-sainte-marie/

11 Ibid.

12 Colin Irwin, "Buffy Sainte-Marie on a rollercoaster career that even the FBI kept an eye on," *The Guardian,* July 30, 2009.

13 Stephen Pevar, interview with Antonio D'Ambrosio, ACLU, February 19, 2016, website accessed September 5, 2021. https://www.aclu.org/blog/racial-justice/american-indian-rights/where-are-your-guts-johnny-cashs-little-known-fight

14 Ibid.

15 Antonio D'Ambrosio, *A Heartbeat and a Guitar: Johnny Cash and the Making of Bitter Tears*, New York: Nation Books, 2009, 16.

16 Christopher Klein, "How Selma's 'Bloody Sunday' Became a Turning Point in the Civil Rights Movement: The assault on civil rights marchers in Selma, Alabama helped lead to the Voting Rights Act," History.com, Mar 6, 2015, accessed August 19, 2021.https://www.history.com/news/selma-bloody-sunday-attack-civil-rights-movement

17 Staple Singers, *Freedom Highway,* Track 1, "Freedom Highway," Roebuck Staples, Epic, 1965, CD.

18 "Malcolm X Sees Rise in Violence: Says Negroes Are Ready to Act in Self-Defense," *New York Times,* March 13, 1964.

19 Malcolm's murder was carried out by members of the Nation

of Islam in retaliation for his breaking with Elijah Muhammad, though it is now clear the state prosecuted the wrong men for the crime. Ashley Southall and Jonah E. Bromwich, "2 Men Convicted of Killing Malcolm X Will Be Exonerated After Decades," *New York Times*, Nov 17 2021. Evanzz, Karl. *The Messenger: The Rise and Fall of Elijah Muhammad*. New York: Vintage Books, 1999, 320–327.

20 Archie Shepp, "Malcolm, Malcolm, Semper Malcolm," Track 3. Impulse! Records, 1965, CD.

21 "Watts Rebellion," History.com website, accessed January 15, 2020. https://www.history.com/topics/1960s/watts-riots

22 Wallace Turner, "Experts Divided on Rioting Cause," *New York Times*, Aug 14, 1965.

23 John Israel, "How Lyndon Johnson Responded to Baltimore's Last Riots," *Think Progress* website, April 28, 2015, Accessed August 19, 2021. https://archive.thinkprogress.org/how-lyndon-johnson-responded-to-baltimores-last-riots-f3c0378909c/

24 Tom Maxwell. Longreads, "A History of American Protest Music: When Nina Simone Sang What Everyone Was Thinking," April 2017, website accessed January 15, 2020. https://longreads.com/2017/04/20/a-history-of-american-protest-music-when-nina-simone-sang-what-everyone-was-thinking/

25 Pete Seeger, Video Interview, Smithsonian Folkways, YouTube channel, February 20, 2014, accessed October 7, 2021. https://www.youtube.com/watch?v=-4wYiShPEyo. Also, *King James Bible*, accessed October 8, 2021. https://www.kingjamesbibleonline.org/Ecclesiastes-Chapter-3/

26 Charlee Champlin, "Byrds Have Yet to Lay an Egg," *Los Angeles Times*. Jun 7, 1965.

27 Mary Campbell, "Drug and Drink Lyrics Rock Record Industry," *Los Angeles Times*, Sep 25, 1966.

28 Irwin Silber, "An Open Letter to Bob Dylan," *Sing Out!* November 1964.

29 David Hajdu, *Positively 4th Street: The Lives and Times of Joan Baez, Bob Dylan, Mimi Baez*. New York: Bloomsbury, 2002, 240.

30 For more on the debates circulating in the folk world, see Wald, *Dylan Goes Electric*, chapter 8, "Electricity in the Air."

31 Dylan could be quite harsh in this period as Michael Schumacher writes, "Dylan still held court at some of his old Village haunts, but he was now turning his anger and resentment on his friends, engaging them in cutting games of dirty dozens that, on any given night could reduce a victim to tears." Schumacher, *There But for Fortune*, 104–105.

32 "Pete Seeger on Dylan Going Electric at Newport Folk Festival," *Democracy Now!* Posted July 24, 2015, accessed August 20, 2021.https://www.democracynow.org/2015/7/24/video_pete_seeger

33 Elijah Wald suggests Seeger's later memory might have been clouded by the attention given to his reaction, pointedly noting a comment from the stage by Peter Yarrow, between Dylan's electric and acoustic sets when fans were calling for his return, "He's [Dylan] going to get his axe." Overall Wall offers a valuable account, including noting that, because of the organizers plan of shunning a "celebrity billing system," Dylan — who had just released "Like a Rolling Stone" and was riding the charts — was slotted to do a short set, early in the Sunday evening finale — this to the disappointment of fans who came specifically for him. Wald, *Dylan Goes Electric*, 262 & 256.

34 Seeger, *Democracy Now!* Dylan quoted in Scorsese, *No Direction Home,* 2:52:40.

35 Scorsese, *No Direction Home*, 2:52.

36 Schumacher, *There But for Fortune*, 103.

37 Ralph Gleason, "Dylan Places Poetry in the Hands of Youth," *San Francisco Chronicle,* September 19, 1965.

38 "Three Negroes Lynched After Attack on Girl," *San Francisco Chronicle*, June 16, 1920 and "They're Selling Postcards of the Hanging: The Real Lynching in Dylan's 'Desolation Row,'"

chimesfreedom.org, June 14, 2016, accessed August 9, 2020. http://www.chimesfreedom.com/2016/06/14/theyre-selling-postcards-of-the-hanging-the-real-lynching-in-dylans-desolation-row/

39 "1965 Grammy Winners," Grammy website accessed August 2021. https://www.grammy.com/grammys/awards/8th-annual-grammy-awards-1965; "Grammy's 1966," Awards & Shows website, accessed, October 8, 2021. http://www.awardsandshows.com/features/grammy-awards-1966-241.html

40 Vincent Bevins. *The Jakarta Method: Washington's Anti-Communist Crusade & the Mass Murder Campaign That Shaped the World.* New York: Hachette, 2020, 267 and Hannah Beech, "U.S. Stood By as Indonesia Killed a Half-Million People, Papers Show," *New York Times,* October 18, 2017.

41 Ibid., 142.

Chapter 6: God, Country, and the Beatles (1966)

1 Interview with John Lennon, *London Evening Standard,* March 4, 1966.

2 "Comment on Jesus Spurs a Radio Ban Against the Beatles," *New York Times*, August 5, 1966.

3 "Adult Contemporary," Week of March 5, 1966, *Billboard* online, accessed July 30, 2021. https://www.billboard.com/charts/adult-contemporary/1966-03-05

4 Barry Sadler appearing on Jimmy Dean show, February 11, 1966, YouTube clip, site accessed October 8, 2021. https://www.youtube.com/watch?v=Ri6ZLWIQjVs

5 *Sir! No Sir!* A film by David Zeiger, accessed July 18, 2020. https://www.youtube.com/watch?v=jULC3SCX9wE

6 Los Angeles FBI, Form FD-122 (Security Index). Re: Donald Walter Duncan, Racial Matters, 5/15/70. Duncan FBI file, section 1, 29. SAC Washington, Subject: Donald Walter Duncan, SM-New Left. 1/28/72, Duncan FBI file, Section 1, 85.

7   Phil Ochs FBI file 100-HQ-441378, Author's scan, page 110. Memo page not available.

8   Vietnam War Allied Troop Levels 1960–73, Americanwarlibrary.com, accessed March 2, 2022. https://www.americanwarlibrary.com/vietnam/vwatl.htm

9   Leonard, *Folk Singers & the Bureau*, 46.

10 Jeff Tamarkin, *Got A Revolution! The Turbulent Flight of Jefferson Airplane,* New York: Atria Books, 2003, 9,17, & 29.

11 Tamarkin 84–85.

12 Gary Hawes, "United States Support for the Marcos Administration and the Pressures that made for Change," *Contemporary Southeast Asia*, June 1986, Vol. 8, No. 1 (June 1986), 18–36.

13 Report of an Amnesty International Mission to the Republic of the Philippines: 22 November -5 December, 1975, *Philippines International Report*, September 1, 1976, 21.

14 Oliver X. Reyes, "The Beatles' Worst Nightmare in Manila," *Esquiremag.ph*, May 24, 2017, site accessed July 30, 2021. https://www.esquiremag.ph/long-reads/notes-and-essays/remember-the-beatles-nightmare-in-manila-a1542-20170524-lfrm10.

15 Ibid.

16 Ibid.

17 Ibid.

18 Ibid.

19 Maureen Cleave, "How Does a Beatle Live? John Lennon Lives Like This," *London Evening Standard,* March 4, 1966. http://headsup.freeshell.org/beatles-articles/standard.html Ruth Graham, "50 Years After John Lennon's 'Bigger Than Jesus' Quote, We Forget How Shocking the *Rest* of That Interview Was," *Slate*, March 4, 2016, accessed October 10, 2021. https://slate.com/culture/2016/03/it-s-been-50-years-since-john-lennon-s-bigger-than-jesus-quote-but-the-rest-of-that-interview-was-even-more-shocking.html

20 "More Critics Board Beatle 'Ban' Wagon," *Chicago Tribune*, August 6, 1966.

WHOLE WORLD IN AN UPROAR

21 "Quote on Jesus Stirs Ban-Beatles Drive," *AP/Los Angeles Times*. Aug 3, 1966.

22 "Beatle Mania Hits Sour Note," *Chicago Tribune*, Aug 5, 1966.

23 Jordan Runtagh, "Remembering Beatles' Final Concert," *Rolling Stone*, August 29, 2016.

24 "Ban Beatles Disks on Air in South Africa," *Chicago Tribune*, Aug 9, 1966.

25 Brian Wawzenek, "When John Lennon Apologized for 'More Popular Than Jesus' Comment," Published August 11, 2016. Ultimate Classic Rock website accessed January28, 2020. https://ultimateclassicrock.com/john-lennon-apologizes/

26 Shirley Thelma Hunt, CONFETTI column, *Chicago Daily Defender*. Aug 16, 1966. For more on the "Black Power" slogan, see Carson, *In Struggle*, 215–228.

27 Jack Anderson, "Beatles Let Hair Down: John, George, and Paul Talk About the Pope, Vietnam and What-Not," *The Washington Post*. Aug 28, 1966.

28 Ibid.

29 Ibid.

30 See for example, Ella Atcheson, "The Beatles never intended to quit touring for good," *NME* online, accessed, August 2, 2021. https://www.nme.com/news/music/the-beatles-4-1191035; Jordan Runtagh, "Remembering Beatles' Final Concert," *Rolling Stone*, August 29, 2016.

31 Olivia *Harrison, George Harrison: Living in the Material World. New York: Harry N. Abrams. 2011, 204.*

32 Evidence of the US efforts to keep Harrison and Lennon out of the country comes via the Immigration and Naturalization Service, which compiled a 91-page file on George Harrison. In it is a memo to the file, dated February 25, 1970, From: "Assistant Commissioner Adjudications." The memo outlines that "Mr. Bob Precht [Ed Sullivan's son-in-law] telephoned to advise that the services of the 'Beatles' were no longer needed or desired by Ed Sullivan Productions. Mr. Precht stated he was calling to notify the Immigration and Naturalization

Service so that the subjects would not use the petition filed by Ed Sullivan Productions to enter the United States." The memo continues, noting that after their London embassy had advised that "since petitioner [Sullivan] did not desire their services the visas would be refused." It is unclear what the nature of the group's interactions with Sullivan was aimed at — it suggests an appearance — however the group was in the process of breaking up. Regardless, the report makes clear, short of a Sullivan appearance, the government was not going to let Lennon and Harrison into the country. The two, however, would be issued visas later that spring. https://www.uscis.gov/sites/default/files/document/foia/George_Harrison.pdf

33 Robert Shelton, "The Folk Rock Rage," *New York Times,* January 30, 1966.

34 "A Symposium: Is Folk Rock Really 'White Rock?'" *New York Times*, Feb 20, 1966

35 Ibid.

36 Greil Marcus, *Like a Rolling Stone: Bob Dylan at the Crossroads*, New York, Public Affairs, 2006, 179.

37 Ibid.

38 Shelton, *No Direction Home*, 147. For more on Guthrie's Party membership see, Aaron J. Leonard, "Woody Guthrie's Communism and 'This Land Is Your Land,'" History News Network, November 20, 2020, website accessed October 10, 2021. https://hnn.us/article/177412

39 John Pareles, "When Dylan's Genius Burned Brightest," *New York Times*, October 11, 1998.

40 Bob Dylan Interview with Ed Bradley, *60 Minutes*, December 5, 2004. *CBS*, accessed October 10, 2021. https://www.cbsnews.com/news/60-minutes-bob-dylan-rare-interview-2004/

41 Ibid.

42 Mary Campbell, "Drug and Drink Lyrics Rock Record Industry," *Los Angeles Times*, Sep 25, 1966.

43 Ibid.

Chapter 7: More Than the Summer of Love (1967)

1   Mick Jagger, Keith Richards, Charlie Watts, Ron Wood, *According to the Rolling Stones*, San Francisco: Chronicle Books, 2003, 112.

2   Martin Douglas, "Robin Olds, 84, Fighter Ace; Hero of Big Vietnam," *New York Times*, June 20, 2007.

3   "On 24 February, the Commune was officially suspended and renamed as the Shanghai Revolutionary Committee by Mao himself, who declared that it was too early to set up a Commune." See, Shanghai Peoples Commune (1967), ChinesePosters.net, accessed April 9, 2022. https://chineseposters.net/themes/shanghai-commune

4   Joel Selvin, *The Summer of Love*. New York, Plume, 1994, 106–107, "48 Years Ago: Human Be-In at the Polo Fields," Richmond District Blog, Posted by Sarah B., January 15, 2015, accessed March 27, 2021. https://richmondsfblog.com/2015/01/15/48-years-ago-human-be-in-at-the-polo-fields/

5   Richmond Blog, "48 years ago..."

6   Dan Sullivan, "Village Begins Antiwar Festival: Actors, Artists and Films Part of Angry Arts Week," *New York Times*, January 30, 1967.

7   Art Seidenbaum, "Pick Peace Group, Get into Fight," *Los Angeles Times*, Jun 3, 1967.

8   "Vietnam Summer: Activism during the Vietnam War," Sep 25, 2017, American Friends Service Committee website, accessed, February 22, 2021 https://www.afsc.org/story/vietnam-summer-activism-during-vietnam-war#:~:text=Vietnam%20Summer%20was%20a%20time,our%20group%20formed%20Philadelphia%20Resistance.

9   Mat Callahan, *The Explosion of Deferred Dreams: Musical Renaissance and Social Revolution in San Francisco, 1965–1975*. Oakland, PM Press, 2017, 102.

10 Conversation with Mat Callahan, May 2017.

11 Elliott died of heart failure in 1974. "Cass Elliott Death Linked to Heart Attack," *New York Times*, August 6, 1974.

12 Joe Livernois, "Beach Boys a No Show at Monterey Pop," Voices of Monterey website accessed July 23, 2021.https://voicesofmontereybay.org/2019/12/12/monterey-rocks-7/

13 Reporting Office, Los Angeles Carl Dean Wilson, 7/7/67. Wilson FBI file, 26–28.

14 "1967: Two Rolling Stones on Drug Charges," *BBC*, On This Day, site accessed October 12, 2021. http://news.bbc.co.uk/onthisday/hi/dates/stories/may/10/newsid_2522000/2522735.stm

15 Mick Jagger, Keith Richards, Charlie Watts, Ron Wood, *According to the Rolling Stones*, San Francisco: Chronicle Books, 2003, 112.

16 Ray Davies, *X-Ray: The Unauthorized Autobiography of Ray Davies*, New York: Overlook Press, 1995, 251.

17 Thomas Kitts, *Ray Davies: Not Like Everybody Else*, New York: Routledge, 2008, 60–61.

18 Roberts, *Tell Tchaikovsky*, 188.

19 Kitts, *Not Like Everybody Else*, 61.

20 Ibid.

21 "Revisit: Monterey International Pop Festival: Music, Love, and Flowers, 1967," Grammy Awards website, June 26, 2020, accessed October 13, 2021. https://grammymuseum.org/museum-at-home/monterey-international-pop-festival-music-love-and-flowers-1967/

22 Davies, *X-Ray*, 252.

23 Jack Gould, "Quartet Continues to Agitate the Faithful," *New York Times*. Feb 10, 1964.

24 John Dreyfuss, "Busy Day for LBJ," *Los Angeles Times*. June 23, 1967.

25 Schumacher, *There But for Fortune*, 145.

26 "The Riots of the Long, Hot Summer," *Encyclopedia Britannica* online, site accessed July 25, 2021. https://www.britannica.com/story/the-riots-of-the-long-hot-summer

27 See Rick Rojas and Khorri Atkinson, "Five Days of Unrest That Shaped, and Haunted, Newark," *New York Times,* July 11, 2017, and Siddhartha Mitter, "The Newark race riots 50 years on," *The Guardian,* July 11, 2017, site accessed March 15, 2021. https://www.theguardian.com/cities/2017/jul/11/newark-race-riots-50-years-rebellion-police-brutality

28 Gene Roberts, "Detroit Is Swept by Rioting and Fires," *New York Times*, July 24, 1967, Gene Roberts, "U.S. Troops Sent into Detroit," *New York Times*, July 25, 1967, and Gene Roberts, "Troops Battle Detroit Snipers," *New York Times,* July 26, 1967.

29 This work does not confine itself to a single term to describe the urban violence that took place in this period, this in accord with the spontaneous, often contradictory, character of the violence which took place. For examples of the debate in definition of riot or rebellion, see, Bill McGraw, "Riot or rebellion? The debate on what to call Detroit '67," *Detroit Free Press,* July 4, 2017, accessed online October 14, 2021. https://www.freep.com/story/news/2017/07/05/50-years-later-riot-rebellion/370968001/ Also, Elizabeth Hinton, *America on Fire*: *The Untold History of Police Violence and Black Rebellion Since the 1960s.* New York: Liveright, 2021, 4.

30 Otis Redding comments, "Respect," from *Jimi Hendrix and Otis Redding, Historic Performances Recorded at the Monterey International Pop Festival*, Reprise, 1970. Vinyl. Franklin also garnered a 270-page FBI file. While most of it deals with matters such as copyright infringement and threats against her, it pointedly records her support for the civil rights movement and of Angela Davis. Franklin FBI file, FBI website, accessed September 15, 2022. https://vault.fbi.gov/aretha-franklin/aretha-franklin-part-01/view

31 David Brown, "Grace Slick's Festival Memories: Fearing Orgies and Getting Lit. Jefferson Airplane singer recalls her first experiences Monterey, Woodstock and Altamont," *Rolling Stone*, May 23, 2014.

32 Tamarkin, *Got A Revolution!* 149–150.

33 Tamarkin, *Got A Revolution!* 124.

34 Tamarkin, *Got A Revolution!* 125.

35 Tamarkin, *Got A Revolution!* 158, and Nicole Meldahl, "Who Saw the Summer of Love: Part I Merchants & Diggers," accessed July 26, 2021. https://summerof.love/who-saw-the-summer-of-love-merchants-diggers/

36 Adam Sweeting, "Obituary: Bruce Palmer," *The Guardian*, October 16, 2004, accessed July 26, 2021. https://www.theguardian.com/news/2004/oct/16/guardianobituaries.artsobituaries1

37 Raffi Khatchadourian, "High Anxiety: LSD in the Cold War," *New Yorker*, December 15, 2012.

38 Jesse Jarnow, "LSD: How the Psychedelic Renaissance Changed Acid," *Rolling Stone*, October 6, 2016.

39 DEA Drug Fact Sheet, LSD, DEA.gov, April 2020. https://www.dea.gov/sites/default/files/2020-06/LSD-2020_0.pdf

40 "Stop The Draft, October 1967 — Harvey Richards Media Archive," February 16, 2013, accessed, October 14, 2021. https://web.archive.org/web/20201102023321/https://hrmediaarchive.estuarypress.com/stop-the-draft-october-1967/.

41 "Joan Baez Barred from D.A.R.'s Hall," *New York Times*, August 13, 1967, and B. Drummond Ayres Jr., "30,000 in Capital at Free Concert by Joan Baez," *New York Times*, August 15, 1967.

42 Supv. Albert P. Clark, to SAC San Francisco, Subject Margarita Mimi Farina. Mimi Baez Farina FBI File, October 1967.

43 "U.S. Attorney Deplores the Arrest of Five on the Coast of Not Carrying Draft Cards: Joan Baez Arrested," *New York Times*, December 20, 1967.

44 Thomas Karamessines, Deputy Director of Plan to Walter Rostow, Special Assistant to the President. Subject: Beheiren and the Four U.S. Navy Deserters, January 20, 1968. https://www.maryferrell.org/showDoc.html?docId=54192&search=Joan_Baez#relPageId=1&tab=page

45 Ibid., 12.

46 Ben A. Franklin, "War Protestors Defying Deadline Seized in Capital," *New York Times,* Oct 23, 1967, E.W. Kenworthy, "Thousands Reach Capital to Protest Vietnam War," *New York Times,* Oct 21, 1967, and "The March on the Pentagon: An Oral History," *New York Times*, October 20, 2017.

47 Ed Sanders, *Fug You: An Informal History of the Peace Eye Bookstore, the Fuck You Press, the Fugs, and Counterculture in the Lower East Side.* Boston: DeCapo Press, 2011, 182–189.

48 Norman Mailer, *Armies of the Night*: *History as a Novel, The Novel as History,* New York: 1968, Plume (reprint), 1995, 122.

49 Katie Mettler, "The day anti-Vietnam War protesters tried to levitate the Pentagon," *Washington Post*, October 19, 2017.; David Smith, "How this 1967 Vietnam war protest carried the seeds of American division," *The Guardian*, October 21, 2017, accessed March 27, 2021. https://www.theguardian.com/us-news/2017/oct/21/1967-vietnam-war-protest-american-division

50 Aaron J. Leonard and Conor A. Gallagher, "Newly Obtained Files Shed Light on the Murder of Fred Hampton," *Jacobin*, March 2021, accessed March 27, 2021. https://jacobinmag.com/2021/03/newly-obtained-fbi-files-fred-hampton

51 Howard Osborn, Director Security, CIA, "Threat to CIA by Some 'Black Power' Elements," 12/11/67. https://www.maryferrell.or/showDoc.html?docId=105904#relPageId=2&search=%22Malvina_Reynolds%22

52 Ibid.

53 Ibid.

54 Harry Belafonte files 1954–1981, NYPL, accessed November 19, 2021.https://archives.nypl.org/scm/20963

55 "BLIND MEMO REGARDING INTERVIEW OF UNIDENTIFIED PERSON," July 21, 1965, Source: CIA. The memo begins stating: "[A] source of this office talked to Mr. Jay Richard KENNEDY at his residence, New York

City, on July 13, 1965," before documenting Kennedy's claims about everyone from Martin Luther King to James Farmer. https://www.maryferrell.org/showDoc. html?docId=13294#relPageId=2&search=BLIND_ MEMO%20REGARDING%20INTERVIEW%20OF%20 UNIDENTIFIED%20PERSON%20belafonte

56 Ray Manzarek, *Light My Fire: My Life with the Doors*. New York: Putnam, 1998, 248–251. Door's guitarist Robbie Krieger disputes Manzarek's telling, offering that singing the original lyrics was a nervous slip on the part of Morrison. Regardless, the result was the same. Jim Farber, "Doors guitarist Robby Krieger: 'The music will outlast the crazy Jim stuff,'" *The Guardian*, accessed December 3, 2021. https://www. theguardian.com/music/2021/dec/03/doors-guitarist-robbie-krieger-the-music-will-outlast-the-crazy-jim-stuff

57 "New Haven Police Close 'The Doors': Use of Mace Reported," *New York Times*, December 11, 1967, and "Rocker Jim Morrison arrested this day in New Haven," *New Haven Register*. December 9, 2019.

Chapter 8: Whole World in an Uproar (1968)

1 "Chicago Mayor Richard Daley speaks on the 1968 Democratic Convention," ABC News, VideoSource, September 9, 1969, Getty Images website, accessed, June 30, 2020.https://www. gettyimages.com/detail/video/mayor-richard-daley-gives-press-conference-following-the-news-footage/450024384

2 Melissa McCaffrey, "Il est interdit d'interdire! (It is forbidden to forbid): The Protests That Defined a Generation," Recto|Verso Blog, May 16, 2018, accessed September 4, 2021. https://www.rectoversoblog.com/2018/05/16/il-est-interdit-dinterdire-it-is-forbidden-to-forbid-the-protests-that-defined-a-generation/

3 Matthew Twombly, Research by Kendrick McDonald, "A Timeline of 1968: The Year That Shattered America," *Smithsonian Magazine* website accessed April 8, 2021.

https://www.smithsonianmag.com/history/timeline-seismic-180967503/

4   Clark Clifford with Richard Holbrooke, *Counsel to the President: A Memoir*, New York: Random House, 1991, 474.

5   "U.S. Involvement in the Vietnam War: The Tet Offensive, 1968," US State Department, Office of the Historian website, accessed March 28, 2021. https://history.state.gov/milestones/1961-1968/tet

6   Ian Shapira, "'It was insanity': At My Lai, U.S. soldiers slaughtered hundreds of Vietnamese women and kids," *Washington Post*, March 16, 2019; Seymour M. Hersh, "My Lai 4: A report on the massacre and its aftermath," *Harpers*, May 1970.

7   Georg Lowery, "A campus takeover that symbolized an era of change," *Cornell Chronicle*, April 16, 2009, website accessed May 8, 2021.https://news.cornell.edu/stories/2009/04/campus-takeover-symbolized-era-change

8   Jennifer Schuessler, "At Columbia, Revisiting the Revolutionary Students of 1968," *New York Times,* March 21, 2018.

9   Hilton Obenzinger, "When the Grateful Dead joined the Columbia strike," *The Sixties: A Journal of History, Politics and Culture*, 2016, Vol. 9, No. 2, 290–294 http://dx.doi.org/10.1080/17541328.2016.1246834

10 Nettanal Slyomovics, "Why Sirhan, a Jerusalem-born Palestinian, Shot Bobby Kennedy," *Haaretz,* May 24, 2018. https://www.haaretz.com/us-news/.premium.MAGAZINE-palestinian-terrorist-or-american-psycho-what-motivated-rfk-s-killer-1.6116114

11 Jordan Scott and Kelly Agan, "Williams, Robert Franklin," NCPEDIA, accessed January 9, 2022.https://www.ncpedia.org/williams-robert-franklin

12 Peter Doggett, *There's a Riot Going On: Revolutionaries, Rock Stars and the Rise and Fall of '60s Counter-Cultures.* Edinburgh: Canon Gate, 2007, 47.

13 Ben A. Franklin, "Capital Put Under 4pm Curfew: Calm is

Restored 9,000 Troops Patrol," *New York Times*, April 7, 1968, and Reed, Roy, "U.S. Troops Sent to Baltimore," *New York Times*, April 8, 1968.

14 Peter B. Levy, *The Great Uprising: Race Riots in Urban America During the 1960s*, Cambridge: Cambridge University Press, 2018, 153.

15 "'Why?': Remembering Nina Simone's Tribute to The Rev. Martin Luther King Jr," *NPR.Org*, April 6, 2008, site accessed October 14, 2021. https://web.archive.org/web/20201102023115/   https://www.npr.org/2008/04/06/89418339/why-remembering-nina-simones-tribute-to-the-rev-martin-luther-king-jr.

16 Songfacts, "Lyrics For 'Why? (The King of Love Is Dead)' By Nina Simone," *Songfacts*, website, accessed November 2, 2020. https://www.songfacts.com/lyrics/nina-simone/why-the-king-of-love-is-dead

17 "Lightfoot Song Black Day in July banned in USA," CMC Radio Program, Metronome, Alan Miller, April 13, 1968, CBC Digital Archives, accessed August 29, 2020. https://www.cbc.ca/archives/entry/lightfoot-song-black-day-in-july-banned-in-the-usa

18 Arwa Haider, "Pata Pata: The world's most defiantly joyful song?" BBC website, September 11, 2019, accessed September 9, 2021.https://www.bbc.com/culture/article/20190911-pata-pata-the-worlds-most-defiantly-joyful-song

19 Peniel E. Joseph, *Stokely: A Life*. New York: Basic Civitas, 2014, Ch. 14, 188.

20 "'Afraid I'll Buy Guns…' Carmichael," *New Journal and Guide*. Norfolk, Va. December 7, 1968.

21 C. Gerald Fraser, "Carmichael Quits the Black Panthers," *New York Times*. July 4, 1969.

22 JC Moore to WC Sullivan, Subject: COUNTERINT-ELLIGENCE PROGRAM, Black Nationalist Hate Groups, Racial Intelligence, February 29, 1968. The other criteria in the Black Nationalist Hate COINTELPRO was the prevention of the coalition of Black groups, preventing violence on the part of such

groups, preventing the leaders of such groups from gaining respectability, and preventing the long-range growth of such groups, especially among youth.

23 SAC, WFO, to Director, FBI. Re: Counterintelligence Program, Black Nationalist Hate Groups, Racial Intelligence. 7/23/68.https://www.maryferrell.org/showDoc. html?docId=216698&relPageId=4&search=%22Makeba%22

24 WFO to Director FBI, December 11, 1968. Makeba FBI file, Section 1, 9–10.

25 Jack Anderson, "Carmichael Appears Guinea-Bound," *The Washington Post*, Nov 29, 1968.

26 Joseph. *Stokely*, see Ch. 14.

27 Lynskey, *33 1/3 Revolutions*, 118 and James Sullivan, *And the Hardest Working Man: How James Brown Saved the Soul of America,* New York: Gotham Books 2008.

28 "Don't Burn James Brown Urges Negroes," *Chicago Tribune,* Apr 7, 1968, "James Brown Answers Emergency Call in D.C," Ethel Payne. *New Pittsburgh Courier,* April 13, 1968, "Singer James Brown Buying a Chain of Radio Stations," *Call and Post,* Cleveland, April 6, 1968.

29 "Lack of Negroes in USO Shows Hit," *Los Angeles Times Jun* 25, 1968.

30 Randall Kennedy, "How James Brown Made Black Pride a Hit," *New York Times,* July 20, 2018.

31 Lynskey, *33 1/3 Revolutions,*124.

32 Richie Unterberger, *Eight Miles High: Folk-Rock's Flight from Haight-Ashbury to Woodstock.* E-book, Copyright, Richie Unterberger, 2015, 79.

33 Ibid, 27.

34 Interview with Eldridge Cleaver, *Frontline.* PBS website accessed September 11, 2021. https://www.pbs.org/wgbh/pages/frontline/shows/race/interviews/ecleaver.html

35 "Three Yippies Beaten at Hotel," *Washington Post,* August 25, 1968.

36 Email from Joe McDonald to Aaron J. Leonard August 4, 20021.

37 David R. Farber, *Chicago '68,* Chicago & London: University of Chicago Press, 1994, 12.

38 Harry Golden, "Daley Orders 'Shoot to Kill' for Arson," *Washington Post,* April 17, 1968.

39 Donald Johnson, "Guard Is Called Up to Protect Chicago During Convention," *New York Times,* August 21, 1968; "McCarthy Hoping for Chicago Peace," *New York Times,* Aug 13, 1968; and J. Anthony Lukas, "Police Battle Demonstrators in Streets," *New York Times.* August 29, 1968.

40 Farber, *Chicago '68,* 177, 218–219.

41 Gregory Daurer, "1968 Convention Rocker to Kick Out Jams in Denver," *HuffPost,* 09/20/2008, accessed September 11, 2021. https://www.huffpost.com/entry/1968-convention-rocker-to_b_120117

42 Lukas, "Police Battle Demonstrators."

43 *Chicago '68,* Farber, 167.

44 Phil Ochs Interview with Izzy Young on returning to New York after the Chicago Convention, insert to Folkways album no. FB5321, Broadside Volume 11. New York, 1976. Posted on Marxists.org accessed April 12, 2021.https://www.marxists.org/archive/ochs/1968/chicago-convention.htm

45 Report of: REDACTED, 7/27/72. Title: Philip David Ochs, Character: Security Matter – Youth International Party, Phil Ochs FBI file, 100-HQ-441378, Form FD-305, Author scan, 125.

46 "Lennon and Friend Charged in Possession of Marijuana," *New York Times.* Oct 19, 1968, and Duncan Campbell, "Detective who busted John and Yoko lifts the lid on corrupt 1960s policing," *The Guardian,* October 18, 2020.https://www.theguardian.com/books/2020/oct/18/norman-pilcher-detective-who-busted-john-and-yoko-grasses-up-1960s-coppers-beatles-rolling-stones

47 Keith Altham, "The Rolling Stones: The Banned Stones Cover," *New Musical Express,* 1968

48 Ibid.

49 Gavin Edwards, "Banned in the U.S.A.: 20 Wildest Censored Album Covers." *Rolling Stone,* August 28, 2019.

50 Robert Ham, "'Street Fighting Man': The Story Behind the Stones' Political Classic," September 18, 2020. Discover Music online, accessed, April 27, 2021. https://www.udiscovermusic.com/stories/the-rolling-stones-street-fighting-man/

Chapter 9: Fire is Sweeping (1969)

1 "Youths Rally for Decency in Alabama," *Chicago Tribune,* April 17, 1969.

2 David Bianculli, *Dangerously Funny: The Uncensored Story of The Smothers Brothers Comedy Hour,* New York: Touchstone Simon & Schuster, 2009, 109.

3 Elizabeth Hinton's *America on Fire* includes an appendix with statistics for riots between 1964 and 1972. Figures from 1964–1967 are drawn from the US Government and list 4 incidents in 1964, 4 in 1965, 17 in 1966 and 75 in 1967. She then lists incidents drawn from Christian Davenport's Radical Information Project at the University of Michigan Center for Political Studies, who in turn drew information from the Lemberg Center for the Study of Violence. That list — which only includes date and city — lists 504 incidents in 1968, 613 in 1969, 632 in 1970, 319 in 1971 and 71 in 1972. Hinton, *America on Fire*, 313–327. By contrast, the *New York Times*, in 1969, reported, "Five 'major' disturbances" and "sixteen 'serious' incidents," for 1969. Tom Wicker, "In The Nation: Not So Hot a Summer," *New York Times*, September 9, 1969. The disparity in the figures suggest the criteria for inclusion in Hinton's lists is broader than that of the government or the *Times* — for example many entries are for a single day. Regardless, it is clear that disturbances in1969, and the immediate years after, in no way approached the intensity of Watts 1965, Newark and Detroit 1967, or those in the wake of Martin Luther King's assassination in 1968.

4   "Today in Metropolitan Police History: turn that racket off! 1969," January 30, 2016, Pastense Blog, accessed April 30, 2021. https://pasttenseblog.wordpress.com/2016/01/30/today-in-metropolitan-police-history-turn-that-racket-off-1969/

5   Renata Adler, "In Which a Filmmaker Discovers the Evil City," *New York Times,* November 20, 1968.

6   Dalya Alberge, "Let him be: how McCartney saved roadie from arrest after Beatles' final concert," *The Guardian*, December 5, 2021. Evans would be killed in a confrontation in Los Angeles by the LAPD in 1976, when he is reported to have pointed a rifle at them. While a later account in the *LA times* stated it was an air rifle, a later correction described it as a real rifle. *Rolling Stone* in 1976 described it as a 30.30. Patrick Snyder and Dolores Ziebarth, "6th Beatle, Mal Evans Killed in Los Angeles," *Rolling Stone,* February 12, 1976. Chris Carter, "Do You Want to Know a Suitcase?" *Los Angeles Times*, July 18, 2004.

7   Peter Jackson's documentary — through editing — suggests the Beatles were able to end the concert on their own terms, after an interruption by police. Peter Jackson, *The Beatles: Get Back*, Disney, 2021, see Part III starting at 2:00.

8   Marisa Lati, "The Beatles played on a London rooftop in 1969. It wound up being their last show," *Washington Post*, January 30, 2019; Runtagh, "Beatles' Famous Rooftop," *Rolling Stone,* January 29, 2016.

9   *Paul McCartney, Mojo, 2001*, "Too Many People," The Paul McCartney Project, accessed September 12, 2021. https://www.the-paulmccartney-project.com/song/too-many-people/

10 Bianculli, David. *Dangerously Funny: The Uncensored Story of The Smothers Brothers Comedy Hour.* New York: Touchstone Simon & Schuster, 2009, 17–18.

11 Shelly Kale, "50 Years Ago: Counterculture Riots on the Sunset Strip," Summer of Love website, accessed November 20, 2021. https://summerof.love/sunset-strip-counterculture-riots/

12   Peter Drier, "Recalling Pete Seeger's Controversial Performance on the Smothers Brothers Show 50 Years Ago," *The American Prospect*, February 28, 2018.

13   "Harry Belafonte: Don't Stop the Carnival," *The Smothers Brothers Comedy Hour*, September 29, 1968. https://www.youtube.com/watch?v=QFE4N57ibUQ

14   Bianculli, *Dangerously Funny*, 132. Notably, while never as controversial as the Smother Brothers, the popular Monkees were also object to scrutiny, this by the FBI. Alison Stine, "Now I'm a believer": Inside the Monkees drummer Micky Dolenz's FBI lawsuit." *Salon*, Sept. 1, 2022.

15   Ibid., 42.

16   Report of SA [Redacted], April 24, 1970, Title: Thomas Frederick Baker, James D Morrison, Continental Airlines, 11/11/69. Character: Crime Aboard Aircraft, Assault Interfering with Inflight Crew, Morrison FBI, file 27.

17   J. Edgar Hoover to [Redacted], March 26, 1969, Doors FBI file. https://vault.fbi.gov/The%20Doors/The%20Doors%20Part%201%20of%201/view

18   See Richard Pollak, *The Creation of Doctor B: A Biography of Bruno Bettelheim*. New York: Simon & Schuster, 1996, Anne C. Roark, "Bettelheim Plagiarized Book Ideas, Scholar Says," *Los Angeles Times*, February 7, 1991, and Shelly Puhak, "The Abuses of Enchantment," *Virginia Quarterly Review*, Fall 2019, accessed January 22, 2022. https://www.vqronline.org/essays-articles/2019/09/abuses-enchantment

19   Statement of Bruno Bettelheim, March 20, 1969, House Committee on Education and Labor "Hearings on Campus Unrest," Washington, USGPO, 1969, 260.

20   Ibid., Bettelheim testimony, 268.

21   Sanders, *Fug You*, 300. Charlie Heinze. "The Beatnik Exorcism of Senator Joe McCarthy's Grave in 1968," Cult of Weird, site accessed November 21, 2021. https://www.cultofweird.com/death/exorcism-of-joe-mccarthy/

22   Bettelheim testimony, 274.

23 Chicago Transit Authority, *Chicago Transit Authority*, side 4, Columbia 1969, vinyl.

24 The Flying Burrito Brothers, *The Gilded Palace of Sin,* "My Uncle," side 1, track 5, A&M, 1969, vinyl.

25 Steppenwolf, *Monster,* "Draft Resister," side 2, track 2, ABC Dunhill 1969, vinyl.

26 Creedence Clearwater Revival, *Willy and the Poor Boys,* "Fortunate Son," side 2, track 1, Fantasy, 1969, vinyl.

27 Plastic Ono Band, "Give Peace a Chance," Apple, 1970, Single.

28 Jefferson Airplane, *Crown of Creation.* RCA, 1969, Vinyl.

29 Jane Wilson, "Gracie: The style and motto of the lead singer and prettiest member of the Jefferson Airplane," *Los Angeles Times*, February 18, 1968.

30 John Sundstrom, "Up Against the Wall Motherfuckers," The Outlaw Page, published in the *East Village Other*, 1968.

31 Jefferson Airplane, *Volunteers.* "We Can Be Together," side 1, track 1; "Volunteers," side 2, track 6; "Meadowlands," side 2, track 5, and liner notes, Vinyl, RCA 1969.

32 Tamarkin, *Got A Revolution!* 208.

33 Tamarkin, *Got A Revolution!* 200, Jimi Hendrix was also arrested in May 1969, this at the Toronto airport after inspectors found heroin and hashish in his luggage. Hendrix would claim the drugs were likely gifted to him by a fan, without his knowledge, and was acquitted. Annette York, "Heroine to the Rescue: Jimi Hendrix is Innocent," *Rolling Stone*, January 21, 1970.

34 Report of Brent T. Palmer. San Francisco, FBI. Re: "Steven Charles Hamilton — Security Matter Revolutionary Union," 4/10/70 — Appendix Page 26 — Description of SDS. BU file, Steve Hamilton, 100-45639. Document release p. 163.

35 Aaron J. Leonard, "The FBI and the Shattering of Students for a Democratic Society," *Truthout,* October 2, 2014. https://truthout.org/articles/the-fbi-and-the-shattering-of-students-for-a-democratic-society/

36 The Weatherman tried to make ties with the counterculture,

their name was in fact drawn from a line in Bob Dylan's "Subterranean Homesick Blues" ("you don't need a weatherman to know which way the wind blows").

37 See Leonard & Gallagher, *Heavy Radicals*.

38 See, Leonard & Gallagher, *Heavy Radicals*, especially chapter 4, "Protracted War or Protracted Struggle."

39 "Stonewall Riots," History.com, May 31, 2017, updated June 25, 2021, accessed September 16, 2021. Dennis Eskow, "3 Cops Hurt as Bar Raid Riles Crowd," *Sunday News*, June 29, 1969. https://www.history.com/topics/gay-rights/the-stonewall-riots

40 Dave Van Ronk FBI file, 100-NY-136446 v. 3, 164–176.

41 See Matt Callahan's, *The Explosion of Deferred Dreams*, 175–76, David Boaz, "RIP Elliot Tiber, One of the Capitalists Who Created Woodstock," August 10, 2016, Cato Institute, accessed September 17, 2021. https://www.cato.org/blog/rip-elliot-tiber-one-capitalists-who-created-woodstock

42 Allan Parachini, "Selling Woodstock," Los Angeles Times, May 25, 1989, Brad Tuttle, "Here's How Much Woodstock Performers Got Paid 50 Years Ago — and Who's the Richest Star Now," *Money*, August 15, 2019, accessed September 17, 2021. https://money.com/woodstock-1969-bands-richest-how-much-paid/

43 Richard F. Shepard, "Woodstock Festival Vows to Carry On," *New York Times*. July 18, 1969.

44 "845 Life: Wallkill Judge Sent the Woodstock Fest Packing in 1969," *Recordonline.Com*, April 28, 2019, accessed October 20, 2021. https://www.recordonline.com/news/20190428/845-life-wallkill-judge-sent-woodstock-fest-packing-in-1969

45 Makower, Joel. *Woodstock The Oral History 40th Anniversary Edition*. Albany: State University of New York Press, 2009, 247–248.

46 Michael Wadleigh, *Woodstock: Various Artists,* Warner Bros., 1970, and Janet Serjeant, "How 'Woodstock' movie shaped festival's place in countercultures," *Reuters*, August 13, 2019.

47   Terry Gross, Fresh Air, Interview with Questlove, NPR, September 1, 2021, accessed September 17, 2021. https://www.npr.org/2021/09/01/1033238644/questlove-revives-black-woodstock-in-summer-of-soul-documentary

48   *Summer of Soul,* Questlove, Director, Searchlight Pictures, Hulu, 12:56. In similar fashion, in 1972, Stax sponsored a concert in LA, ostensibly to commemorate the 7th anniversary of the Watts riots but prominently promoting Stax artists, including then popular Isaac Hayes. That event too was dubbed a "Black Woodstock," though its dissimilarities were even more drawn than the Harlem event. *Wattstax*, PBS/POV website, accessed January 5, 2022. http://archive.pov.org/wattstax/film-description/

49   FBI Memo: Phonograph Record Entitled "Rehearsals for Retirement," By Phil Ochs, Threat Against the President October 22, 1969, Ochs FBI file, author scan page 176.

50   Steven Roberts, "Charlie Manson: One Man's Family," *New York Times*, January 4, 1970.

51   David Smith, "Charles Manson was a nightmare from the 'summer of love,'" *Washington Post,* November 20, 2017.

52   Robert A. Wright, "Grand Jury Votes to Hear Evidence in Tate Slaying," *New York Times*, December 3, 1969, Jerry Cohen, "Wild Cult Blamed in Tate Slayings," *Los Angeles Times*, December 2, 1969, Charles Powers, "Crippled Hippy Bus in Desert Led to Arrests," *Los Angeles Times*, December 2, 1969, Tom O'Neil and Dan Piepenbring, "Five myths about Charles Manson." *Washington Post,* August 23, 2019.

53   Jerry Cohen, "Savage Mystic Cult Blamed for 5 Tate Murders, 6 Others," *Los Angeles Times,* December 2, 1969.

54   An unromanticized, "smaller-than-life," and ultimately more accurate account of Manson's life and crimes can be found in Jeff Guinn's *Manson. The Life and Times of Charles Manson*, New York: Simon and Schuster, 2013.

55   See Jeremy Varon, *Bringing the War Home: The Weather Underground, the Red Army Faction, and Revolutionary Violence*

in the Sixties and Seventies, Berkeley: University of California Press, 2004. Dohrn's "dig-it" quote, *Fifth Estate,* January 22–February 4, 1970, 13. Dohrn, "Crazy Motherfuckers" from Todd Gitlin, *The Sixties: Years of Hope, Days of Rage.* New York: Bantam, 1993, 222. Dohrn's later explanation, "Professor Bernardine Dohrn remarks on her Manson Family remarks," CSPAN July 26, 2013. https://www.c-span.org/video/?c4460430/user-clip-professor-bernardine-dohrn-remarks-manson-family-remarks .

56   David Browne, "The Rock Counterculture Had a Dark Side," *Rolling Stone,* December 24, 2019.

57   Seymour M. Hersh, "My Lai 4: A report on the massacre and its aftermath," *Harper's,* May 1970.

58   John Herbers, "250,000 War Protestors Stage Peaceful Rally in Washington: A Record," *The New York Times.* Nov 16, 1969.

59   Rae Alexandra, "Brando, Fonda and Beyond: How Celebs Rallied Around the Alcatraz Occupation," KQED, website accessed Nov 20, 2021. https://www.kqed.org/arts/13869074/brando-fonda-and-beyond-how-celebs-rallied-around-the-alcatraz-occupation

60   Evan Andrews, "When Native American Activists Occupied Alcatraz Island," History.com, Nov 20, 2014, accessed September 7, 2021. https://www.history.com/news/native-american-activists-occupy-alcatraz-island-45-years-ago

61   Aaron J Leonard and Conor A. Gallagher, "Newly Obtained FBI Files Shed New Light on the Murder of Fred Hampton," *Jacobin,* March 2021, accessed May 16, 2021. https://jacobinmag.com/2021/03/newly-obtained-fbi-files-fred-hampton

62   Joel Selvin, *Altamont: The Rolling Stones, the Hells Angels and the Inside Story of Rock's Darkest Day,* New York: Dey St, 2016, 1. "Brian Jones Fined in Dope Case," *Rolling Stone,* October 26, 1968. "Obituary: Brian Jones," Greil Marcus, *Rolling Stone,* August 9, 1969.

63   Selvin, *Altamont,* 96.

64 Ibid., 112.

65 Altamont was not alone in displaying the darker aspects of such festivals. The Isle of White Festival in 1970 and the Newport Jazz Festival in 1971 both had to close down in the wake of gate-crashing incidents by crowds incensed by the ticket prices and the general aura of profit-making. Laura Barton, "Joni Mitchell, Isle of Wight 1970: the day the music nearly died," *The Guardian,* July 7, 2020, accessed, October 3, 2021. https://www.theguardian.com/music/2020/jul/07/joni-mitchell-isle-of-wight-1970-iconic-festival-sets ; "Disturbance Cancels Newport Festival," Leonard Feather, *Los Angeles Times*, July 5, 1971.

66 *Rolling Stone* committed significant resources to covering Altamont, garnering them a National Magazine Award — the first of two that year, the other being for an interview with Charles Manson — giving what had been a quasi-underground publication a seat at the table of mainstream journalism. David Browne, "Rolling Stone at 50: Shaping Contrasting Narratives of Woodstock, Altamont." *Rolling Stone*, February 7, 2017, accessed November 30, 2021. https://www.rollingstone.com/music/music-features/rolling-stone-at-50-shaping-contrasting-narratives-of-woodstock-altamont-196583/

Chapter 10: Feel the Future Tremble (1970)

1   Ronald Reagan, San Francisco Hilton Speech, May 12, 1970 Bay Area Television Archive, accessed July 9, 2020. https://diva.sfsu.edu/collections/sfbatv/bundles/189601

2   John Sundstrom, "Up Against the Wall Motherfuckers," The Outlaw Page, published in the *East Village Other*, 1968.

3   *Chicago '68,* Farber, 205.

4   Donald Janson, "16 Indicted by US in Chicago Tumult," *New York Times*, March 21, 1969, Donald Janson, "8 Leaders of Protest During the Democratic Convention Plead Not Guilty to Incite a Riot," *New York Times*, April 10, 1969, and "The

Chicago Seven go on Trial," History.com website, accessed September 19, 2021. https://www.history.com/this-day-in-history/the-chicago-seven-go-on-trial

5   Arlo Guthrie Testimony, Famous Trials, accessed September 19, 2021. https://famous-trials.com/chicago8/1325-guthrie ; J. Anthony Lukas, "Song by Guthrie Barred at Trial," *New York Times*. January 16, 1970.

6   Testimony of Judy Collins, "Famous Trials," accessed October 21, 2021. https://famous-trials.com/chicago8/1320-collins

7   Judy Collins, *Sweet Judy Blue Eyes: My Life in Music*, New York: Three Rivers Press. 2012, 272.

8   J. Anthony Lukas, "Chicago 7 Cleared of Plot; 5 Guilty on Second Count," *New York Times,* February 19, 1970, William E. Farrell, "Chicago Seven Start New Trial Today," *New York Times*, October 29, 1973 and David Stout, "William Kunstler, 76, Dies; Lawyer for Social Outcasts," *New York Times*, September 5, 1995.

9   Graham Nash, *Songs for Beginners*, "Chicago," side 2, track 6, Atlantic, 1971.

10   Peter Doggett, *CSNY: Crosby, Stills, Nash & Young.* New. York: Atria Books, Kindle Edition, 189–190.

11   Marc Meyers, "She Went Chasing Rabbits," *Wall Street Journal*, April 29, 2011. https://www.wsj.com/articles/SB10001424052748703778104576287303493094530

12   "Abbie Hoffman Barred From White House Tea," *New York Times*, 4/25/1970.

13   Grace Slick, with Andrea Cagan, "Somebody to Love?: A Rock-and-Roll Memoir, New York: Warner Books, 1998, 190.

14   "Abbie Hoffman Barred..."

15   SAC San Francisco, to Director FBI. Subject: Abbot Howard Hoffman, SM-ANA [anarchist], Key Activist. Abbie Hoffman FBI file 100-449923, section 7, 136.

16   Memo, GRACE W. SLICK, aka, Grace Barnett Wing, August 14, 1970, Jefferson Airplane FBI file retrieved from the FBI Vault, page 10, accessed January 8, 2022. https://vault.fbi.

gov/Jefferson%20Airplane%20/Jefferson%20Airplane%20
Part%201%20of%201/view

17 David Felton, "Blood, Sweat & Tears Turn Backs on
    Communism," *Rolling Stone*. September 3, 1970.

18 Steve Katz, *Blood, Sweat, and My Rock 'n' Roll Years: Is Steve
    Katz a Rock Star*, Lanham, MD: Lyons Press, 2015, 152.

19 Felton, "Blood, Sweat & Tears Turn Backs on Communism."

20 William Beecher, "128 U.S. Planes Carry Out Attack in North
    Vietnam," *New York Times*, May 3, 1970 and Robert B. Semple,
    "Nixon Describes Cambodian Drive as Great Success," *New.
    York Times* June 4, 1970.

21 John Kifner, "4 Kent State Students Killed by Troops." *New
    York Times*, May 5, 1970.

22 Crosby, Stills, Nash & Young, "Ohio," writer, Neil Young,
    Atlantic, 1970.

23 "Jackson Police Fire on Students," May 15,1970, *New York
    Times*, May 15, 1970; Steve Miller Band, *Number 5*, "Jackson
    Kent Blues," side 2, track 4, Capitol, 1970.

24 Quicksilver Messenger Service, *What About Me*, "What About
    Me," side 1, track 1, Capitol, 1970.

25 David Paul Kuhn, *The Hardhat Riot: Nixon, New York City, and
    the Dawn of the White Working-Class Revolution*, New York-
    London: Oxford University Press, 2020, 150.

26 Ibid.

27 "N.Y. Workers beat up students," Associated Press story, *Boston
    Globe* May 9, 1970.

28 Kuhn, *The Hardhat Riot*, 231–232.

29 Merle Haggard, "Sing Me Back Home," Capitol, 1967, single
    and Merle Haggard, "Mama Tried," Capitol, 1968.

30 Earl Gottschalk, "Love It or Leave It: New Patriotic Music Wins
    Fans, Enemies," *The Wall Street Journal*, August 18, 1970.

31 Ibid.

32 Robert Hilburn, "Haggard Wins 5 Country Music Awards,"
    Los Angeles Times. April 15, 1970. Later in life Haggard would
    reflect on how the song had come to identify him and would

walk it back to a degree — even turning it into satire in live performances. Other times, however, he would embrace its core message. Martin Chilton, "Merle Haggard: Sometimes I wish I hadn't written Okie from Muskogee," *The Telegraph*, April. 8, 2016. Also, author attendance at Bob Dylan/Merle Haggard concert, Beacon Theatre, NY, 2005.

33 Ronald Reagan "San Francisco Hilton Speech, May 12, 1970," Bay Area Television Archive, Accessed. July 9, 2020. https://diva. sfsu.edu/collections/sfbatv/bundles/189601

34 Crosby, Stills, Nash & Young, *Deja Vu*, "Almost Cut My Hair," side 1, track 3, Atlantic, 1970.

35 "Spiro T. Agnew speech. September 14, 1970, Las Vegas, Nevada. Nevada Republican Dinner," John R. Coyne Jr., *The Impudent Snobs: Agnew vs. the Intellectual Establishment*. New Rochelle: Arlington House, 1972, 371–372.

36 Thomas Powers, "Nixon's Drug Crusade," *New York Times*, Sep 4, 1977, and James M. Markham, "President Calls for 'Total War' On US Addiction," *New York Times*, March 21, 1972.

37 Dan Baum, "Legalize It All. How to win the war on drugs," *Harpers*, April, 2016.

38 German Lopez, "Was Nixon's War on Drugs a Racially Motivated Campaign? It's a Bit More Complicated," *Vox*, accessed January 16, 2022. https://www.vox. com/2016/3/29/11325750/nixon-war-on-drugs

39 "New Orleans Cops & the Dead Bust," *Rolling Stone*, March 7, 1970.

40 "Arrest Jefferson Airplane Singer," *The Capital Times*, May 21, 1970.

41 Everett True, "Joe Cocker on being deported from Australia: we were used as guinea pigs," *The Guardian,* December 23, 2014; "Marijuana Charges Against Six Rock Musicians Dropped," *Los Angeles Times*, July 19, 1972; "Guitarist for Rock Group Accused of Having Drugs," *New York Times*, March 30, 1973; "Drug Arrest 'Probably Illegal," *San Francisco Chronicle*, February 23, 1973.

42 "Goodbye, Janis Joplin: Superstars just fade, but cultural heroines die hard," *Rolling Stone*, October 29, 1970.

43 Jack Batten, "Janis Joplin: Sex, drinking added to image of blues-rock singer," *The Globe and Mail,* Oct 6, 1970.

44 Fred Sparks, "Rock — The Drug Scene," *San Francisco Examiner*, September 30,1971.

Chapter 11: The Sixties End (1971–1972)

1   Richard Nixon, Acceptance speech at 1972 Republican National Convention, C-Span, accessed January 17, 2022. https://www.c-span.org/video/?3911-1/richard-nixon-1972-acceptance-speech.

2   John Prine, *John Prine*, "Your Flag Decal Won't Get You Into Heaven Anymore," side 2, track 1, Atlantic, 1971.

3   "Somebody to shove: Paul Kantner, Jefferson Airplane bandmates got arrested at 1972 Rubber Bowl concert," *Akron Beacon Journal*, August 19, 2002.

4   Tamarkin, *Got A Revolution!* 257, and "Arrest Grace Slick," *Kenosha News,* August 23, 1972.

5   Medsger, Betty. *The Burglary: The Discover of J. Edgar Hoover's FBI*. New York: Vintage, 2014, 263. Donald Janson. "F.B.I. File Theft Stirs Anger and Joy Among the Residents, of Media, Pa." *New York Times,* March 29, 1971, "FBI Spies on Blacks, New Left," *Chicago Tribune*, April 8, 1971.

6   Medsger. *The Burglary*, 309.

7   Memorandum, Pittsburgh FBI Office, November 3, 1971. Makeba FBI File, File 1, Section 2, 22.

8   SAC Washington Field Office, to Director FBI, November 11/11/71, Makeba FBI file 1 Section 2, 35–36.

9   Memorandum FBI Office Boston, Mass. November 13, 1971. Makeba FBI File 1, Section 2, 43–44.

10 SAC New York to Acting Director FBI, Stokely Carmichael, Extremist Matters, Key Black Extremist, Miriam Makeba, Extremist Matters, 9/1/72. Miriam Makeba FBI file, File 1, Section 2, 71.

11   Miriam Makeba and James Hall. *Makeba: My Story*, New York and Scarborough, Ontario: New American Library, 1987, 162.

12   Interview with Swedish journalist Elisabeth Frankl, *Stockholm, Expressen*, 15. February 1970. Transcript in Makeba FBI file. Sec 1, 87.

13   Ibid.

14   "U.S. Says Stokely, Wife Owe $48,000 in Back Taxes." *Jet Magazine*, March 11, 1970.

15   Peter Richardson, *No Simple Highway: A Cultural History of the Grateful Dead*, New York: St. Martin's Press, 2014, 168.

16   "Newton Attacks Sexual Fascism," *San Francisco Chronicle*, March 6, 1971. The Lumpen served mainly as a vehicle to promote the particular campaigns of the BPP. While musically accomplished, their lyrics tended toward sloganeering, as can be seen in their songs "Free Bobby Now" and "No More." For more on the Lumpen, see Ricky Vincent, *Party Music: The Inside Story of the Black Panther's Band and How Black Power Transformed Soul Music*, Chicago: Lawrence Hill Books, 2013. Also Eric Arnold, "A Brief History of the Lumpen, the Black Panthers' Revolutionary Funk Band," February 25, 2019. KQED website, accessed, October 12, 2021. https://www.kqed.org/arts/13851531/a-brief-history-of-the-lumpen-the-black-panthers-revolutionary-funk-band

17   Flores Forbes, *Will You Die With Me? My Life and the Black Panther Party,* New York, Atria Books, 2010, 95.

18   Leslie Oelsner, "Charges Dropped Against Seale," *New York Times,* May 26, 1971.

19   Magee, who was initially put on trial with Davis, would later plead guilty to kidnapping, garnering a life sentence—he remains imprisoned. Lasey Fosburgh, "Ruchell Magee, Once Angela Davis' Co-Defendant, Gets Life for Kidnapping," *New York Times,* January 24, 1975

20   For more on Jonathan Jackson and the Marin raid as well as the killing of George Jackson see, Gregory Armstrong, *The Dragon Has Come*, New York: Harper Row, 1974, Jo Durden-

Smith, *Who Killed George Jackson*, New York: Knopf, 1976, and Paul Liberatore, *The Road to Hell*, New York: *Atlantic Monthly Press*, 1996.

21 Meagan Day, "The Attica demands," September 8, 2016, Meagan Day, Medium site, accessed October 1, 2021. https://medium.com/@meaganday/the-attica-demands-50f9b6af8501; *Dog Day Afternoon*, Sidney Lumet, dir., Warner Brothers, 1975.; Heather Thompson, *Blood in the Water: The Attica Prison Uprising of 1971 and its Legacy,* New York: Pantheon, 2016, 260. Also, "Attica: Then and Now" National Lawyers Guild, website accessed October 1, 2021. https://nlgnyc.org/attica-50/

22 Archie Shepp, *Attica Blues*, Impulse, 1972.

23 Sarah King, "Free The Army: How Celebrities and Entertainers Mobilized to Challenge Pro-War Entertainment During the Vietnam War," US History Scene website, accessed June 16, 2021 https://ushistoryscene.com/article/fta/

24 "Winter Soldier Investigation," The Sixties Project website, accessed September 24, 2021. http://www2.iath.virginia.edu/sixties/HTML_docs/Resources/Primary/Winter_Soldier/WS_entry.html

25 Richard Stacewicz, *Winter Soldiers: An Oral History of the Vietnam Veterans Against the War.* Twayne Publishers, 1997, 234; *Winter Soldier*, 1972. Winter Film Collective, Vietnam Veterans Against the War. American Film Institute Catalog. https://www.proquest.com/artistic-aesthetic-works/winter-soldier/docview/1746211214/se-2?accountid=14521 (accessed September 24, 2021).

26 Scott Camil, Sgt. (E-5), 1st Bn., 11th Marine Regt., 1st Marine Div., Winter Soldier Investigation [WSI] transcript, 1st Marine Div., p. 2.

27 Graham Nash Mines His Catalog for Some Person Performances, *PBS*, accessed January 24, 2022. https://www.pbs.org/newshour/show/graham-nash-mines-his-catalog-for-some-personal-performances

28 Peter Doggett, *CSNY: Crosby, Stills, Nash & Young*, New York: Atria Books, Kindle Edition, 289–290.

29 "Vets' History: Operation 'Dewey Canyon III,'" by VVAW, *The Veteran*, April 1977, Vol. 7, No. 2, VVAW website, accessed. September 24, 2021. http://www.vvaw.org/veteran/article/?id=1656

30 Lawrence Roberts, *May Day 1971: A White House at War, a Revolt in the Streets, and the Untold History of America's Biggest Mass Arrest*, Boston: Mariner Books, 2020, 129–140.

31 Roberts, *May Day 1971*, 160.

32 "Washington, DC protests against the war in Vietnam (Mayday), 1971," Global Non-Violence Database, accessed, September 24, 2021. https://nvdatabase.swarthmore.edu/content/washington-dc-protests-against-war-vietnam-mayday-1971

33 Vietnam War Allied Troop Levels 1960–73, Americanwarlibrary.com.

34 Stacia Friedman, "Remembering Phil Ochs and a revolution interrupted," WHYY/PBS, April 18, 2016, accessed January 16, 2022. https://whyy.org/articles/remembering-phil-ochs-and-a-revolution-interrupted/

35 Schumacher, *There But for Fortune*, 244–251.

36 Ibid., 295–297.

37 Manzarek, *Light My Fire*, 8–9.

38 Elizabeth Goodman, "Jim Morrison's Death May Be Reinvestigated," *Rolling Stone*, July 10, 2007.

39 Manzarek, *Light My Fire*, 333.

40 In 2010, Florida's governor pardoned Morrison, prompting the surviving members of the Doors to issue a statement. It read in part, "Every city The Doors were booked into canceled their engagement," and that "a circus of fire-and-brimstone 'decency' rallies, grand jury investigations and apocalyptic editorials followed." It concluded, "If the State of Florida and the City of Miami want to make amends for the travesty of Jim Morrison's arrest and prosecution 40 years after the fact,

an apology would be more appropriate." "The Doors respond to Florida's pardon of Jim Morrison: 'We don't feel Jim needs to be pardoned for anything,'" *Los Angeles* blog, accessed October 22, 2021. https://latimesblogs.latimes.com/music_blog/2010/12/the-doors-respond-to-floridas-pardon-of-jim-morrison-we-dont-feel-jim-needs-to-be-pardoned-for-anyth.html

41   John Lennon & Yoko Ono, *The Mike Douglas Show* February 17, 1972. Rhino, 1999, VHS. https://www.youtube.com/watch?v=Q-HES64-D7w

42   SAC New York, to Director FBI, Subject: John Winston Lennon, 8/30/72, In Jon Wiener, *Gimme Some Truth: The John Lennon FBI Files*, Berkeley: University of California Press, 1999, 295.

43   Ibid.

44   Lennon's immigration situation would go on for many years. He was finally able to obtain a Green Card in 1976. Leslie Maitland, "John Lennon Wins Residency in US," *New York Times*, July 28, 1976.

45   In 1966 only 31% of respondents to a Gallup poll said it was a mistake to send US troops to Vietnam, by 1971 that number had risen to 60%. Frank Newport and Joseph Carroll, "Iraq Versus Vietnam: A Comparison of Public Opinion," August 24, 2005, Gallup website, accessed September 23, 2021. https://news.gallup.com/poll/18097/iraq-versus-vietnam-comparison-public-opinion.aspx.

46   "Terry Skinner," Alabama Hall of Fame website, accessed January 24, 2022. https://web.archive.org/web/20110520071314/http://alamhof.org/terryskinner.html and "Terry Skinner" Discogs, accessed October 25, 2021. https://www.discogs.com/artist/441177-Terry-Skinner

47   "Calley 'obeyed orders,'" *The Guardian*, February 23, 1971.

48   Louis Harris, "Public Divided on Calley Guilt," *Chicago Tribune*, April 5, 1971.

49   "Tex Ritter Critical Over Capitol Move," *Los Angeles Times*,

April 13, 1971, Alan Shuster, "U.S. Command in Vietnam Bars 'Battle Hymn of Calley,'" *New York Times.* May 1, 1971.

50   James Ryan, "Those Weren't the Days: The 1950s Revival of the 1970," *Rebeat*, accessed April 24, 2022. http://www.rebeatmag.com/those-werent-the-days-the-1950s-revival-of-the-1970s/

51   See for example, "Jesus Freaks Seen as Test of Christian Belief," *Los Angeles Times*, Jan 15, 1972.

52   Clive Barnes, "The Theater: Godspell," *New York Times*, May 18, 1971.

53   Gus Flatley, "They Wrote It: And They're Glad," *New York Times*, October 31, 1971.

Conclusion: Yesterday and Today

1   Spiro T. Agnew speech. September 14, 1970, Las Vegas, Nevada. "Nevada Republican Dinner," Coyne Jr., *The Impudent Snobs*, 371.

2   "Phil Ochs Discusses Politics of Songwriting, Kablegram 41 no. 4 (15 December 1967)," *I'm Gonna Say it Now: The Writings of Phil Ochs Back Guilford,* Edited by David Cohen, Connecticut: Beat Books, 2020, 205.

3   Clifford's remarks were in regard to the immediate situation after the Tet Offensive. Clifford, *Counsel to the President*, 476.

4   Leonard, *Folksingers*, 235.

5   For more analysis on the Cold War / Sino-Soviet split, see Lorenz M. Lüthi's, *The Sino-Soviet Split: Cold War in the Communist World, World*, Princeton, NJ: Princeton University Press, 2008, Mingjiang Li, *Mao's China and the Sino-Soviet Split: Ideological Dilemma,* London, and New York: Routledge, 2012 and Anhui Li and Yafeng Xia. *Mao and the Sino-Soviet Split: 1959–1973, A New History*. Washington: Lexington Books, 2020.

6   See, for example, Mary L Dudziak, "Desegregation as a Cold War Imperative," *Stanford Law Review* 41, no. 1 (1988): 61–120. Accessed July 4, 2021. "At a time when the U.S. hoped to reshape the world in its own image, the international

attention given to racial segregation was troublesome and embarrassing. The focus of American foreign policy at this point was to promote democracy and to 'contain' communism. However, the international focus on U.S. racial problems meant that the image of American democracy was tarnished."

Appendix: The FBI Files

1 David Hardy, FBI to Aaron J. Leonard. June 14, 2016.

INDEX

A

Agnew, Spiro T. 203, 204, 229
Albert, Richard (Baba Ram Das) 128
Ali, Muhammad 91
Allende, Salvadore 220
Almanac Singers, the 30, 113
Altamont 130, 186, 189–91, 229
American Friends Service Committee 129, 280
American Graffiti 225
amphetamines 205
Anderson, Jack 119, 120, 155, 156
Armstrong, Louis 12, 233
Aspinall, Neil 117
Australia 22, 206

B

Baez, Joan 31, 32, 60, 61, 74, 81, 82, 88, 104, 139–41, 171, 182, 218, 222
Baldwin, James 39
Balin, Marty 113, 114, 137, 177, 205
Bay of Pigs 34, 35, 94
Beach Boys, the 83, 131, 184
Beatlemania 74, 75
Beatnik Riot 39, 40
Beats 9–11, 13

Beherien (Peace for Vietnam Committee) 141
Belafonte, Harry 27–30, 144, 145, 153, 171
Berry, Chuck 13, 18, 22, 76, 121
Bettelheim, Bruno 174
Big Brother and the Holding Company 129
Blackboard Jungle 19
Black Panther Party (BPP) 86, 126, 143, 150, 156, 160, 162, 188, 189, 193, 213–15, 222, 223
Blood, Sweat & Tears 197
Bosch, Juan 94
Boyer, Elisa 90, 91
Boyle, Peter 217
British Invasion 74, 75, 78, 132, 133
Broadside 62, 73, 123
Brown, James 156–58
Brown, Peter 117
Brown v. Board of Education 102
Bryant, Anita 4
Buffalo Springfield 131, 138, 170, 229
Burroughs, William S. 9
Byrds, the 102, 103, 105, 122, 125, 176, 204, 225

C

Caen, Herb 10

ACKNOWLEDGEMENTS

To the friends who offered insights and encouragement in undertaking this project, I want to give a warm thank you: Mat Callahan, Dennis O'Neal, Steve Garabedian, Trevor Griffey, Andras Jones, and the wonderful group of friends and family who gathered for my presentation on "How Bob Dylan & the Beatles Upset the Status Quo" — and offered their questions and thoughts. Also, a special thanks to Terri Thal for her memories and insights on Dave Van Ronk, and to Joe McDonald for his recollections of Chicago '68, and to Barbara Dane for her recollections of a life well lived.

Also, much appreciation to the students and administrators in the Osher Life Long Learning programs at Boise State University, CSU Channel Island, CSU Monterey Bay, University of the Pacific, Stockton, and UC Riverside, where I was able to evolve this book up from "Music, Rebellion & Repression" into the volume it has since become. A special thanks in that regard to Michele Compton, Jennifer Juanitas, Sandra Richards, Dana Thorp Patterson, and Laura Mehlaff. Also, thanks to Kate Blalack at the Woody Guthrie Center for her generous assistance in obtaining a copy of Phil Ochs's FBI file.

A special thanks to Tariq Goddard for his continued support, and the entire team at Repeater Books: Josh Turner, Christiana Spens, and Johnny Bull.

And an extra special thanks to Ron Cohen, Conor Gallagher, and Carl Neville, for giving of their time reading through the manuscript and offering their thoughts and much needed corrections. And finally, as always, to Irka Mateo for her enduring capacity to hear me out and offer her loving thoughts. That said, in the end, all opinions, oversights, and otherwise written here are my own.

REPEATER BOOKS

is dedicated to the creation of a new reality. The landscape of twenty-first-century arts and letters is faded and inert, riven by fashionable cynicism, egotistical self-reference and a nostalgia for the recent past. Repeater intends to add its voice to those movements that wish to enter history and assert control over its currents, gathering together scattered and isolated voices with those who have already called for an escape from Capitalist Realism. Our desire is to publish in every sphere and genre, combining vigorous dissent and a pragmatic willingness to succeed where messianic abstraction and quiescent co-option have stalled: abstention is not an option: we are alive and we don't agree.